49.95

DATE DUE

DEMCO, INC. 38-2931

THE HISTORY OF NICARAGUA

ADVISORY BOARD

THE HISTORY OF NICARAGUA

Clifford L. Staten

The Greenwood Histories of the Modern Nations
Frank W. Thackeray and John E. Findling, Series Editors

 GREENWOOD

AN IMPRINT OF ABC-CLIO, LLC
Santa Barbara, California • Denver, Colorado • Oxford, England

Library of Congress Cataloging-in-Publication Data
Staten, Clifford L.
    The history of Nicaragua / Clifford L. Staten.
        p. cm. — (The Greenwood histories of the modern nations)
    Includes bibliographical references and index.
    ISBN 978-0-313-36037-4 (hard copy : alk. paper)—ISBN 978-0-313-36038-1 (ebook)
1. Nicaragua—History. I. Title.
    F1526.S78   2010
    972.85—dc22   2010000950

ISBN: 978-0-313-36037-4
EISBN: 978-0-313-36038-1

14   13   12   11   10   1   2   3   4   5

This book is also available on the World Wide Web as an eBook.
Visit www.abc-clio.com for details.

Greenwood
An Imprint of ABC-CLIO, LLC

ABC-CLIO, LLC
130 Cremona Drive, P.O. Box 1911
Santa Barbara, California 93116-1911

This book is printed on acid-free paper ∞

Manufactured in the United States of America

To the love of my life, my wife Shan

Contents

Series Foreword

The Greenwood Histories of the Modern Nations series is intended to provide students and interested laypeople with up-to-date, concise, and analytical histories of many of the nations of the contemporary world. Not since the 1960s has there been a systematic attempt to publish a series of national histories, and as series advisors, we believe that this series will prove to be a valuable contribution to our understanding of other countries in our increasingly interdependent world.

Some 40 years ago, at the end of the 1960s, the Cold War was an accepted reality of global politics. The process of decolonization was still in progress, the idea of a unified Europe with a single currency was unheard of, the United States was mired in a war in Vietnam, and the economic boom in Asia was still years in the future. Richard Nixon was president of the United States, Mao Tse-tung (not yet Mao Zedong) ruled China, Leonid Brezhnev guided the Soviet Union, and Harold Wilson was prime minister of the United Kingdom. Authoritarian dictators still controlled most of Latin America, the Middle East was reeling in the wake of the Six-Day War, and Shah Mohammad Reza Pahlavi was at the height of his power in Iran.

Since then, the Cold War has ended, the Soviet Union has vanished, leaving 15 independent republics in its wake, the advent of the computer age has radically transformed global communications, the rising demand for oil makes the Middle East still a dangerous flashpoint, and the rise of new economic powers like the People's Republic of China and India threatens to bring about a new world order. All of these developments have had a dramatic impact on the recent history of every nation of the world.

For this series, which was launched in 1998, we first selected nations whose political, economic, and socio-cultural affairs marked them as among the most important of our time. For each nation, we found an author who was recognized as a specialist in the history of that nation. These authors worked cooperatively with us and with Greenwood Press to produce volumes that reflected current research on their nations and that are interesting and informative to their readers. In the first decade of the series, more than 40 volumes were published, and as of 2008, some are moving into second editions.

The success of the series has encouraged us to broaden our scope to include additional nations whose histories have had significant effects on their regions, if not on the entire world. In addition, geopolitical changes have elevated other nations into positions of greater importance in world affairs, and so, we have chosen to include them in this series as well. The importance of a series such as this cannot be underestimated. As a super-power whose influence is felt all over the world, the United States can claim a "special" relationship with almost every other nation. Yet many Americans know very little about the histories of nations with which the United States relates. How did they get to be the way they are? What kinds of political systems have evolved there? What kind of influence do they have on their own regions? What are the dominant political, religious, and cultural forces that move their leaders? These and many other questions are answered in the volumes of this series.

The authors who contribute to this series write comprehensive histories of their nations, dating back, in some instances, to prehistoric times. Each of them, however, has devoted a significant portion of their book to events of the past 40 years because the modern era has contributed the most to contemporary issues that have an impact on U.S. policy. Authors make every effort to be as up-to-date as possible so that readers can benefit from discussion and analysis of recent events.

In addition to the historical narrative, each volume contains an introductory chapter giving an overview of that country's geography, political institutions, economic structure, and cultural attributes. This is meant to give readers a snapshot of the nation as it exists in the contemporary world. Each history also includes supplementary information following the narrative, which may include a timeline that represents a succinct chronology of the nation's historical evolution, biographical sketches of the nation's most important historical figures, and a glossary of important terms or concepts that are usually expressed in a foreign language. Finally, each author prepares a comprehensive bibliography for readers who wish to pursue the subject further.

Readers of these volumes will find them fascinating and well written. More importantly, they will come away with a better understanding of the contemporary world and the nations that comprise it. As series advisors, we hope that this series will contribute to a heightened sense of global understanding as we move through the early years of the twenty-first century.

Frank W. Thackeray and John E. Findling
Indiana University Southeast

Acknowledgments

In writing a book for the general public and young students, I am indebted to scholars who have spent most of their professional lives studying Nicaragua. These include Craig Auchter of Butler University with whom I traveled to Nicaragua and John Booth who taught at the University of North Texas when I was completing my doctoral program. Other scholars who have had a tremendous influence on how I interpret events in Nicaragua include Thomas Walker of Ohio University, Laura Enriquez of the University of California at Berkeley, Jeffrey Paige of the University of Michigan, Stephen Kinzer of Northwestern University, Leslie Anderson and Lawrence C. Dodd of the University of Florida, and Charles D. Brockett of the University of the South. Others who have influenced this book in different but significant ways include the late Neal Tate of Vanderbilt University, the late Clair Matz of Marshall University, Linda Gugin of Indiana University Southeast, John Findling of Indiana University Southeast, George Aldridge of the United States State Department, Robert Harding of Spring Hill College, Allen Maxwell of Indiana University Kokomo, Stephanie Bower of Indiana University Southeast, and Tim Ambrose of Indiana University Southeast. I am also indebted to the students of Indiana University Southeast over the past 20 years who have made me a better teacher of Latin American politics.

During my visits to Nicaragua I met many people who helped shape my views of this beautiful and tragic country. I would like especially to thank Kathy McBride and Mark Lester of the Center for Global Education in Barrio Martha Quezada in Managua who showed us much of the country and arranged interviews with influential *Nicas* such as José Rico Castellon, Ricardo Oliu, Father Fernando Cardenal, Father Ernesto Cardenal, Luis Carrion, and Rene Nuñez. Kathy also managed to somehow get our group into the Olaf Palme Center in Managua to attend the inauguration ceremony of the Sandinista Renovation Movement. I had a wonderful talk one very warm summer evening in Managua with Sister Ani who told me the story of how her friend and United States citizen Benjamin Linder was murdered by the Nicaraguan resistance or *contras*. She explained why and how she came to be a believer in liberation theology and the progressive Catholic Church in Nicaragua. Leana Tiffer and Ruth at the Olofito Center in Managua helped me with my Spanish one summer and told me many personal stories of their lives as students under the Somoza dictatorship and the Sandinista nationwide literacy campaign in which they participated. Leana's father was the driver for ABC television correspondent Bill Stewart whose execution by Somoza's National Guardsmen was caught on film. Señora Jasmina Morales, a seamstress living in Barrio Riguero in Managua, and her son opened their house to me one summer and gave me a taste of everyday life for the working class in Managua. The city dump, called *La Chureca*, is home to a community of the poorest of the poor in Managua. Two young men, who were sifting through the mountains of trash for anything of value, took time over a couple of days to tell me how they and their families managed daily survival under such unbelievable conditions.

Señor Juan José Lezcano and Señora Rafaela graciously opened their house to me in the colonial city of Granada. I fondly remember Señora Rafaela's sweet *café con leche* and her *gallo pinto* in the mornings, as well as her *nacatamales* at the end of the week. Maria Haydee, also of Granada, who helped me with my Spanish on the second floor of the old social club overlooking the plaza, told me stories about the history of this beautiful city that rests on the western shore of Lake Nicaragua. She spoke candidly of the hardships faced by her family during the revolutionary years of the 1980s. Miguel, whom I met while hiking up the volcano Mombacho, told me all about the fine Nicaraguan coffee grown on the *finca* that he and several other families run as a cooperative. Finally, I would like to thank all of my fellow international travelers and scholars at the café near the *Casa de Los Tres Mundos* on the plaza in Granada with whom I shared stories and drank more than a few beers and at least a couple of bottles of rum.

Without my secretaries—Mary Ann Braden, Leslie Deal, and Brigette Adams—finding time in my daily schedule and running interference for me, this book would never have been written. I am most appreciative to the editors of this series, Frank Thackeray and John Findling, who had the confidence in me to write such a book. Finally, I would like to thank my children Josh, Ryan, Anna, and Glenn for their continued support, proof-reading, understanding, and love. I am especially thankful for their patience with my monopoly of the home computer.

Timeline of Historical Events

1633	Bluefields established on the Mosquito Coast
1664, 1666	English buccaneers led by Henry Morgan attack and loot Granada
1678	British establish a protectorate over the Mosquito Coast and create the Miskito Kingdom
1735	Charles Marie de la Condamine suggests building a canal between Lake Nicaragua and the Pacific Ocean
1786	British agree to leave the Mosquito Coast
1788	Count Louis-Hector de Segur suggests building a canal between Lake Nicaragua and the Pacific Ocean
1791	Martin de Labastide suggests building a canal between Lake Nicaragua and the Pacific Ocean
1804	Alexander von Humbolt suggests building a canal between Lake Nicaragua and the Pacific Ocean
1811	First Nicaraguan uprising against Spain occurs in city of Rivas
1821	Central America gains independence from Spain; Nicaragua becomes part of independent Mexico
1823	Central America declares its independence from Mexico and forms the United Provinces of Central America
1838	Nicaragua becomes an independent country
1847	British re-establish the Mosquito Coast as a protectorate
1848	British seize San Juan del Norte and rename the port city Greytown
1849	United States negotiates commercial treaty with Nicaragua
1850	Clayton-Bulwer Treaty confirmed; British-U.S. cooperation for any canal built across Central America
1851	Cornelius Vanderbilt establishes a cross-isthmus transit route consisting of a steamship route up the San Juan River and into Lake Nicaragua followed by a brief overland trip from Rivas to the Pacific Ocean
1854	Fruto Chamorro Pérez becomes the first President of the Republic of Nicaragua
1855–1856	William Walker, supported by the Liberal Party, arrives in Nicaragua, takes over the city of Granada, and becomes president

1857	William Walker is ousted by an army of both the Conservative and Liberal Parties
1860	William Walker is captured and executed
1870s	Coffee becomes the principle crop in Nicaragua and foreign investment is encouraged
1893	Liberal revolt brings José Santos Zelaya to power
1894	Last British intervention on Mosquito Coast
1902	United States decides to build a cross-isthmus canal in Panama rather than Nicaragua
1909	Zelaya is overthrown by the conservatives with the support of the United States
1912–1925	U.S. military forces occupy Nicaragua
1926–1933	U.S. military forces reoccupy Nicaragua
1927–1933	Augusto César Sandino leads Nicaraguan nationalists against U.S. occupation army
1932	Earthquake destroys Managua
1933	Anastasio Somoza García named director of the National Guard; U.S. Marines withdraw from country; Sandino agrees to peace settlement
1934	Somoza assassinates Sandino
1936	Somoza with the support of the Guard becomes president of Nicaragua
1955	Cotton becomes the primary export of the country
1956	Anastasio Somoza García is assassinated; Luis Somoza Debayle becomes president
1959	Fidel Castro comes to power in Cuba
1961	Nicaragua supports U.S. invasion at the Bay of Pigs, Cuba
1963	First communiqués signed by the Sandinista Front for National Liberation (FSLN) are issued
1972	Earthquake devastates Managua; corruption by Anastasio Somoza Debayle associated with the relief effort turns many elites and middle class against Somoza
1976	Carlos Fonseca, founder of the FSLN, is killed
1978	Assassination of Pedro Joaquín Chamorro, leader of the conservative opposition to Somoza; opposition to

	Somoza expands dramatically; United States suspends military support to Somoza
1979	Sandinistas lead a broad-based coalition of forces which overthrows the Somoza government and comes to power; revolutionary junta established consisting of three Sandinistas, Violeta Chamorro, and businessman Alfonso Robelo, but in reality it was the nine-member Sandinista National Directorate that held power in the country
1979–1981	*Contra* resistance forces formed from former National Guardsmen in Honduras; President Reagan assists in organizing and arming them
1981–1988	Reagan administration wages a "low-intensity" war against the Sandinistas
1982	Boland Amendment to the 1973 War Powers Act prohibits U.S. funds from being used to overthrow government of Nicaragua; Nicaragua unable to get loans from World Bank due to U.S. pressure
1984	CIA places mines in harbor at Corinto and damages at least 9 ships; CIA carries out commando raids against Sandinista targets; Daniel Ortega elected as president of Nicaragua
1985	United States enforces full trade embargo against Nicaragua
1986	World Court condemns the mining of Nicaraguan harbors as a violation of international law and fines the United States; President Reagan ignores the court's decision; United States supplies *contra* forces with land mines and Stinger anti-aircraft missiles; CIA supply plane flown by Eugene Hasenfus shot down and provides evidence of extensive CIA supply network to the *contras*; Hasenfus publicly revealed that, contrary to the Boland Amendment, the United States was supplying military aid to the *contras* in an attempt to overthrow the Sandinista government; precipitates "Iran-contra scandal" in Washington
1990	Violeta Chamorro, wife of assassinated Pedro Joaquín Chamorro, defeats Ortega in the presidential election
1992	Peace accords implemented in Nicaragua

1996	Arnoldo Alemán Lacayo elected as president
1998	Hurricane Mitch destroys much of infrastructure of the country and 10,000 people die
2002	Enrique Bolaños Geyer elected as president
2004	Central American Free Trade Agreement implemented
2006	Daniel Ortega elected as president for the second time
2008	Sandinistas dominate the municipal elections, many of the Sandinista mayors who were elected are critics of Daniel Ortega

Acronyms Used in this Book

ALBA—Bolivarian Alternative to the Americas
ALN—Nicaraguan Liberal Alliance
ALN-PC—National Liberal Alliance
AMNLAE—Association of Nicaraguan Women "Luisa Amanda Espinoza"
APRE—Alliance for the Republic
ATC—Association of Rural Workers
BANAMERICA Group—group of Nicaraguan economic elites associated with the Bank of America
BANIC Group—group of Nicaraguan economic elites associated with the Bank of Nicaragua
CAFTA—Central American Free Trade Agreement
CEB—Christian Base Community
CEPA—Evangelistic Committee for Agrarian Reform
COSEP—Superior Council of Private Enterprise
COSIP—Superior Council of Private Initiative
CPC—Citizen Power Councils
CPT—Permanent Congress of Workers
CST—Sandinista Worker's Central
DN—Sandinista National Directorate
EPS—Sandinista People's Army

FAO—Broad Opposition Front
FER—Federation of Revolutionary Students
FJD—Democratic Youth Front
FLN—National Liberation Front
FNT—National Workers Front
FSLN—Sandinista Front for National Liberation
FUAC—Andres Castro United Front
GPP—Prolonged People's War
HIPC—Highly Indebted Poor Country
IMF—International Monetary Fund
JDN—Democratic Youth Movement
JPN—Patriotic Nicaraguan Youth
JRN—Revolutionary Nicaraguan Youth
JRS—Sandinista Revolutionary Youth
MDN—Nicaraguan Democratic Movement
MNN—Movement for a New Nicaragua
MPDC—Popular Christian Democratic Movement
MPRS—Movement for the Restoration of Sandinismo
MR—Republican Mobilization
MRS—Sandinista Renovation Movement
OAS—Organization of American States
PCN—Nicaraguan Conservative Party
PETRONIC—Nicaraguan State Oil Company
PLC—Liberal Constitutionalist Party
PLI—Independent Liberal Party
PLN—Liberal Nationalist Party
PLO—Palestine Liberation Organization
PRN—Party of Nicaraguan Resistance
PSC—Social Christian Party
PSN—Nicaraguan Socialist Party (communist party)
P—Proletariat Tendency
PTN—Nicaraguan Workers Party
SAIMSA—Industrial Agricultural Services of Masaya
TI—Third Tendency or *terceristas*
UDEL—Democratic Union of Liberation
UN—United Nations
UNAG—National Union of Farmers and Ranchers
UNO—National Opposition Union
UPCA—United Provinces of Central America
USAID—United States Agency for International Development

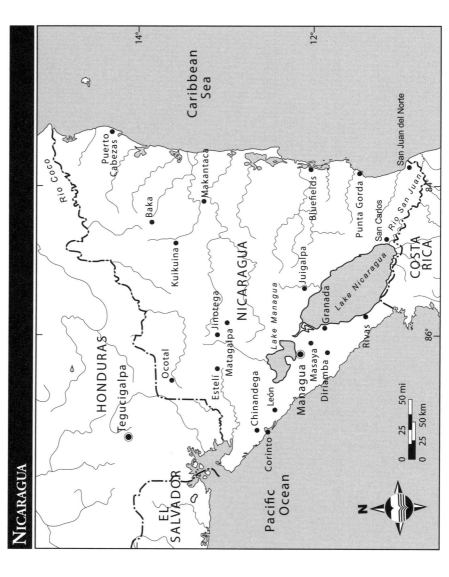

1

Nicaragua and Its People

On January 10, 2007, a balding Daniel Ortega Saavedra of the Sandinista National Liberation Front (FSLN) was sworn in as president of Nicaragua for the second time in 22 years. Dressed in his now signature white shirt with the sleeves rolled up to his elbows, Ortega's once radical rhetoric was nearly absent as he promised moderate economic policies and a desire to work with the United States. His second inauguration received little attention in the United States. This was in stark contrast to the almost daily front-page coverage that the fatigue-clad Ortega and his fellow Sandinistas received during the political upheavals in the late 1970s and throughout the 1980s. In 1979 a broad-based revolution led by the Sandinistas toppled a corrupt, U.S.-supported, family dynasty that had ruled the country since the 1930s. Ortega was elected to the presidency for the first time in 1984 in the middle of a brutal civil war. The civil war devastated the Nicaraguan economy, exhausted its people, divided families, and fueled one of the last Cold War struggles. President Ronald Reagan and the United States intervened politically, economically, and militarily for eight years and failed in an overt attempt to topple the Sandinista-led government.

Since those times the country has changed significantly. Civil war has been replaced by political stability and periodic, competitive, and free national and local elections. Peaceful transfers of power between different parties have become the norm. In 1990 *Nicas* rejected the revolutionary rule of Ortega and the FSLN and turned to the matriarch of the country, Violeta Barrios de Chamorro, leader of a 14-party National Opposition Union (UNO). In 1996 the country elected the populist but corrupt José Arnoldo Alemán Lacayo, the leader of the right wing alliance. In 2001 the country elected Enrique José Bolaños Geyer, also leader of the right wing alliance, to the presidency. In November 2006 *Nicas* once again turned to the FSLN with its new motto of "without hunger, without poverty." In a country that lacks many of the characteristics typically found in stable democracies, it is clear that a "democratic consciousness has taken hold."[1]

Yet, in other ways Nicaragua has not changed. Stephen Kinzer states that ". . . the great challenge of Nicaraguan national life—how to provide people with decent lives—remains unanswered."[2] Widespread, chronic poverty has never been solved and tremendous economic inequality is most evident. Much of the history of this beautiful, yet tragic country can be summed up by Leonardo Zeledon, a former Nicaraguan resistance or *contra* leader during the 1980s civil war, who stated in an interview with the author in 1995 that, "No one here [in Nicaragua] breathes without the lung of the United States." Whether it is because of the Americans, the British, or the Spanish, Nicaragua has rarely been able to control its own destiny. The search for gold, silver, and emeralds brought the Spanish. The California gold rush, the development of a cross-isthmus trade route, and growing interest in the development of a canal connecting the Caribbean to the Pacific Ocean brought both the U.S. and British interests. The periodic civil wars between the liberal and conservative parties brought the United States as political arbiter, occupier, and stabilizer. The U.S. occupation of the country between 1912 and 1933 left a legacy of overt intervention, served to mobilize Augusto César Sandino's peasant and worker army against the United States, and provided both a national hero and a symbol for the 1979 Sandinista-led revolution. The cotton boom of the 1950s and 1960s and the Cold War brought the United States even more closely associated with the Somoza family dictatorship. The Sandinista revolution that toppled the youngest son of the Somoza dynasty, Anastasio Somoza Debayle, brought the country more overt intervention from the United States. Nicaragua has become more independent of the major powers than at any time in its history with the end of the Cold War and the post 9/11 terrorist threat to the United States. Ironically, the market and financial forces of today's global economy have entangled and limited the possibilities of the country probably more than at any time in its history.

THE GEOGRAPHY OF NICARAGUA

Nicaragua, slightly smaller than the state of New York, is the largest country in Central America. Its name is taken from the words *Nicarao* and *agua*. *Nicarao* was the name of the chief of a group of indigenous peoples living between Lake Nicaragua and the Pacific Ocean in the early 1500s near what is today the city of Rivas. *Agua* is the Spanish word for water and refers to Lake Nicaragua. The country is bordered by Honduras and the Gulf of Fonseca to its north, Costa Rica to its south, the Pacific Ocean to its west, and the Caribbean Sea to its east. Managua, located on the southern shores of Lake Managua, became the capital as a result of a political compromise between the rival political groups from the cities of León and Granada. Today, the Managua region is home to 27 percent of the country's 5.8 million people.

There are three primary geographic regions in the country. The Pacific coastal plains or lowlands are the most economically developed region and home to the vast majority of the country's population and its major cities. The more temperate climate with moderate and seasonal rains coupled with rich soils derived from volcanic ash allowed for the development of commercial agriculture such as cotton, coffee, sugar, and rice. The soils of the central highlands or mountains that run from the northwest to the southeast of the country are suitable primarily for the growth of coffee. The Caribbean lowlands make up more than one-half of the country, yet are home only to about 8 percent of the total population. It is the least economically developed area of the country. The region receives a tremendous amount of rainfall and is made up of hot and humid tropical rain forests, savannahs, and swamps. The rivers are subject to heavy flooding during the rainy season from May through October and tropical storms are common from July through October. The Caribbean coast of Nicaragua is often referred to as the Mosquito Coast.

Nicaragua is home to the two largest lakes in Central America, both believed to have been part of the Pacific Ocean at one time. Lake Managua, often referred to as Lake Xolotlan, with an area of 400 square miles is polluted with sewage, pesticides, and other toxic contaminants including mercury. From 1968 to the early 1990s, the U.S.-based Penwalt Corporation dumped more than 90 tons of mercury into the lake.[3] Lake Managua empties into the Tipitapa River which flows into Lake Nicaragua. Lake Nicaragua, often referred to as Lake Cocibolca, with an area of 3,100 square miles is the largest body of fresh water in Central America and the second largest in all of Latin America. It is much like an inland sea with many islands, winds blowing from the northeast, and large waves. It is also known for its periodic, large, and intense storms. The lake is home to freshwater sharks, swordfish, tuna, and tarpon. It empties into the San Juan River and eventually spills into the Caribbean Sea. The western shore of Lake Nicaragua near Rivas is about 14 miles from the Pacific Ocean, and British and U.S. interest in the construction of a cross-isthmus canal in this area can be traced to the 1840s.

In addition to its lakes, the country is known for its volcanoes and earthquakes. A chain of active and nonactive volcanoes is located along the Pacific coast. Consiguina volcano is located in the far northwest of the country and one can see across the Gulf of Fonseca to El Salvador and Honduras from the edge of its crater. Its eruption in 1835 was so powerful that ashes came down as far away as Mexico City and Jamaica. Nicaragua's national symbol, the cone-shaped volcano Momotombo located on the northwestern shore of Lake Managua, was celebrated by the country's most famous poet and literary figure, Rubén Dario. Its eruption in 1610 forced the inhabitants of the original city of León to physically move the city westward to a new location. It last erupted in 1905. Other volcanoes of note include Mombacho located near the city of Granada on the western shore of Lake Nicaragua and Masaya which is surrounded by a national park and is easily accessible. Samuel Clemens, better known as Mark Twain, traveled across Nicaragua in 1867 and introduced Americans to the volcanoes Concepcion and Maderas located on Ometepa Island in Lake Nicaragua. He described them as "two magnificent pyramids, clad in the softest and richest green . . . so isolated from the world and its turmoil."[4] There were significant earthquakes on the Pacific side of the country in 1931, 1951, 1972, 1992, 2004, and 2005. The 1931 earthquake and subsequent fires destroyed Managua and the city had to be rebuilt. The massive December 1972 earthquake destroyed much of the downtown area of Managua, killed an estimated 10,000 people, and left more than 300,000 homeless.

THE PEOPLE, CULTURE, AND SOCIETY OF NICARAGUA

Most of the country is sparsely populated with the majority of the people living on the Pacific coastal plains. Fifty-eight percent of the population lives in urban areas. Nicaragua's ethnic makeup is 69 percent mestizo (mixed indigenous peoples and white European), 17 percent European or white, 9 percent black, and 5 percent indigenous peoples. The vast majority (97.5 percent) speak Spanish although English and other languages, such as Miskito, can be found in the Caribbean lowlands. Although most (73 percent) Nicaraguans are Roman Catholic, there is a growing Evangelical presence (15.1 percent) with a variety of other religions being practiced. Those *Nicas* who live in the Caribbean lowlands have always been geographically, religiously, linguistically, culturally, ethnically, and politically distinct from the Spanish-heritage majority who live in the Pacific plains and central highlands. Many, such as the Miskito, Sumu, and Rama, are descended from the indigenous peoples or the Africans who were brought to the area as slaves by the British. Many are Protestant, primarily Moravian, and many speak English.

The Roman Catholic Church has historically played a major role in the shaping of Nicaraguan culture, society, class structure, education, and the political processes. The most important national religious festival is *La Purisima*. The weeklong celebration ends on December 8 and honors the Immaculate Conception of Mary. People construct altars in honor of the Virgin Mary and place them in front of or just inside their homes. Children will often walk from house to house visiting these altars and singing songs to the Virgin. In return they receive gifts of food or sweets. Almost all cities and towns in Nicaragua have their own patron saint. City festivals to honor these saints, such as the Feast of Saint Dominic in Managua and the Saint Jerome Festival in Masaya, are common and are characterized by colorful parades, fireworks, dancing, music, food, bullfights, horseracing, cockfight tournaments, and crowded streets. They often involve mock battles and imitations of characters in Spanish folklore. *Nicas* typically view saints as mediators between themselves and God. Pictures and small shrines dedicated to particular saints are commonly found in many homes.

For much of the history of Nicaragua the Roman Catholic Church supported policies that favored the wealthy elite over the poor. It tolerated or supported many of the repressive and unjust policies put in place by the country's political elites. Yet, there is a history of priests speaking out against injustice dating back to the early 1500s with Bartolomé de las Casas and Antonio de Valdivieso. More recently Jesuit priests Fernando and Ernesto Cardenal and Edgar Parrales, Maryknoll priest Miguel D'Escoto, and former Archbishop of Managua Miguel Obando y Bravo of the Salesian order played major roles in the struggle against the Somoza family dynasty. Obando then came to speak out against the revolutionary government of the Sandinistas and its policies.

It is often said that all *Nicas* are considered to be poets until they prove differently and Nicaragua has a very distinguished literary tradition. The country's most famous satirical play and its first pre-Columbian literary work (author unknown), *El Gueguense*, which reflects the clash of Spanish and indigenous cultures, can be observed during the Festival of San Sebastian in the city of Diriamba each January. The play, consisting of music, dance, and theater, is recognized internationally and has become a symbol of Nicaraguan defiance, resistance, and nationalism. In addition to Dario, the father of Latin America's first literary tradition "modernism," and José Coronel Urtecho, who led the Vanguardia Literary Movement of the 1920s, writers such as Alfonso Cortés, Pablo Antonio Cuadra, Pedro Joaquín Chamorro, Ernesto Cardenal, Sergio Ramirez, and Gioconda Belli are also recognized worldwide.

Even with this significant literary tradition, the lack of access to education for all *Nicas* and the problem of illiteracy have been historical constants. At the time of the Sandinista revolution in 1979, the national illiteracy rate for those older than 15 years of age was estimated to be at 50 percent. By 1982 the "Literacy Crusade" led by Fernando Cardenal had reduced illiteracy to about 12 percent nationally. Today the illiteracy rate is about 32 percent. It is worth noting that one-third of the country's 5.8 million people are under the age of 14. Although schooling is free and mandatory for both elementary and high school students, the majority only finish elementary school. Hidden costs consisting of school uniforms, books, and other materials often make it difficult, if not impossible, for *Nica* families who typically have several children.

Family life can be very difficult in Nicaragua largely due to poverty. Children work at a very early age selling gum or trinkets on street corners or in the local, open-air markets. Many work before and after attending school. Households are typically large and the presence of a grandmother, uncle, godchild, or a daughter with her own child in addition to the nuclear family is quite common. Family and extended family or kinship ties are extremely important in Nicaraguan society. In difficult economic times, extended family networks may provide a security net such as access to a small piece of land in the countryside or employment in the urban areas. Family networks also determine social class and economic and political ties. It is for this reason that lower-class families will attempt to select godparents who are from a higher social or economic class. Thus, they are in a position to help pay for schooling or to find employment that could possibly raise the child out of poverty. In return, godparents receive personal loyalty, prestige, and political support if needed.

This informal, mutual exchange of benefits between a person or family of more power or higher status and another person or family of less power or lower status is often referred to as a patron-client relationship and is a characteristic that one can find throughout the social, economic, and political systems of Nicaragua and Latin America in general. For example, a peasant family is allowed to live on a small piece of land on a large estate. On that land the family has access to housing, can grow its own crops for food, and possibly receive medical care, religious training, and schooling for the children through the "kindness" of the landowner. The landowner may even become a godparent to the children. In return, the landowner receives prestige, labor for his estate agriculture, and political support during elections. These relationships promote stability in the rural areas. Also, there are local party bosses who live in virtually all urban neighborhoods or *barrios* in Nicaragua. The party boss has ties to a major party which gives him access to resources. He is able to dole out resources to his neighbors. These resources may be jobs, scholarships for students, or obtaining trash pick-up, clean water, or other basic services for the neighborhood. In return, the local party boss receives prestige and political support. These patron-client relationships tend to create security and stability with each person or family getting what it needs or wants. Secure patron-client relationships tend to bring about stability in the social, economic, and political systems. When these relationships break down, insecurity and instability often follow. For example, in the 1950s and 1960s Nicaragua shifted to modern agricultural techniques that required the shift to wage labor on the large estates. Peasant families became insecure because they lost access to housing, land, and food on which they depended. This insecurity was a cause of the increasing political instability and the growing opposition to the Somoza dynasty throughout the 1960s and 1970s.[5]

National heroes are often born during periods of instability and military conflict. *Nica* national heroes include the Indian chief Diriangen who fought the Spanish in the early 1500s, Benjamin Zeledón and Augusto César Sandino who fought the U.S. occupying forces in the early part of the twentieth century, and more recently Pedro Joaquín Chamorro and Carlos Fonseca Amador who fought against the U.S.-supported, Somoza family dictatorship. *Nicas* are typically hard-working, warm, outgoing, and extremely generous. They love to poke fun at political leaders, priests, Americans, and just about anyone in a powerful position. They can be most irreverent, yet at the same time quite often will use the title *don* or *doña* in front of the names of people for whom they have respect.

Cockfighting is common and draws people from virtually every segment of Nicaraguan society, rich and poor, powerful and weak, to small arenas throughout the country on weekends. The violent sport was brought to the country by the Spanish and is very much still a part of the *Nica* culture today. Many members of the National Assembly are *galleros* or those who raise, train, and fight game roosters. *Nicas* are also passionate baseball fans and the first teams were organized by U.S. businessmen in the 1880s. Almost every town has a baseball field and there is a professional league in the country. It is not uncommon to see kids playing ball in the street, in an alley, or in an open field. They are extremely proud of their countrymen who have been able to play major league baseball in the United States with the most famous being Denis Martinez. Others include Marvin Benard, Vicente Padilla, and Albert Williams. Many baseball fans remember that former Pittsburg Pirate and Hall of Fame member Roberto Clemente, although not a *Nica*, died in a plane crash trying to fly relief supplies to the earthquake victims in Managua in 1972. The baseball stadium in Masaya is named after Clemente.

THE POLITICAL SYSTEM OF NICARAGUA

For much of its history, politics in Nicaragua reflected the competition for control of the government between the elite families of León and Granada. The families of León came to be represented by the Liberal Party and the families of Granada came to be represented by the Conservative Party. Control of the government was often settled by force and the families were not above asking the United States or Great Britain to intervene in support of one or the other. Granada, because of its key location on Lake Nicaragua, quickly became the commercial center of the country. The list of elite families of Granada reads like a who's who of Nicaragua: Cuadra, Chamorro, Cardenal, Carrion, Lacayo, Guzman, Pellas, Zavala, and others. Even the revolutionary Sandinistas had ties to the conservative families of Granada who for so many years had opposed rule by the Liberal Party and, in particular, the Somozas who ruled from 1937 to 1979.[6] León, which for much of the history of the country was unable to compete with the commercial power of Granada, became the legal, intellectual, educational, and ecclesiastical center of the country. Families such as Sacasa and Somoza are the best known elite families but the Gurdian, Icaza, Vijil, and Teran families became prominent around León and Chinandega with the cotton boom of the 1950s. Although the competition between León and Granada no longer defines the politics of the country, elite families still play primary roles in the political parties, governing institutions, and major businesses.

Nicaragua has largely been under authoritarian governments since its colonial era and it has a long history of violent, repressive governments. Mass poverty, a history of elite conflict and elite-led civil wars, a history of authoritarianism, and a major socialist-oriented revolution have made the country a very unlikely candidate to develop a democratic political system. Interestingly enough, it was the Sandinista-led revolution with its grassroots, mobilized participatory political processes that helped to set the stage for the transition to the stable, largely democratic government of today.[7] The country has held successful elections since 1984 with different parties coming to power and leaving peacefully when defeated in the next election. Defying the odds, democratic practices have taken hold in Nicaragua despite the tremendous poverty and economic and social inequalities.

Today the country is a republic and functions under the constitution adopted in 1987 and amended in 1995, 2000, and 2005. It is divided into 15 departments and two autonomous regions located in the Caribbean lowlands. The president is elected to a five-year term and is eligible for a second term as long as it is not consecutive. The Council of Ministers or cabinet is appointed by the president. The unicameral or one-house National Assembly consists of 92 members. One seat is reserved for the previous president and one seat for the runner-up in the presidential election. The other 90 seats are based on a proportional representation scheme in which each party or coalition receives the percentage of seats equal to the percentage of votes that its presidential candidate receives in the election. Currently the FSLN holds 38 seats, the Liberal Constitutionalist Party (PLC) holds 25 seats, the Nicaraguan Liberal Alliance (ALN) holds 22 seats, and the Sandinista Renovation Movement (MRS) holds 5 seats. There are 18 minor parties that did not receive enough votes to be able to hold seats in the National Assembly. In 2005 the constitution was amended to allow the National Assembly to override a presidential veto by a simple majority vote. The 16-member Supreme Court is selected by the National Assembly. Labor groups in the country are represented by the National Worker's Front (FNT) which is a group of eight Sandinista unions and the Permanent Congress of Workers (CPT) consisting of four non-Sandinista unions. The National Workers Central is an independent union. Business groups are represented through the Superior Council of Private Enterprise (COSEP).

THE ECONOMY OF NICARAGUA

Tomás Borge, one of the founders of the FSLN, referred to Nicaragua not only as the "land of corn . . . corn that grows in unfertile soil, corn that rises up to defy the sun" but also as the "land of coffee . . . red coffee, black coffee."[8] The economy of the country has always been based on agriculture. For most peasants living in rural areas corn, rice, and beans are the basic subsistence crops. The wealthy elites of the country have traditionally pursued what is known as the agro-export model of development. Agricultural crops such as coffee, sugar, rice, and cotton are grown on large estates almost exclusively for export. These are often referred to as cash crops. To be successful this requires access to large amounts of land, control of the labor force, and a large foreign market for the crops. Since colonial times land had been distributed unequally in the country and as cash crops became increasingly important to the growth of the economy, the elites found both legal and illegal ways to claim more and more land, at the expense of the Catholic Church, the rural poor, and indigenous peoples. The coffee boom of the late 1800s and the cotton boom of the 1950s witnessed a growing concentration of land in the hands of the wealthy.[9] This contributed to the growing number of Nicaraguans who joined the ranks of the low wage, seasonally employed, landless poor. In a country in which most wealth is determined by the ability to grow cash crops, income inequality is primarily a reflection of the inequality found in land owner-ship. It is precisely this land and income inequality that helped to fuel the revolution of 1979 and the land redistribution programs of the Sandinistas in the 1980s.

The revolutionary Sandinistas seized the vast properties of the Somoza family and its most ardent supporters. In an attempt to create a more egali-tarian economy and society, the FSLN created state-run farms and redis-tributed land to peasants in the form of both cooperatives and private property. Faced with opposition to some of these reforms from within the country, a trade embargo by the United States, the loss of international credit, a costly and brutal civil war that destroyed much of the economic infrastructure, an opposition army supported by the United States, and its own economic mismanagement, some of the primary beneficiaries of the land reform turned against the FSLN in the 1990 presidential election.[10] With a new U.S. president in 1989, the election of Chamorro as president in 1990, the negotiated end to the civil war, an end to the U.S. embargo, and renewed access to international credit, the country returned to the more orthodox agro-export model of development in 1990.

The major products of Nicaragua today are coffee, bananas, sugarcane, cotton, rice, corn, tobacco, beef, veal, pork, poultry, dairy products, shrimp, and lobsters. The country has some light industries including food process-ing, chemicals, textiles, clothing, beverages, and footwear. Its primary exports are coffee, beef, shrimp and lobster, tobacco, and sugar. Most of its exports go to the United States, El Salvador, and Honduras although its primary imports are consumer goods, machinery and equipment, and petroleum products from the United States, Mexico, Venezuela, Costa Rica, Guatemala, and China.

Like many of the poorer countries of Latin America and the remainder of the world, Nicaragua has established several export trade zones as part of a national economic development strategy. The purpose of these so-called *zonas francas* is to encourage foreign investment and to provide employment in the country. There are about 120 mostly U.S. and Asian firms in the state-run Las Mercedes export trade zone located near the air-port in Managua and several other privately run export trade zones. Firms that invest in these *zonas francas* receive significant tax advantages. Most firms are textile and apparel assembly plants called *maquiladoras*. Textiles and apparels exported to the United States are not subject to taxes. These *maquiladoras* employ mostly young females. Workers typically make more than the minimum wage of the country but the wage will not pay the basic monthly food costs for a family.

Nicaragua has one of the lowest per capita incomes in the western hemisphere with an unemployment and underemployment rate estimated to be greater than 50 percent. Today it is estimated that 45 percent of the population survives on less than one dollar a day. Income inequality is dramatic with the United Nations (UN) reporting that the top 10 percent of the population receives almost 50 percent of the national income while the bottom 40 percent of the population receives less than 10 percent of the national income. One-third of the children suffer from malnutrition.

THE FUTURE

Nicaragua continues to face an uncertain future. Although democratic processes have been developing for more than 20 years, the country has been unable to solve its pervasive poverty. It continues to be at the mercy of international economic forces that it cannot control. While the Central American Free Trade Agreement has been in effect since 2004, the current decline in global demand for its products has caused incomes to fall. Economic infrastructure projects such as roads and bridges are largely funded through foreign aid from countries such as the United States, Germany, and Japan. The current downturn in the world economy is a threat to continued access to this aid. Although published in 1888, Dario's first book of poems and prose, *Azul*, is as relevant today as it was then. Reading it one feels the sadness, the sense of the frustrations of those who fight against the status quo and seek the ideal, yet Dario still conveys a sense of hope. *Nicas* continue today to struggle against the status quo, the pervasive poverty, with little change, yet somehow they remain ever hopeful and resilient.

NOTES

1. Stephen Kinzer, *Blood of Brothers: Life and War in Nicaragua* (Cambridge: Harvard University Press, 2007), 404. See also Leslie Anderson and Lawrence C. Dodd, *Learning Democracy: Citizen Engagement and Electoral Choice in Nicaragua, 1990–2001* (Chicago: University of Chicago Press, 2005), 39–40.

2. Kinzer, *Blood of Brothers: Life and War in Nicaragua*, 395.

3. Jennifer Clapp, *Toxic Exports* (Ithaca: Cornell University Press, 2001), 117.

4. This quote was taken from an article first published on March 16, 1867, in the newspaper *San Francisco Alta California*. The quote was found at the Web site, Mark Twain: Quotations, Newspapers, Collections, and Related Sources. http://www.twainquotes.com/18670316.html (accessed February 20, 2009).

5. Charles D. Brockett, *Land, Power, and Poverty*, 2nd ed. (Boulder, CO: Westview Press, 1998), 68–98.

6. Carlos M. Vilas, "Family Affairs: Class, Lineage and Politics in Contemporary Nicaragua," *Journal of Latin American Studies* 24:2 (May 1992): 322.

7. Anderson and Dodd, *Learning Democracy*, 32–75.

8. Tomás Borge, *The Patient Impatience* (Willimantic, CT: Curbstone Press, 1992), 22.

9. Laura Enriquez, *Harvesting Change* (Chapel Hill: University of North Carolina Press, 1991), 26–27, 34–35.

10. Laura Enriquez, *Agrarian Reform and Class Consciousness in Nicaragua* (Gainesville: University Press of Florida, 1997), 31–57.

2

Pre-colonial, Colonial, and Early Independence (4000 BC–1856)

Many of the continuing characteristics of Nicaraguan history, politics, economics, and society were developed during this time period. The indigenous peoples of Nicaragua were almost wiped out after the first century of colonial rule by the Spanish. Ignored by the Crown, Nicaragua quickly became a sleepy colonial backwater with two major cities, León and Granada. Granada quickly established itself as the commercial center of the country largely due to its location on Lake Nicaragua. The cities became political rivals and virtual city-states engaged in a constant struggle to control the country. It was during this period that the dramatic cultural, political, and economic separation between western Nicaragua and its Caribbean coast developed. The Spanish settled in the more hospitable and economically viable Pacific coastal plains and lowlands and ignored the largely inhospitable Caribbean lowlands. The agro-export strategy of economic growth began to take shape. The significance of the geographic position of Nicaragua was recognized by the Spanish as soon as they discovered that one could travel from the Caribbean at San Juan del Norte, up the San Juan River, and into Lake Nicaragua. The western shore of Lake Nicaragua near the city of Rivas is approximately 14 miles from the Pacific Ocean. The

Spanish recognized the possibility of building a canal but never carried out the idea. Independence from Spain did not change the primary contours of the liberal-conservative struggle for power to control Nicaragua and this struggle would eventually draw in both the United States and Great Britain.

PRE-COLONIAL NICARAGUA AND ITS INDIGENOUS POPULATION

The so-called Ancient Footprints of Acahualinca found near the crater lake of Acahualinca in Managua provide evidence of humans inhabiting Nicaragua at least 6,000 years ago. The tracks consist of well-preserved human footprints in petrified volcanic ash and mud. Little is known about the original inhabitants. Peoples in western Nicaragua migrated southward from Mexico and arrived several centuries prior to the Spanish. They spoke the Pipil language which is closely related to the Nahuatl language spoken by the Aztecs. Similar to the early inhabitants of Mexico, they drank chocolate, raised turkeys and dogs for their meat, and their staple foods were corn, beans, squash, chili peppers, and avocados. There is some dispute as to the origins of the early inhabitants of the Caribbean lowlands. Some argue that they migrated from South America although other evidence indicates that they migrated from Mexico.[1] These semi-nomadic groups lacked permanent settlements and engaged largely in hunting and fishing. They cultivated limited amounts of arrowroot, manioc, and dates. Later these groups in the Caribbean lowlands engaged in slash-and-burn agriculture. Their staple foods were cassava, sweet potatoes, plantains, and pineapples. They traded with and were influenced by the peoples of the Caribbean which was evident in the thatched round huts in which they lived and the canoes that they used.

There were three principal groups of indigenous peoples living in the western part of the country when the Spanish arrived: the Choretegano or Chorotegas (sometimes referred to as Mangues), the Niquirano or Nicaraos, and the Chontal. The Chorotegas arrived in Nicaragua between the fourth and ninth centuries from Mexico. The cities of the Chorotegas had central plazas with market places and religious centers. They had an organized military and sacrificed slaves for religious purposes. Entire family clans lived in long houses consisting of wood with thatched roofs. They left large basalt figures on the islands of Zapatera and Ometepe in Lake Nicaragua. The cities of Diria and Diriamba both claim to be the home of the legendary Chorotega warrior chief Diriangen who was immortalized in Carlos Mejía Godoy's famous revolutionary love song *Nicaragua, Nicaraguita*. The Nicaraos arrived around the thirteenth century. They were successful in agriculture and developed trade ties with other indigenous peoples in

Mexico and Peru. The most famous of the Nicaraos, chief Nicarao for whom the country is named, lived in the city of Nicaraocali, now called Rivas. It is not known when the Chontal arrived in Nicaragua.

When the Spanish arrived, the Nicaraos were found on the isthmus of Rivas between Lake Nicaragua and the Pacific Ocean. The Chorotegas lived largely in the central part of the country between Lake Managua and Lake Nicaragua. The Chontal lived east of Lakes Managua and Nicaragua in the central highlands of the country in what are today the departments of Boaco, Chontales, and Matagalpa. The best estimate of the number of indigenous peoples living in Nicaragua at the time of the conquest is about 825,000.[2] By 1581 there were only 50,000 to 60,000 remaining.[3] Although mistreatment and cruelty by the Spaniards and death from fighting contributed to this dramatic depopulation, the primary reasons were slavery and exposure to "European" diseases such as measles and influenza.

Nicaragua's primary economic activity from 1527 to 1542 was the export of indigenous peoples as slaves to Panama and Peru. The Spanish Crown's policy toward the enslavement of the indigenous peoples was ambiguous. When Pope Alexander VI gave Spain the right to colonize the New World in 1493 he stated that the Spanish should convert the indigenous peoples to Christianity and he prohibited their enslavement. At the same time he stated that if the indigenous peoples refused to convert to Christianity or once converted they reverted back to their old religious practices they could be enslaved. This ambiguity allowed the power-seeking Spanish conquistadors to enslave hundreds of thousands of indigenous peoples via the *encomienda* system that had originally been used by the Spanish against the Moors (Muslims). The Crown gave the conquistadors some of the land that they conquered including its inhabitants, and this was referred to as *encomienda*. The inhabitants provided labor for the conquistador in return for religious instruction and safety. The Spanish also viewed the forced labor practiced by the indigenous peoples in Nicaragua to be a form of slavery, and this provided another justification for their own expansion and export of slavery. It is estimated that 500,000 indigenous peoples were exported from the country as slaves from 1527 to 1542.[4] When the slave trade ended in 1550, "there were simply no Indians left" to export.[5] The Dominican Friar Bartolomé de las Casas and Bishop of León Antonio de Valdivieso spoke out against the mistreatment, cruelty, and slavery to which the Spanish subjected the indigenous peoples.

THE SPANISH CONQUEST AND EARLY COLONIAL NICARAGUA

As many have pointed out the primary motives for the Spanish conquest of the Americas were to enrich the Crown, its colonial administration, and the colonists and to convert people to Christianity. In 1501 Rodrigo de Bastidas and Vasco Núñez de Balboa arrived in Panama. Pedro Arias de Ávila or Pedrarias came from Spain in 1514 as the new Governor of Panama or the area that was then called *Castilla del Oro*. On orders from Pedrarias, Gil Gonzalez Davila left Panama in 1522 with a small group of Spaniards and traveled through Costa Rica into the isthmus of Rivas and southwestern Nicaragua. Gonzalez converted thousands of people to Catholicism, found Lake Nicaragua, and received quantities of gold from some of the indigenous peoples. He met and spoke with chief Nicarao. Not all the indigenous peoples submitted to the Spanish. Chief Diriangen and approximately 3,000 Chorotega warriors chased Gonzalez and his men back to their ships along the Pacific. In 1524 Pedrarias then sent Francisco Hernández de Córdoba into Nicaragua and he founded the cities of León and Granada. Rather than reporting back to Pedrarias in Panama, Córdoba plotted with Hernán Cortés in Mexico to be appointed the Governor of Nicaragua. Pedrarias heard of the plan and charged Córdoba with treason. He was arrested and executed. This was just the beginning of the political intrigue that characterized the early colonial years of Nicaragua.

León became the capital of the province of Nicaragua and housed all the major political appointees and the Catholic Bishop. Pedrarias was appointed Governor of Nicaragua in 1527 and arrived in León the following year. He had agricultural machinery brought in and began cultivating grains and fruits. He introduced pigs, sheep, mules, and cattle to the region. Pedrarias ruled with great cruelty toward the indigenous peoples and came to be known as "God's Wrath." By 1530 many Spanish settlers had left Nicaragua to join Francisco Pizarro in the colonization and pillage of the Incan Empire in Peru. Pedrarias died in 1531 and Francisco de Castaneda became Governor. Castaneda ruled for three years and continued the mistreatment and cruelty toward the indigenous peoples. Because of these abuses, the Spanish Crown appointed Rodrigo de Contreras as Governor and ordered Castaneda to be put on trial. Contreras attempted to stop the most blatant abuses toward the indigenous peoples held *encomienda*.

In 1542 the Spanish Crown passed a series of laws designed to protect the indigenous peoples from abuses. They could no longer be taken as slaves or used as beasts of burden, and could no longer be held *encomienda*. The Crown put Contreras under investigation for his mistreatment of indigenous peoples at the insistence of Bishop Valdivieso. Contreras traveled to Spain in 1548 in a failed attempt to defend himself, retain control of his *encomienda*, and retain much of his wealth. In his absence Contreras' wife encouraged his sons, Hernando and Pedro, to seize power. They were also supported by several conquistadors who had supported Gonzalo Pizarro in his ill-fated rebellion in Peru in 1546. Hernando Contreras murdered Bishop Valdivieso in 1550. The brothers, now in control of Nicaragua, moved into Panama and defeated the loyalist forces at Panama City. The Panamanian militias refused to yield, rose up against the Contreras brothers, and defeated and killed them in battle.

In 1543 Spain reorganized its colonies in the Americas. It created the Viceroyalty of New Spain which covered all the land from northern Panama into the United States as well as the Caribbean and part of Venezuela. Its capital was Mexico City. New Spain was further divided into smaller geographic units called *audiencias* or courts and Nicaragua was under the *Audiencia de los Confines* which covered most of Central America. The head of each *audiencia* was appointed by the Spanish Crown and was referred to as the Captain General. Each province was headed by a local Governor. One should note that because of the vast distance between Spain and its colonies, government in Spanish America was largely a local affair and decrees from the Crown were often ignored.

One of Balboa's men, Álvaro de Saavedra Cerón, surveyed the area from 1517 through 1529 and was the first to discuss the possibility of a canal from Lake Nicaragua to the Pacific Ocean. He died before he could recommend it to King Charles V (also known as Charles I or Carlos I of Spain). Pedrarias had also investigated the possibility of a canal to the Pacific Ocean but never followed up on the idea. It was during Contreras' rule in 1539 that the Spanish made the significant discovery that Lake Nicaragua spilled into the San Juan River which emptied into the Caribbean Sea. This was significant because it paved the way for the development of a trade route across the isthmus and the growth of Granada as the commercial center of Nicaragua. Phillip II (son of Charles V) ordered an investigation into the possibility of constructing a canal from Lake Nicaragua to the Pacific. He abandoned the idea in 1567 because it was feared that a water route across the isthmus would make it easier for the Portuguese and the French to cause trouble with Spain's gold and silver mines in Peru. Phillip II also believed that the construction of a canal would somehow upset the divinely who ordained balance of nature in the region.

Nicaragua had already become a colonial backwater by 1570 when it came under the *Audiencia de Guatemala*. It lacked the riches found in the other Spanish colonies and it had been depopulated of most of its indigenous peoples by this time. The decision not to pursue a canal to the Pacific meant that it would not attract a large number of Spanish settlers. Those who remained began carving out a living for themselves on ranches or *fincas*. Much of what they produced such as corn, beans, and cattle was for their own consumption although some products were for export such as cacao which is used to make cocoa, indigo which is used to make blue dye, cochineal which is used to make red dye, and animal hides. By the end of the 1600s the cacao boom ended largely due to increasing competition, depleted orchards, and the lack of knowledge concerning the preservation of orchards and the development of new orchards by the Spanish. The trade in indigo and cochineal was also severely limited because the small Spanish market and Spanish trade policies made it illegal to trade directly with larger markets in other European countries.

In 1610 the city of León was destroyed when the volcano Momotombo erupted. The city was literally rebuilt 20 miles to the west of the original site. The plains around the city of León made it the center of ranching in the early years. Because of the city of Granada's location, it became the logical choice for many merchants who were engaged in trade with the West Indies and Spain. The primary economic activities around the city were the tobacco and cacao plantations, as well as cattle and donkey breeding.

Throughout the 1600s, England, France, and the Dutch competed with Spain for control of the Caribbean and for colonies. The European countries created their own buccaneers (mercenaries who engaged in piracy during nonwar periods) and attacked each other's settlements and colonies. Spanish cities were under threat of attack and even a backwater colony like Nicaragua was not immune, especially the small settlements on the Caribbean or Mosquito Coast and the city of Granada. In 1633 a Dutch buccaneer, Abraham Blaauvelt, built a settlement on the Mosquito Coast and allied with the local indigenous peoples who did not like the Spanish. These people came to be known as the Miskito Indians and the settlement came to be known as Bluefields. It became a rendezvous point for both British and Dutch buccaneers. The British had established a thriving trade in logwood (used to make dyes) along the Mosquito Coast by the mid-1600s and the trade grew considerably to the point that it generated considerable conflict with Spain. The British created a protectorate along the Mosquito Coast in 1678 with Bluefields as its capital. They introduced slaves into the area and appointed the Indian Chief Oldman I as the first monarch of the Miskito Kingdom. Ongoing conflict between Britain and Spain (and later Britain and Nicaragua) over control of the Mosquito Coast would continue until the end of the 1800s.

In 1664 the English buccaneer Henry Morgan and others aided by the Miskito Indians attacked and looted the city of Granada. Morgan returned with Edward Mansvelt in 1666 and traveled up the San Juan River and across Lake Nicaragua in a fleet of canoes. They looted and burned the city. Granada was attacked in 1685 by the French buccaneer Le Sieur Raveneau de Lussan. By the end of the century Spain, England, and France had recognized the loss in potential revenues and agreed to end the buccaneer era, although this did not end their competition for the economic resources of the region.

COLONIAL NICARAGUA—LEÓN AND GRANADA AND WAR

By the 1700s one could see the growth of an agriculturally based economy in Nicaragua. The area around León and Chinandega came to be associated with cattle and the export of animal products such as hides. León came to trade primarily with the other Spanish colonies along the Pacific. The economy of León was also associated with government service, pine products, and ship building. Granada became a center of regional trade with Spain via Lake Nicaragua and the San Juan River. Cattle increasingly became its major export as well. León and Granada came under control of competing elite families. Families in León came to oppose the restrictive trade policies of the Spanish Crown. They preferred a more open, free trade system and came to be known as liberals. The families in Granada who were the primary beneficiaries of the restrictive Spanish trade policies resisted change. They came to be known as conservatives. Over time conservatives also wanted to maintain the pervasive role of the Catholic Church in society with the liberals pushing for a more secular society. Competition between the conservative families of Granada and the liberal families of León became the political norm. This competition, often violent, would last well into the twentieth century and come to define Nicaraguan politics.

Throughout the 1700s, Spain was almost constantly at war and this placed tremendous financial strains on its treasury. With the Bourbon family replacing the Hapsburgs on the Spanish throne in the early 1700s, Spanish trade policies became less restrictive. Under the Treaty of Utrecht in 1713 the British were able to send one ship a year to trade with the Spanish colonies. This spurred a growing black market trade with British merchants and their North American colonies. By the middle of the 1700s many Spanish colonies had already established illegal trade ties with other European countries and North America. In 1749 the Spanish Crown sent officials, called *intendentes*, to each province in Spanish America. This new official was not only to oversee the treasury but also promote agricultural exports and development. As trade expanded, creoles (Spaniards born in the colonies) began to see the dramatic potential of expanded economic trade and wanted to have greater control over their trade decisions. This brought them into political conflict with the Spanish Crown and the local *peninsulares* (governing authorities in the colonies who were born in Spain). In 1778 the Bourbon monarch of Spain Charles III liberalized trade policies even more by allowing colonial ports to trade freely among themselves and with any Spanish port. Spanish American trade ties to the United States expanded. In 1797 and again in 1801 the Crown authorized trade between its colonies and neutral countries (countries not at war with

Spain). This allowed an even greater U.S. economic presence in Spanish America.

Conflict continued with the British over its logwood trade on the Mosquito Coast. Spanish naval weakness made it difficult to prevent and, it recognized British access to the tropical woods in the Treaty of Paris in 1763. In an attempt to split the Spanish colonies in the New World, a British force under the leadership of a young Captain Horatio Nelson failed to capture the cities of Granada and León in 1780. By this time the logwood trade had died out and the British agreed to leave the Mosquito Coast in 1786 with the Spanish promise of autonomy for the Miskito Kingdom. The British would return to the coast in the 1840s with the goal of establishing a cross-isthmus trade route.

Never completely forgotten, the idea of a cross-isthmus trade route resurfaced in the 1700s. Charles Marie de la Condamine, the French surveyor of the Amazon River, after visiting the area in 1735 suggested the construction of a canal connecting Lake Nicaragua with the Pacific Ocean. In 1777 the British investigated the idea and in 1779 Charles III of Spain revisited the idea. Count Louis-Hector de Segur of France proposed construction of a canal in 1788, as did the Frenchman Martin de Labastide in 1791. In 1804 the German scientist Alexander von Humbolt also suggested a plan. None of these ideas or plans came to fruition.

INDEPENDENCE, EARLY NICARAGUA, BRITISH AND U.S. INFLUENCE

From 1810 through the mid-1820s Spanish America fought for its independence. Several factors contributed to this struggle for independence. One was the growing resistance to the restrictive trade policies practiced by the Spanish Crown. The gradual reduction in these restrictions throughout the 1700s coupled with a growing black market trade allowed many in Spanish America to see the benefits of trading with the North Americans and other Europeans. Related to this was the increasing desire of the Spanish colonial Creole elite to have a greater say over its political and economic destinies. By 1808 Napoleon Bonaparte of France occupied Spain and placed his brother Joseph on the Spanish Crown. Provincial *juntas* or governing groups and a Central *Junta* were created to lead the Spanish resistance to the French. In 1809 representatives from the colonies were asked to serve on the Central *Junta*. This was the first time that Creoles had been asked to come to Spain and participate in governing. In 1810 a *cortes* or parliament of elected deputies was created. This further raised the political expectations of the Creoles in the colonies. Complaints about the lack of equal representation on the *cortes* and the refusal to adopt policies of free trade contributed to the frustrations among the Creole elite. The new Constitution of 1812 created a constitutional monarchy, even though Ferdinand was not yet back on the throne. When Ferdinand was restored to the throne in 1814 the dreams of Spanish Creoles exercising real political power were dashed when he abrogated the 1812 Constitution. Ferdinand sent troops to Spanish America in 1814 in an attempt to quell the growing independence movement. Eventually all of Spanish America would gain its independence by the mid-1820s.

In Nicaragua, the city of Rivas staged the first uprising against Spanish rule in 1811. The rebellion was brutally repressed by troops from Costa Rica. That same year Miguel Lacayo led a revolt in Granada. Once again the rebellion was defeated and the residents of Granada bore the brunt of the repression. Ironically, the liberals in León remained loyal to the Spanish Crown during these rebellions. In 1821 the *Audiencia de Guatemala* which included Nicaragua declared its independence from Spain. León declared itself independent of Guatemala, while Granada remained loyal. Although they conpeted with each other for control of Nicaragua, León and Granada accepted union with the Mexican Empire under the monarchy of Agustin de Iturbide the following year. With the fall of Iturbide's government in 1823, a large army from León was sent to Granada to prevent its attempt to establish an independent republic. Finally, Central America declared its independence from Mexico that same year and created a government to rule the United Provinces of Central America (UPCA) consisting of Guatemala, Honduras, El Salvador, Nicaragua, and Costa Rica.

The UPCA agreed that the provinces would govern their own internal affairs. Slavery was abolished, suffrage was granted only to the members of the upper class (large landowners and merchants), and the Catholic Church retained its privileges as the official established religion. Salvadoran Manuel José Arce, a conservative, was elected as its first President in 1825. Guatemala City, dominated by conservatives, served as the first capital city. Civil war broke out almost immediately between liberals who favored political and economic systems like the United States and Western Europe and the conservatives who looked to Spain for their political and economic models. Arce sided with the conservatives and attempted to centralize power by removing the heads of state in El Salvador, Honduras, and Guatemala. Honduran General Francisco Morazán led the liberal struggle against the federal forces. He captured Guatemala City in 1829 and the conservatives capitulated. Morazán was elected as President in 1830 and initiated several liberal reforms that were met with immediate hostility from the conservatives. He attempted to deny the Catholic Church some of its privileges such as the monopoly on education. Morazán defeated conservative uprisings in 1831 and 1832 and in 1834 he moved the capital to San Salvador. In 1834 conservative José Cecilio del Valle was elected President. His death that year brought Morazán back to the presidency. Church leaders hysterically blamed outbreaks of cholera and smallpox and the eruption of Consiguina volcano on the liberal government of Morazán. In 1838 the conservative governments of Honduras, Guatemala, and Nicaragua declared their independence from the UPCA and waged a war against Morazán, who was exiled and eventually executed by the government of Costa Rica in 1842.

Life in Nicaragua mirrored the liberal-conservative struggle of the UPCA. Liberal León and conservative Granada, which had become virtual city-states, fought for control of the political processes. The outcome was near political chaos and constant warfare. Nicaragua became an independent state on April 30, 1838. By the 1840s cattle and hides became the primary exports as the western slopes of the central highlands were ideal for raising cattle and other livestock. Vast ranches could be found around Chontales, Matagalpa, and Segovia. The agriculturally based economy produced sugar, cotton, coffee, tobacco, rice, and maize. The liberal-conservative struggle for control of the political system continued. From 1838 through 1854 Nicaragua had 24 different Supreme Directors (the title of chief executive officer at that time). Lawlessness and banditry were common. One of the most notorious bandits was Bernabe Somoza, the great uncle of the head of the future dynasty to rule the country Anastasio Somoza Garcia. E.G. Squier, U.S. envoy to Nicaragua, in his travel commentary in 1849 described Bernabe Somoza as "a tall, graceful man, with a feather in his hat, a red Spanish cloak hanging over his shoulder" a "gentlemanly cutthroat."[6]

By the late 1840s U.S. and British influence in the area had increased dramatically with a renewed focus on a cross-isthmus trade route. An early attempt to construct a canal across the isthmus from the Pacific to Lake Nicaragua in 1826 by the Central American and the American Atlantic and Pacific Canal Company never got started due to lack of funding. The instability of the UPCA, the ongoing political conflict in Nicaragua, the war between Texas and Mexico in the 1830s, and the U.S. war with Mexico in 1848 were the main reasons the U.S. government acted ambivalently toward the development of a cross-isthmus route until 1848. This, by default, paved the way for greater British presence that had surveyed the area in 1823. The British sent Frederick Chatfield in 1834 to negotiate commercial treaties and agreements. In 1847 the British once again declared the Miskito Kingdom a protectorate and the following year they occupied San Juan del Norte and renamed it Greytown. This was significant because the town was the Caribbean point of entrance to the cross-isthmus transit route and proposed canal across Nicaragua. This, coupled with the California gold rush, renewed U.S. interest in Nicaragua, and President Zachary Taylor sent Squier to negotiate a commercial treaty with Nicaragua in 1849. Squier was successful and Cornelius Vanderbilt's American Atlantic and Pacific Ship-Canal Company developed a transit route which consisted of a steamship route up the San Juan River and into Lake Nicaragua. This was followed by a brief overland trip from Rivas to the Pacific Ocean. Between 1851 and 1855 Vanderbilt's cross-isthmus transit route generated nearly 2,000 passengers a month and had become extremely profitable.

In 1850 the United States and Britain negotiated the Clayton Bulwer Treaty in which both agreed that neither would negotiate exclusive rights to any cross-isthmus canal in the region. This treaty was negotiated without consulting the Nicaraguans. After witnessing an American killing a Nicaraguan on a steamer on the San Juan River in 1854, U.S. consul Solon Borland refused to allow the Greytown police to have jurisdiction over the matter. Believing that Americans were not safe in Greytown, Borland convinced the U.S. government and President Pierce to send a warship to the harbor. In July the American warship bombarded the town after its demands for reparations were not met by the local officials. This was an early example of U.S. gunboat diplomacy that would become commonplace in the early 1900s.

In an attempt to resolve the liberal-conservative divide in Nicaragua the conservative Supreme Director José Laureano Pineda Ugarte decided to move the capital city to Managua in 1852. A short-lived liberal revolt returned the capital to León. The revolt was crushed when Pineda received help from the troops of the conservative president of Honduras. In 1854 the conservative Fruto Chamorro Pérez became the first president of the new Republic of Nicaragua. The Chamorro family remains a fixture in Nicaraguan politics today. A new constitution was also adopted which greatly strengthened the powers of the chief executive and the central government. In particular, it gave the president the ability to suppress civil rights in times of national emergency. Liberals in León refused to accept the new constitution and civil war broke out once again. The conservatives relied on their supporters in Guatemala while the liberals decided to find help elsewhere.

Financed by two of Cornelius Vanderbilt's agents who wanted to seize control of the profitable cross-isthmus transit route, San Francisco journalist Byron Cole conspired with the Nicaraguan liberals to defeat the conservatives. They recruited William Walker, a southerner from the United States, and about 60 other filibusters to defeat the conservatives. A filibuster refers to a nonauthorized military incursion into another country for the purpose of seizing power. They were a reflection of the Manifest Destiny ideology held by many U.S. citizens of the era.[7] Walker arrived at Realejo on the Pacific Coast in June 1855, took command of the liberal forces, attacked and captured Granada by October, and worked out a power sharing agreement with the conservatives. In effect, the "Grey-Eyed Man of Destiny" was now in charge of Nicaragua.

William Walker (1824–1860)

Walker hardly looked like a filibusterer at 5'2" and 120 pounds. He was born to a family of Scottish Calvinists in Tennessee in 1824 and was a devout supporter of the institution of slavery. Extremely bright, Walker graduated from the University of Nashville at the age of 14 and by the time he was 19 years old he had earned a medical degree from the University of Pennsylvania. He also studied at several universities in major European cities including Edinburg, Gottingen, Heidelberg, and Paris. While in Europe he witnessed the major revolutions of 1848. After briefly practicing medicine in Philadelphia, he studied law in New Orleans where he worked as a journalist with Walt Whitman. He moved to California and led a brief filibuster into northern Mexico in Baja. The purpose of this expedition or filibuster was to annex Sonora and Baja to the United States and to extend slavery to the region. On returning to the United States, he was tried in federal court in San Francisco for violation of U.S. neutrality laws and acquitted. He was later recruited by the liberals of Nicaragua in their ongoing war with the conservatives. Walker recruited an army which he called "the Immortals" and set out to "liberate" Nicaragua. By the time he had seized power, his exploits had become very popular in much of the United States. In July 1856 a new musical opened at New York's Pardy National Theatre entitled, *Nicaragua or General Walker's Victories*. The *New York Evening Post* declared that with Walker in power the "destiny of Central America is now more manifestly than ever placed in the Anglo-American hands."[8]

NOTES

1. Until recently, most scholars accepted the claim that the early inhabitants of the Caribbean lowlands—the Caribisi—migrated from South America. This was based primarily on observations by George Squier, the American consul to Nicaragua, who in 1849 noticed the similarities between these groups and the Chibcha of Colombia. One should see the Michigan Historical Reprint Series of E. G. Squier, *Travels in Central America, Particularly in Nicaragua* (originally published in 1853) (Ann Arbor: University of Michigan Library, 2005). This claim is found in most of the current literature

about the origins of these peoples. Yet, there is some evidence that these peoples actually migrated from Mexico in the fourth century and originally settled in the western part of Nicaragua along the Pacific Coast before migrating to the Caribbean lowlands. See Julian Guerrero and Lola Soriano, *Las 9 Tribas Aborigenes de Nicaragua* (Managua, 1982), 13–25.

2. Linda Nelson, "The Depopulation of Nicaragua in the Sixteenth Century," *Journal of Latin American Studies* 14:2 (November 1982): 284–85.

3. Ibid.

4. Ibid., 285. See also Mark Burkholder and Lyman Johnson, *Colonial Latin America*, 6th ed. (Oxford: Oxford University Press, 2008), 141–42.

5. Murdo MacLeod, *Spanish in Central America: A Socioeconomic History, 1520–1720*. (Berkeley: University of California Press, 1973), 54.

6. E. G. Squier, *Travels in Central America, Particularly in Nicaragua* (Michigan Historical Reprint Series) (Ann Arbor: University of Michigan Library, 2005), 166.

7. John Findling, *Close Neighbors, Distant Friends* (Westport, CT: Greenwood, 1987), 26.

8. Ibid., 28.

3

The Coffee Boom, Zelaya, and United States Intervention (1856–1925)

Modern Nicaragua came into existence during this period. The coffee boom of the mid-to-late 1800s and early 1900s firmly established the agro-export model of economic development as the preferred choice of both the liberal and conservative elites. Both liberal and conservative Nicaraguan governments and foreign investors subsidized the growth of the coffee industry and other export crops. The growing need for large estates to promote the growth of coffee and other export crops was achieved, for the most part, by the seizure of land occupied by peasants, indigenous peoples, and the church. Foreign investors and the government played primary roles in the development of economic infrastructure, such as roads and ports, to meet the needs of export agriculture. The country became further integrated into the global economy. Increasing U.S. intervention and dominance of both the economic and political systems of the country became a constant in the early 1900s, yet it awakened a deep and growing sense of nationalism and resistance to foreign occupation. While the traditional elite conservative and liberal parties continued to compete for control of the country, Augusto César Sandino injected a class-based, nationalistic politics into the political processes. This period laid the groundwork for the rise of the Somoza dynasty and the Sandinista revolution.

THE WILLIAM WALKER AFFAIR

After taking Granada in October 1855, the American filibusterer William Walker established a coalition government with the conservative Patricio Rivas but the real power in the country was Walker. Without consulting the Secretary of State, the U.S. representative to Nicaragua, John Hill Wheeler, also a southerner, recognized the new government on November 10. Walker began implementing several liberal reforms designed to open up Nicaragua to foreign investment. Believing Walker to be a threat, the Central American countries of Costa Rica, Guatemala, Honduras, and El Salvador declared war on Nicaragua on March 1, 1856. Rivas fled the country and Walker became President in June 1856. He confiscated the landholdings of his conservative enemies for release to U.S. citizens, declared English as the official language, and legalized slavery. The legalization of slavery spread the fear among all *Nicas*, conservative and liberal, that the United States was planning to annex the country. U.S. financier Cornelius Vanderbilt began organizing the opposition to the Walker government. Walker had confiscated his cross-isthmus transit company and given it to two of his former employees, Cornelius Garrison and Charles Morgan, who had financed the filibuster. After initially supporting the Walker government, U.S. President Franklin Pierce reversed his recognition policy despite continued support from many southern politicians. From November 1856 through May 1857 allied forces from the other Central American countries and Nicaraguan conservative and liberal forces supported by the British fought a drawn out and destructive war against Walker's army. Whenever he was forced to retreat, Walker purposely destroyed and looted the surrounding areas. Rather than surrendering to the Central American forces, Walker and his cholera-ridden army surrendered to the U.S. Navy Commander C. H. Davis in Rivas. Davis returned Walker and the remnants of his army to New Orleans. Walker attempted to return to Nicaragua two other times. The last was in 1860 when he was captured by the British, turned over to authorities in Honduras, and executed.

CONSERVATIVE RULE AND THE COFFEE BOOM

Even though the liberals were discredited because of their initial association with Walker, a period of relative political stability between the conservative and liberal *Nica* elite families followed. Conservative presidents ruled the country until 1893. Liberals tended to be urban professionals and merchants and as a group they were more secular than the conservatives from Granada. Conservatives represented the large landowners that produced coffee, sugar, and beef or cattle. As a whole they tended to be protective of the role of the Catholic Church in society. There was a growing convergence on economic policy as conservatives and, like their liberal counterparts, began to promote free trade and coffee exports.

Conservative Tomas Martínez Guerrero became president in November of 1857 and served until 1867. It was under Martínez that the capital was finally moved to Managua. Martínez was followed in the presidency by conservatives Fernando Guzmán Solórzano, José Vicente Cuadra Lugo, Pedro Joaquín Chamorro, Joaquín Zavala Solis, Adán Cárdenas del Castillo, Evaristo Carazo Aranda, and Roberto Sacasa Sarria. It was these conservative governments that laid the groundwork for the Nicaraguan coffee boom.

By the late 1800s coffee had become one of the most valuable crops in the world. It was fueled by the growing demand in both Europe and the United States. The coffee boom in Nicaragua played a major role in changing the social, economic, and political landscape of the country. Although it was first introduced in the 1820s and its growth as a crop expanded during the 1840s, coffee did not take off and transform the country until the Nicaraguan governments promoted the crop to meet the expanding European and American demand in the mid-to-late 1800s. To develop coffee as a major export product, the various *Nica* governments had to address the need for transportation infrastructure (roads, ports, railroads, steamship lines), land, capital (start-up money), expertise, and a large labor pool.

With Vanderbilt's steamship line across Lake Nicaragua and the end of the Walker affair, coffee production expanded dramatically in the area known as the southern Uplands—the area from Managua to Granada to Jinotepe. This was aided by government reforms in the 1840s which included tax subsidies to coffee producers, the provision of coffee seedlings at cost, cash awards to growers, easy access to land for coffee production, and the development of roads. Owners of the large coffee plantations were granted exemptions from military service. By the mid-1860s Nicaragua was exporting coffee to the world market for the first time. The completion of a railroad line from the northwestern port city of Corinto to Lake Managua near Momotombo volcano in 1886 coupled with the development of a steamship line to Managua made it easier for coffee growers of this region to get their crop to the world market.

In the 1870s the government actively promoted the growth of coffee in the North-Central Highlands which range from a line running south of Matagalpa through Estelí to the Honduran border and then to the northeast through the mountains. The climate and soils of this region are the best for the production of coffee but the lack of roads and transportation to the area made the commercial production impossible without active government promotion. Foreign immigration was encouraged by giving away parcels of land up to 350 *manzanas* (1 *manzana* is the equivalent of 1.73 acres) in size and allowing them to retain their native citizenship even if they became landowners. Coffee growers in the region were given tax breaks and extensive subsidies. In 1889 the land "giveaway" was expanded to 500 *manzanas* if one planted at least 25,000 trees.[1] These reforms led to an influx of immigrants from Germany, Great Britain, and the United States, many of whom were quite wealthy and knowledgeable about coffee. One should note that *Nicas* could also take advantage of these reforms as well and this led to a growing number of nationals who settled in the region. All of this led to the development of large-scale coffee estates.

Land in the North-Central Highlands for coffee expansion came largely at the expense of the indigenous peoples. The Nicaraguan governments used various policies to gain access to the communally owned (owned as a group) land of the indigenous peoples. These policies included privatization of communal land, land auctions, and outright confiscation. Those indigenous peoples working the land at the time were given the opportunity to purchase it. Those who could not pay had their land auctioned to the highest bidder. Indigenous peoples resisted and in 1881 they attacked the government offices in Matagalpa. The resistance was met with swift and brutal repression by the government and their lands were lost to the coffee estates. Coffee production changed the nature of landownership in the region from indigenous communal property and state-owned property to the dramatic expansion of private property holdings. This also meant that many peasants who were squatters and had no legal right to the land on which they were living and working lost their lands as well.

The development of the larger coffee plantations required access to finance. Many of those who immigrated brought their own wealth with them. Since commercial banking institutions were almost nonexistent at the time, many *Nicas* financed their coffee through the so-called *pactos de retroventa*. Under this system a farmer sold his land to a buyer and then leased it back from the buyer for a period of time with the idea of eventually repurchasing the land at a later date. This gave the farmer access to financing to cover the substantial start-up costs of the coffee plantation. Conservative President Chamorro also encouraged British banks to help finance coffee plantations and during the 1880s the British began investing in infrastructure projects and agricultural enterprises. German investment in the Nicaraguan coffee industry was especially noticeable.

Labor shortages also made it difficult for the coffee plantations to be successful. The conservative governments passed labor laws that allowed plantation owners to bind laborers contractually for specific periods of time or to specific plantations. Agricultural justices were created and given the authority to arrest and levy fines against laborers who were in violation of these labor contracts. Laborers included peasants who had been forced off the land on which they had been living and working and the indigenous peoples.

By 1885 to 1890 coffee exports had reached 9.3 million pounds and it had become the principal export of Nicaragua.[2] With a population of about 423,000 in 1890, Nicaragua was tied by coffee further into the world economy. In addition to coffee other major exports included cotton, gold and silver, rubber, leather, sugar, and tobacco. By 1890 the political stability and conservative dominance that had characterized the country for more than 30 years began to change as a new class of coffee producers based in Managua and allied with the liberals began aggressively pushing for economic reforms that would more rapidly facilitate the agro-export model of national development in Nicaragua.[3] In 1891 Roberto Sacasa Sarria, a conservative from León rather than Granada, was elected to the Presidency. Sacasa, who could trace his family roots back to the early 1500s, produced a split in the ruling conservative party. When he attempted to retain power in 1893, a coalition government was created by dissident conservatives and liberals under the leadership of José Santos Zelaya López. The coalition failed and the liberals under Zelaya seized power in the so-called July Revolution. They called for a constitutional convention and quickly wrote another constitution which attacked the privileges of the Church, provided for free secular education, guaranteed freedom of religion, limited the right of foreigners to claim diplomatic protection, and abolished the death penalty. Zelaya became the first liberal president in nearly a half a century.

CONTINUED INTEREST IN THE CANAL AND GROWING FEARS OF U.S. INTERVENTION

Fearing the possibility of more American filibustering, the conservative Martínez government had refused to ratify a treaty that would have allowed Vanderbilt's company the ability to begin the construction of a canal. By 1862 U.S. interests in a cross-isthmus canal in Nicaragua were revived with the Dickinson-Ayon Treaty that granted the United States the right to build a canal and required it to protect and guarantee its neutrality. Nicaragua was to retain sovereignty over the canal zone. Based on the Clayton-Bulwer Treaty with the British, the United States publicly recognized that the construction of the canal was still not an exclusive right. But in 1872 President Ulysses S. Grant created the Inter-Oceanic Canal

Commission stating that it should be an "American canal, on American soil." In 1889 the Maritime Canal Company began work on a Nicaraguan canal although construction came to a halt in 1893 when the company lost all funding due to the stock market panic in the United States. The U.S. representative to Nicaragua in 1890 pointed out that the "nation that with the Nicaraguan government, on a joint agreement, controls Lake Nicaragua, will then control the destiny of the Western Hemisphere."[4] The political implications of this statement and the issue of ownership rights to a canal and a canal zone were not lost on Nicaraguans and, in particular, the liberal and strident nationalist Zelaya who had just come to power.

JOSÉ SANTOS ZELAYA LÓPEZ (1853–1919)

Zelaya was born in 1853 into a wealthy coffee-growing family in Managua. His father was José Maria Zelaya and his mother Juana López. He was educated at the Instituto de Oriente in Granada. He then studied in France and was influenced by the positivist writings of Auguste Comte and Herbert Spencer. After returning from Europe, Zelaya became the mayor of Managua and set up a lending library which he stocked with the writings of French philosophers.[5] He paved the streets of Managua and put in street lamps. He imported the first, and at that time, the only car in Nicaragua. With a French driver he rode around Managua and waved to the crowds of people. Zelaya was a large man who cast an imposing figure. As president he conducted a national census and created a National Archives and Museum. Zelaya's fervent nationalism combined with his economic policies created conflict with the British and, in particular, a U.S. policy that had become increasingly interventionist focusing on rights to a cross-isthmus canal and the protection of its expanding business interests.

NICARAGUA UNDER ZELAYA

True to his liberal philosophy Zelaya sought to lessen the influence of the Catholic Church in Nicaragua. By 1899 he had confiscated all Church lands. The new constitution not only called for a separation of church and state and the freedom of religion, it also allowed for free secular education. By the end of his first term in office Zelaya was spending 10 percent of his budget on public schools and by the end of his presidency he had constructed more than 140 public schools. He legalized civil marriages and divorce. It was Zelaya who gave political rights to all citizens, including women.

Zelaya continued the coffee reforms and the transformation of the economy of the country at a faster pace. He began extensive programs to build

and improve roads and railroads throughout the country. In 1906 he negotiated a loan for 6 million dollars to construct a railway from the coffee-
growing areas of the west to the Caribbean. He guaranteed free shipment
of coffee on *Nica* railways. To address the ongoing need for labor on the
coffee estates he instituted strict vagrancy laws in 1894 and 1901, with military service as punishment, a national identity card, and an increase in the
power of the agriculture justices. In 1899 he aggressively confiscated virtually all of the communally held land by the indigenous peoples. In 1909 he
abolished all titles to communally held land. Zelaya believed that communally held land was an obstacle to the modernization of Nicaragua. He auctioned off large sections of state-owned land at minimal prices as long as
the buyer promised to grow coffee or other export-only crops. In sum,
Zelaya transferred 1.3 million hectares (a hectare is the equivalent of 10,000
square meters) of land to private owners, almost all of them elite *Nica* families. To illustrate the point, by 1900 only 57 growers received the majority
of the government coffee subsidies and almost one half of all land sales
under Zelaya went to 30 families—all liberals.[6]

As a result of Zelaya's reforms, coffee production in Nicaragua more
than doubled from 9.3 million pounds from 1885 to 1990 to 19.3 million
pounds from 1905 to 1909.[7] Typical of the *Nica* coffee dynasties that were
established at the turn of the century were those of John Bolt and Salvador
Cuadra near Matagalpa. Bolt, an English miner, immigrated to Nicaragua
and purchased the coffee estates Las Canas and La Grecia. By 1930 he had
more than 50,000 trees in production. Cuadra from one of the elite families
of Granada had 60,000 coffee trees in production by 1910 and more than
100,000 by 1930. Processing and exporting coffee came to be associated
with powerful families such as the Baltodanos and the Rappaciolis.[8]

Although Zelaya was a fervent nationalist, he encouraged and recruited
foreign investment on terms that he believed to be beneficial to Nicaragua.
His most-used method of encouraging investment was the granting of a
concession or a monopoly in certain economic areas. For example, in 1904
he granted exclusive rights of navigation on the Escondido River to the
Bluefields Steamship Company, a subsidiary of the United Fruit Company.
In effect this gave the giant U.S. banana company a monopoly on the shipment of Nicaraguan bananas. He also provided concessions to Italian firms
to cut timber, Swiss firms to extract rubber, and a Spanish firm to do all
government printing. Although Zelaya provided concessions to foreigners
he was very quick to cancel them when he believed that Nicaraguan interests were being threatened or contracts were not followed. For example, in
1898 Zelaya gave a canal commission to U.S. businessmen Edward Gragin and
Eward Eyre. They formed the Interoceanic Canal Company. They failed to
deposit the required capital on time, and Zelaya canceled the concession and

kept the $100,000 deposit that the company had made. In 1907 he canceled a mahogany cutting concession to the John D. Emery Company of Boston when it failed to reforest cut areas as contracted.[9]

Zelaya was supported largely by coffee producers and exporters, Managuan businessmen who prospered due to the coffee boom, intellectuals, and urban labor unions. Conservative opposition increased as elections during the period were rigged to support Zelaya and his liberal *zelayistas*. There were conservative uprisings in 1896 and 1899. The opposition consisted of conservative land owners, cattle producers, those who had seen their trade decline due to the economic advantages given to Zelaya's liberal supporters, and British and American businesses located largely along the Mosquito Coast. Leading conservative opponents were jailed or exiled and often had their property confiscated, yet he often granted his jailed opponents amnesty after an appropriate length of time. After an explosion of a government powder magazine in 1903, Zelaya executed several of those allegedly responsible. A major conservative uprising failed that year but it established Emiliano Chamorro Vargas as the party's leader.

ZELAYA, THE BRITISH, AND THE UNITED STATES

Even though the British agreed to leave the Mosquito Coast in 1860 they continued to support the Miskito Kingdom. Zelaya, who had created Nicaragua's first military academy and its first professional and national army, sent troops to Bluefields in 1894. He reasserted Nicaraguan sovereignty and reintegrated the Miskito Kingdom under Nicaraguan sovereignty. British and U.S. merchants complained. They had established a "cozy" relationship with the Miskito Kingdom who had catered to foreign interests by ignoring Nicaraguan tax laws and customs regulations and had granted concessions to foreigners without consulting Managua. U.S. Secretary of State Robert Gresham, still wanting to build a cross-isthmus canal in Nicaragua, supported the Zelaya administration's sovereignty claim against the wishes of both British and American businesses. The British left but Zelaya had taken several British officials back to Managua for trial on charges of inciting an insurrection. The British demanded that their officials be released and that Nicaragua pay compensation for the "arbitrary and violent" actions taken against their officials. British warships appeared in the harbor at Corinto when Zelaya refused to pay. The U.S. State Department intervened and after some intense negotiations, Zelaya paid the compensation and the British left. This event marked the end of the British role in both Nicaraguan internal affairs and the development of a cross-isthmus canal.[10] Seven years later, the Hay-Paunceforte Treaty was ratified by the

U.S. Senate. It, in effect, abrogated the Clayton-Bulwer Treaty, and allowed the United States to build a canal on its own and fortify it if necessary. British influence in Nicaragua had come to an official end, while U.S. influence was dramatically increasing.

U.S. economic influence in Nicaragua, especially along the Mosquito Coast, began to escalate. U.S. citizens had received land grants in the 1880s from the Miskito Kingdom to plant bananas along the coast and the Escondido River. One should note that Bluefields had become the world leader in the export of bananas by this time. Other economic sectors in the area that were dominated by U.S. firms included gold mining which was controlled by the La Luz and Los Angeles Mining Company owned by the Fletcher family of Pittsburg and the mahogany trade controlled by the John D. Emery Company of Boston. Approximately 90 to 95 percent of commerce from Bluefields was under U.S. control by 1894. In effect, Bluefields had actually become an American town.[11] By 1899 the United Fruit Company had secured contracts with most of the banana planters in the region. The U.S. business community along the Mosquito Coast worked with the conservatives in opposition to Zelaya.

Recognizing the tremendous economic significance of a cross-isthmus canal, Zelaya continued to negotiate faithfully with the United States. Always sensitive to *Nica* national interests, he would never grant the United States sovereignty over any land immediately surrounding a proposed canal. In 1897 and 1899 the U.S. Congress appointed canal commissions and both recommended the Nicaraguan site rather than Panama. In 1901 the Isthmian Canal Commission presented its report to Congress and also recommended that the canal should be built through Nicaragua, not Panama. This analysis was based primarily on cost. The French Panama Canal Company had been attempting to construct a canal since 1882. For many reasons this attempt failed and the company lobbied the United States to purchase its equipment and complete the construction of the canal in Panama. Initially the company requested 109 million dollars in compensation for its equipment. After the report to the U.S. Congress recommended the Nicaraguan route, the French company stated that the United States could now purchase its equipment for only 40 million dollars. This made the cost of the Panama route less than the Nicaraguan route. In the spring of 1902 the United States decided that the Panama route should be given priority unless the financial arrangements with the French Panama Canal Company could not be worked out and an agreement with the government of Columbia of which Panama was a part could not be made. Colombia rejected a U.S. offer to construct the canal and a rebellion broke out almost immediately in Panama. It was led by wealthy landowners and the French Panama Canal Company. Aided by a show of force by U.S.

warships, Panama won its independence and granted the United States the right to build the cross-isthmus canal.

By 1903 it was clear that U.S. policy toward Nicaragua no longer had to give priority to gaining access and rights to a canal at the expense of its business interests. It would now give its highest priority to the protection of its business interests under President Theodore Roosevelt's Corollary to the Monroe Doctrine and later under President William Howard Taft's policy of Dollar Diplomacy. The Roosevelt Corollary emphasized the right of the United States to maintain security in the western hemisphere which meant keeping the Europeans out and protecting the Panama Canal. Dollar diplomacy emphasized the right of the United States to promote and protect its extensive economic interests in the region.

Zelaya with the other liberals in Central America liked the idea of a union of some type that would give them more leverage in dealing with countries outside the region, in particular, the United States. Zelaya saw himself as the leader of such a union. In 1902 all the Central American countries except Guatemala agreed that disputes between them would be resolved by themselves rather than involving countries outside of the region. Conservative Manuel Estrada Cabrera of Guatemala, Zelaya's main rival for regional leadership, opposed any such union. When a dispute broke out between Guatemala and El Salvador in 1906, the U.S. government mediated the conflict and a peace treaty was signed in San Jose, Costa Rica, by all countries except Nicaragua. The United States led the countries to sign an agreement to allow U.S. mediation of disputes in Central America. Zelaya believed that this violated the Corinto agreement of 1902 and would pave the way for U.S. dominance in the region. He refused to sign. In 1907 Nicaraguan troops invaded Honduras to support rebels attempting to overthrow the government and in the same year Nicaraguan troops landed in El Salvador. In 1908 further instability in Honduras was fueled by both Nicaragua and El Salvador. A U.S. show of naval force along the Honduran northern coast that year led to a growing chorus of Americans calling for the ouster of Zelaya. In 1909 U.S. Secretary of State Philander Knox, with close ties to the Fletcher family of Pittsburg, put together a list of "Zelayista crimes" that the United States needed to prevent.[12]

Zelaya, who was very upset with the U.S. decision not to build a canal in his country, attempted to obtain an agreement with the Japanese and the Germans. The fear of a competing canal added fuel to the fire in the growing U.S. opposition to the Zelaya administration. Zelaya's insistence on making sure that the agreements with U.S. businesses concerning concessions were strictly adhered to earned him increasing resentment and continued opposition from U.S. businesses. They complained to the U.S. government and plotted with the conservatives of Nicaragua. In 1909

Zelaya received two loans from the British-based Ethelburga syndicate in the amount of 1.25 million pounds. The United States was disturbed by the possibility of a Nicaraguan default on the loan and the possible reappearance of British intervention in Nicaragua. The U.S. government then let it be known to the conservatives of Nicaragua that it would support the removal of Zelaya.

Another revolt in Bluefields occurred in 1909 this time led by Juan Estrada, the opportunistic liberal governor of the region; Adolfo Díaz, the secretary of the La Luz and Los Angeles Mining Company; and conservative leader Emiliano Chamorro. It was supported by U.S. business interests and conservatives from Granada. Zelaya sent 4,000 troops to quell the rebellion and it looked like Estrada was defeated until U.S. Major Smedley Butler and 400 marines arrived in Bluefields. Saved by the marines, Estrada announced the establishment of a new Nicaraguan government in October. The next month two U.S. mercenaries who were fighting with the conservatives attempted to blow up government troop transports on the San Juan River. Zelaya had them executed. U.S. Secretary of State Philander Knox condemned the executions and made the decision to end diplomatic relations on December 1.

THE RETURN OF CONSERVATIVE RULE AND U.S. OCCUPATION

Zelaya resigned on December 16, 1909, and went into exile in Mexico. He turned over power to the liberal José Madriz who led *zelayista* troops against Estrada in Bluefields early the next year. It looked like Madriz would defeat Estrada when a truce was enforced by the U.S. Naval Commander William Gilmer. U.S. ships prevented *zelayista* ships from attacking Bluefields. Unable to defeat Estrada and lacking recognition from the United States, Madriz resigned and fled the country. Under the Dawson Pact of 1910 the United States installed Estrada as the president and Díaz as vice-president. Emiliano Chamorro became the leader of the Constituent Assembly and an ambitious conservative Luis Mena became Secretary of War. The country was financially broke and could not pay its foreign creditors. The United States moved quickly and offered a financial package to Nicaragua. New York bankers, Brown Brothers and J. W. Seligman, would pay all of its British and European debts and provide the Nicaraguan government with money to get the country up and running again. In return for this new loan, the U.S. government would provide a collector of customs (taxes). This collector-general would run the Nicaraguan treasury making sure that the country paid off both its old and new debts to the United States. This American official would even control the dispersal of money for domestic programs. Colonel Clifford Ham became the collector-general and stayed in that position until 1928.

In an attempt to shore up his power, Estrada shut down the National Assembly, driving Emiliano Chamorro into exile while Mena came to oppose him over the financial agreement with the United States. Fearing a *golpe* or military takeover of the government by Mena, Estrada ordered his arrest. In response, troops loyal to Mena marched on Managua and Estrada resigned in favor of Díaz in May 1911. Díaz, who had little popular support in Managua and was exceedingly pro-American, not only signed the financial agreement with the United States but also gave the United States a controlling interest in the state-owned railroad and the Nicaraguan National Bank. Mena broke with the government of Díaz over the agreement and took his army to Masaya and then Granada. Taking advantage of the situation, a liberal *zelayista*, Benjamin Zeledón, moved to seize power from what he referred to as "the traitors to the Fatherland." Zeledón, a former teacher, journalist, judge, minister of defense, and general in the military, seized León and then moved to set up camp near Masaya.

When Mena's forces captured some U.S. steamships on Lake Nicaragua, Díaz, now with Emiliano Chamorro's support, requested U.S. intervention. By September 1912 there were about 1,100 U.S. Marines in Managua under the command of Major Butler and U.S. warships controlled the Pacific Coast of Nicaragua. Marines marched on Granada and forced Mena, who was sick with dysentery, and his troops to surrender. The Marines and Nicaraguan forces loyal to Díaz then defeated Zeledón's outmanned and outgunned troops in a major battle at Coyotepe Hill near Masaya on October 3 and 4. Zeledón's dead body was paraded through the streets of cities throughout the country. Emiliano Chamorro, the only other possible political threat to Díaz, was immediately made ambassador to the United States. The United States had finally achieved its foreign policy goals in Nicaragua: political stability or at least the illusion of political stability, with pro-American conservatives in power; the removal of any pretext for a British or European intervention; guaranteed payments on its loans made to Nicaragua; and a pro-American business environment. Major Butler, a two-time recipient of the Congressional Medal of Honor and who commanded the Marines in Nicaragua admitted in a speech later in his life that most of his time in Nicaragua was spent "being a high class muscle man for big business, for Wall Street, and for the bankers." A force of 100 to 150 Marines remained in Nicaragua until August of 1925.

NICARAGUA: OPEN FOR U.S. BUSINESS AND U.S. PATERNALISM

Colonel Ham of the United States, the new collector-general for Nicaragua, began to move on the country's financial matters in 1912. A new unit of currency, the cordoba, was introduced. A Nicaraguan National Bank was founded and managed by Americans. From 1912 to 1920 conservative governments continued to sell national lands to promote the export of agricultural products, especially coffee. Some of these lands were actually being worked by squatters who did not have legal titles to the land. In 1914 the Bryan-Chamorro Treaty was signed and ratified in 1916. The treaty gave the United States the exclusive rights, in perpetuity, to build a canal in Nicaragua; a lease to the Great and Little Corn Islands off the Mosquito Coast; and the option to build a naval base in the Gulf of Fonseca. El Salvador and Costa Rica challenged the provisions of the treaty in the Central American Court of Justice. The court, which the United States had played a primary role in creating, ruled against Nicaragua and the United States. Both ignored the ruling.

With liberals unable to find a candidate and with strong U.S. support, Emiliano Chamorro, the author of the Bryan-Chamorro Treaty, was elected president in 1916. Diego Chamorro, Emiliano's aging uncle, was elected president in 1920 through rigged voting. The liberals cried foul and the United States promised them fair elections in 1924 by rewriting the national electoral laws. Diego Chamorro died in 1923 and the U.S. administration of Calvin Coolidge took a less interventionist role in the presidential election of 1924. With the Panama Canal secure and Nicaragua at peace, the American public pushed to bring the U.S. Marines home. The Marines, who had been in Managua since 1912, were thought to be no longer necessary, yet continued to be an irritant to the majority liberals in the country. President Coolidge made the decision to remove the Marines from Nicaragua after the inauguration of a new president in 1925. A coalition ticket of conservative Carlos Solorzano and liberal Juan Bautista Sacasa defeated Emiliano Chamorro. Solorzano appointed Alfredo Rivas, his brother-in-law, as commander of La Loma, the fort which stood on the hill overlooking Managua. He appointed another brother-in-law, Luis Rivas, as commander of the arsenal at Managua known as Campo de Marte. Before the Marines left in August 1925, the United States made the decision that Nicaragua should create its own National Guard and brought in Army Major Calvin B. Carter to organize it. Major Carter began this task at Campo de Marte.

Conservatives immediately pressured Solorzano to get rid of the liberals in his cabinet. The liberal Minister of War José María Moncada and Minister of Finance Victor Roman y Reyes were dismissed. When Emiliano Chamorro seized control of the conservative-dominated army in October 1925, Vice President Sacasa fled the country. The conservative-dominated Congress replaced Solorzano with Emiliano Chamorro. Solorzano resigned in January 1926 and Emiliano Chamorro assumed the presidency. The liberal uprisings against the conservatives began in May 1926 at Bluefields. The Marines landed at Bluefields. Nicaragua was at civil war again and U.S. Marines were in the country again. The stage was set for Nicaraguan politics to change forever with the appearance of Augusto César Sandino and Anastasio Somoza Garcia.

AUGUSTO CÉSAR SANDINO (1895–1934)

An illegitimate son, Sandino was born in 1895 in Niquinohomo to Margarita Calderon. His father, Gregorio Sandino, who was his mother's employer, was a local businessman and farmer. His mother worked as a domestic and in the coffee fields but made barely enough money for them to survive. His mother abandoned him in 1904 and he stayed briefly with his maternal grandmother. His father then took him into his house, provided for him, and sent him to school—a school opened by President Zelaya. Sandino worked for his father and his father passed on to him his own liberal philosophy and the love of classic literature. He witnessed Benjamin Zeledón's dead body being dragged through the streets of his home town in 1912 and attended Zeledón's funeral. Years later Sandino wrote that "Zeledón's death gave me the key to understanding our country's situation in the face of Yankee piracy."[13] He witnessed the arrest of his father who protested the Bryan-Chamorro Treaty which he believed gave the United States control over Nicaragua's government and violated its sovereignty. These events and others in the future played a role in the development of his intense nationalism and his desire to end U.S. dominance over his country.

After some traveling Sandino returned home to Niquinohomo in 1919 and opened a successful grain business independent of his father. He met and planned to marry his cousin Mercedes Sandino. In 1921 Sandino shot Dagoberto Rivas, the son of a prominent conservative. The details are not really known but according to Sandino, Rivas hit him in the head while in church because he mistakenly believed that he (Sandino) was dating his sister. Sandino shot and wounded him in a "spontaneous and thoughtless act." He fled to the Atlantic Coast and then to La Ceiba, Honduras, where he took a job at the Montecristo Sugar Plantation. He then moved to Guatemala and worked on a plantation owned by United Fruit Company of Boston. He ended up working near the port of Tampico, Mexico, for the Huasteca Petroleum Company, a subsidiary of the Mexican Petroleum Company of California. His work in Mexico allowed him to discuss politics with union organizers and others who opposed U.S. dominance in the region. With the statute of limitations on his attempted murder charge expiring, Sandino returned home in May 1926. He ended up working in the North American-owned gold mine of San Albino. It was at San Albino that Sandino realized his talent for mobilizing workers to political action. Many of these workers formed the basis for his anti-imperialist army that would fight the U.S. Marines that occupied their country.

Although his army was made up of workers and poor peasants, Sandino's political ideology was shaped primarily by the humiliation imposed on Nicaragua by U.S. intervention dating back to the 1840s, in particular, the overthrow of the Zelaya government in 1909 and the subsequent occupation by the Marines. His primary goal was to free Nicaragua from both the United States, the so-called "barbarian colossus of the North," and any Nicaraguans or "*vendepatrias*" who had cooperated with the United States. His red and black flag symbolized a free country or death. His speeches verged on an "uncontrollable anti-Yankee phobia."[14] Sandino did not espouse socialism or Marxism in any of his writings. He provides neither the hint of the government taking over the major industries nor a public discussion of land reform. Interviews with his followers indicate an absence of class-based themes with virtually no references to land, labor, and relations between the rich and the poor. Very simply, Sandino's political ideology was based on an unabashed Nicaraguan nationalism.[15]

Sandino's nationalism and hatred toward the United States and conservative *Nica* leaders can be illustrated from the following portion of a letter written in 1926 in which he remembers a conversation with other nationalists in Mexico in 1925:

I discussed the submission of our Latin American peoples before the hypocritical or forceful advance of the murderous Yankee empire. One of those days I told my friends that if in Nicaragua there were a hundred men who loved their country as much as I do, our nation would restore its absolute sovereignty, threatened by that same Yankee empire . . . From that moment I wanted to search for those hundred men . . . those hundred legitimate sons of Nicaragua . . .[16]

After recruiting his "legitimate sons of Nicaragua" which came to be called his Army for the Defense of the National Sovereignty of Nicaragua, he writes:

I realized that the political leaders [of Nicaragua], both Conservatives and Liberals, are a pack of dogs, cowards and traitors, incapable of guiding a patriotic and courageous people . . . they are fighting to reach the Presidency on the basis of a foreign supervision that we would not accept. Spiteful people say that Sandino and his army are bandits, which means that within a year all of Nicaragua will be converted into a nation of bandits, because, before then, our army will have taken the reins of national power, for the greater welfare of our country. Nicaragua will be freed only by bullets, and at the cost of our own blood.[17]

Sandino often used the word *vendepatria* as an epithet to refer to those *Nicas* who had "sold out" to the United States. Under Sandino's red and black flag with the words "Liberty or Death" written on it, the stage was set for the politics of Nicaragua to change forever.

NOTES

1. There is a large literature on how the Nicaraguan government promoted the growth of coffee. In particular one should see *Coffee and Power: Revolution and the Rise of Democracy in Central America* (Cambridge: Harvard University Press, 1997) by Jefferey Paige; *Coffee and Transportation in Nicaragua* (Berkeley: University of California Press, 1964) by David Radell; *Land, Power, and Poverty*, 2nd ed. (Boulder, CO: Westview Press, 1998) by Charles D. Brockett; Jeffrey Gould's 1994 article "El café, el trabajo, y la comunidada indigenade Matagalpa, 1880–1925" in *Tierra, Café y Sociedad: Ensayos Sobre la Historia Agraria del Centroamericana,* edited by H. P. Brignoli and M. Samper (San Jose: FLACSO). For an excellent summary one should see "Coffee in Nicaragua: Introduction and Expansion in the Nineteenth Century" by Craig Revels at http://sites.maxwell.syr.edu/clag/yearbook2000/revels. htm (accessed October 30, 2008).

2. Brockett, *Land, Power, and Poverty*, 20.

3. Paige, *Coffee and Power*, 156–57.

4. Eduardo Crawley, *Dictators Never Die* (New York: St. Martin's Press, 1979), 34–35.

5. Thomas W. Walker, *Nicaragua: Living in the Shadow of the Eagle* (Boulder, CO: Westview Press, 2003), 16.

6. Paige, *Coffee and Power*, 157.

7. Brockett, *Land, Power, and Poverty*, 20.

8. Paige, *Coffee and Power*, 20–21.

9. Ibid., 159.

10. John Findling, *Close Neighbors, Distant Friends* (Westport, CT: Greenwood, 1987), 40–41.

11. Paige, *Coffee and Power*, 160.

12. Findling, *Close Neighbors, Distant Friends*, 57.

13. Stephen Kinzer, *Blood of Brothers: Life and War in Nicaragua* (Cambridge: Harvard University Press, 1991), 27.

14. Donald C. Hodges, *Intellectual Foundations in the Nicaraguan Revolution* (Austin: University of Texas Press, 1986), 113.

15. Paige, *Coffee and Power*, 169–73.

16. Robert Edgar Conrad, *Sandino: The Testimony of a Nicaraguan Patriot, 1921–1934* (Princeton: Princeton University Press, 1990), 41–42.

17. Ibid.

4

Sandino and the Rise of the Somoza Dynasty (1925–1959)

The U.S. Marines left Nicaragua in August 1925 only to return the following year. Augusto César Sandino and his small army of miners, peasants, and laborers in northern, mountainous Nicaragua fought a six-year guerrilla war against the occupying Marines until they left in January 1933. Sandino became a hero and the symbol of *Nica* nationalism, independence, and freedom by fighting and defeating a superior enemy. Before leaving the country the United States made sure that Anastasio Somoza García was in charge of the nonpartisan National Guard. Somoza murdered Sandino and then turned the Guard into an instrument of his own personal power. With the support of the Guard, he staged a *golpe* in 1936 and claimed the presidency. From 1936 through 1979, Somoza and his two sons ruled Nicaragua. The dynasty remained in power by amassing a diverse economic empire; by making the most powerful force in the country, the National Guard, an instrument of the family's personal power; by controlling the liberal party which controlled all branches of government; by manipulating both liberal and conservative agro-export elites with both economic and political incentives and disincentives; and by maneuvering to guarantee continued U.S. support of his government.

Somoza continued to promote the traditional agro-export-based economy and further integrated Nicaragua into the U.S. market. With greater access to financial resources and modern technology and improved infrastructure, Somoza modernized agriculture and took advantage of the cotton boom of the 1950s. Three major economic elite networks developed that came to be known as the *Banco de America* or BANAMERICA, the *Banco Nicaraguensa* or BANIC groups, and the Somoza family economic empire. While they represented three different networks of elites, the ties and relationships that developed among them represented a union of interests among the most important *Nica* elites. More and more land came under control of the agro-export elites of the country. More peasants either lost their land or lost access to land. They faced the prospects of migrating to the urban areas, working as seasonal wage-laborers, or moving to marginal land not condu-cive to the growth of crops. Somoza brought economic growth to the coun-try but made economic and political inequality greater.

At the same time Somoza sowed the seeds of opposition due to his *con-tinuismo* (political maneuvers to remain in power), immense corruption, and repression. Opposition to Somoza from dissident liberals, younger con-servatives who refused to be bought off, and radical students who dreamed of a more egalitarian and democratic Nicaragua began to surface throughout the 1950s and early 1960s. The assassination of Somoza García in 1956 was merely the beginning of the growing opposition to Somoza *continuismo*.

RETURN OF THE U.S. MARINES

Exiled liberal Vice-President Juan Bautista Sacasa began courting the support of Mexican President Elias Calles, who was not popular in the United States because he had forced American oil companies in Mexico to exchange the titles to the land on which they operated for 50-year leases. The Calvin Coolidge administration considered Calles to be a Bolshevik (communist) and anti-United States. Secretary of State Frank Kellog simply could not allow *Nica* liberals supported by a Bolshevik Mexican to come to power. The Marines with the U.S. warship *Cleveland* and the Nicaraguan National Guard stopped the liberal rebellion at Bluefields in May 1926. A second liberal rebellion in August occurred in both the west and the north-east. In the west, near Chinandega, the liberals were defeated while attempting to get to the Pacific Coast to receive a shipment of arms from Mexico. However, a liberal army led by José Moncada captured Rio Grande, north of Bluefields. U.S. Marines prevented Bluefields from falling to the liberals under Moncada. That same year another liberal uprising led by Anastasio Somoza García near San Marcos was also defeated by the conservative forces. Somoza chose not to fight on the battlefield again and maneuvered his way into the inner circles of his uncle, the exiled Vice President Sacasa. By this time conservative President Emiliano Chamorro's government was virtually bankrupt.

The United States intervened by sending the warship *Denver* into the harbor at the Pacific port of Corinto and brought the parties together to force an agreement. Chamorro was forced to resign. The United States maneuvered to get its old friend Adolfo Díaz elected to the presidency because Sacasa with his Mexican and "communist" ties was unacceptable. The Liberals responded by forming another government at Puerto Cabezas with Sacasa as president. The Sacasa government was formally recognized by the government of Mexico. In December 1926 Sacasa fled south as U.S. Marines showed up in Puerto Cabezas. Díaz then requested that the U.S. Marines, or the Legation Guard as it had come to be known, return officially to help put down the liberal rebellion. By January 1927 the Marines were officially back in Nicaragua. With liberals seizing Chinandega in early February, a major conservative attack led by the Nicaraguan National Guard and U.S. Marines pushed the liberals back out of the city. U.S. planes bombed the city of Chinandega in the attack on the liberal army. By the end of the month more than 5,400 U.S. Marines occupied strategic cities throughout the country and 11 warships were in Nicaraguan harbors.

U.S. Secretary of War Henry Stimson came to the small town of Tipitapa near Managua to work out another agreement. Stimson made it clear to the liberals that Marines would not allow Díaz to be defeated in a war. Díaz was to remain as president until U.S.-supervised elections could be held in 1928. Stimson promised the liberals that the elections would be fair. Díaz was forced to accept some liberals in his Cabinet. The liberal and conservative armies were disarmed and a new, nonpartisan National Guard was created under the direction of the United States. Moncada and the other liberal leaders agreed to the Espino Negro Pact on May 12, 1927. During these negotiations Somoza acted as interpreter and gained favor with the American leaders. Somoza became increasingly aligned with U.S. interests. Sandino was the only liberal leader who refused to sign the Espino Negro Pact. He stated that he could not sign as long as U.S. Marines occupied the country. Somoza and Sandino were on two different paths that would lead to an inevitable clash.

SANDINO'S WAR

Sandino initially had about 30 followers, most of whom were miners from San Albino. With the money he had saved, he and his men crossed into Honduras and purchased arms. In November 1926 Sandino's men began attacking small outposts along the Coco River in the northeastern part of Nicaragua. His first clash with conservative forces was at El Jicaro. Snubbed by Moncada who denied his requests for guns and ammunition, Sandino captured weapons that Sacasa had left behind in Puerto Cabezas in December of that year. Hoping to win favor with Moncada by providing him with the captured weapons, Sandino was once again snubbed by the liberal general who considered him a "nobody." Moncada finally agreed to give Sandino the weapons he had captured and stated that he should open up a front in the northern mountains. Sandino and his men set up a base at San Rafael del Norte near the Coco River in the mountain province of Jinotega. He then married Blanca Arauz who ran the local telegraph office. She served as the hub for Sandino's military communication network.

Sandino was shocked that Moncada agreed to the Espino Negro Pact negotiated by U.S. Secretary of War Stimson. He viewed Moncada as a traitor to his country. After rejecting the Espino Negro Pact, he and his 300-man army took as many guns as they could find and left to return to the mountains of Segovia. In July 1927 Sandino and his now 700-man army attacked the U.S. Marine base at Ocotal. The Marines were under orders to "gun the bandits down mercilessly." While Sandino attacked the base, his local supporters in town looted and burned the houses and stores of those *Nicas* who were believed to have been collaborating with the Americans. U.S. planes bombed the city and killed at least 300 civilians. Sandino's army suffered a large number of casualties and withdrew from Ocotal to a mountain base on the border with Honduras called El Chipote. Although Sandino did not win the battle, the ranks of his supporters swelled but were probably never more than 1,000 men. In addition to former workers from the mines and peasants with small plots of land, Sandino's men often were former workers from the banana plantations and mahogany operations that were entirely owned by U.S. companies. Coffee workers from the northwest where there were a large number of U.S.-owned estates also joined his army.

After the battle of Ocotal, Sandino learned that his troops could not fight a major head-on battle with the Marines. His army began to wage a classic jungle-guerrilla war against the U.S. Marines. His men were farmers during the day and guerrilla fighters at night. Hit-and-run tactics and ambushes became common. He avoided open confrontations with large U.S. forces and the Nicaraguan National Guard. The local peasants provided information on U.S. troop movements to Sandino. Sandino's men reported that they could always tell when the Marines were nearby because they could smell the smoke from their cigarettes. Sandino attacked U.S. property whenever and wherever possible. He captured the La Luz y Los Angeles Mining Company and confiscated money and goods. He waged a public relations war in the media and received a sympathetic ear from the American journalist Carleton Beals whose articles in *The Nation* began to question the U.S. role in Nicaragua.

Marines burned food warehouses and killed cattle in an attempt to deprive Sandino's army of food. Homes were burned. Showing little mercy to the so-called Sandinista bandits, U.S. Marine documents are full of reports of prisoners "shot while trying to escape."[1] The United States bombed villages in Segovia and destroyed more than 70 villages in the aftermath of the battle for Ocotal.[2] These actions by the Marines rallied even more peasants to Sandino's side. The little man in the large hat had become a hero, the face and symbol of Nicaraguan nationalism and patriotism defending the country against a foreign invader and overwhelming odds.

In 1928 the liberal Moncado was elected president in what most consider the fairest elections ever held in Nicaragua at that point in history.[3] The war against Sandino began to drain the Nicaraguan budget. The global depression made matters even worse and it is estimated that in 1929 more than one-fourth of the Nicaraguan budget was spent on its National Guard and its war against Sandino. Moncada also created a volunteer force of liberals to supplement the Guard. These groups committed atrocities against the local population in the northern areas controlled by Sandino. Some of the National Guard units, one under the command of U.S. Captain Lewis B. (Chesty) Puller, committed several atrocities against the local peasants.[4] Puller recruited a special and unofficial Guard Company of indigenous peoples from the Caribbean region. This unit attacked pro-Sandino villages and used the machete against the locals. Puller then attributed these atrocities to Sandino's men. In 1930, the Guard attempted to relocate most of the people from the province of Segovia to destroy Sandino's base of power. This raised so much opposition that the Guard dropped the policy.[5]

In another relatively fair election in 1932, the liberal Sacasa became president. That same year—the last of President Herbert Hoover's administration—U.S. foreign policy toward Latin America and, in particular, Central America and the Caribbean, began to change. With a global economic depression; a growing fear of the strategic power of the Soviet Union, Germany, and Japan; and increasing U.S. popular opposition to the presence of the Marines in Nicaragua, President Hoover decided in late 1932 to bring the Marines home. With the strong support of U.S. Ambassador Matthew Hanna and the blessing of the U.S. government, President Sacasa appointed Somoza to command the reformed Nicaraguan National Guard. In January 1933 the Marines began to leave Nicaragua. Somoza quickly recognized that the Guard was the most powerful force in the country and he began to make it an instrument of his own rise to power.

ANASTASIO SOMOZA GARCÍA (1896–1956)

Somoza was born in 1896 in San Marcos to Julia García and Anastasio Somoza, a moderately well-to-do coffee grower. He was schooled at the *Instituto Nacional de Oriente* in Granada. He then went to Philadelphia where he attended the Pierce School of Business Administration and lived with relatives. He worked as an auditor for the Page Motor Company. It was in Philadelphia where he met Salvadora Debayle Sacasa, the granddaughter of the former president of Nicaragua Roberto Sacasa Sarria and the niece of Juan Bautista Sacasa. The Sacasa family, one of the oldest and most famous in the country, traced its *Nica* roots back to the early 1500s. The couple was married in 1919 against the wishes of the bride's family. After returning to León, Somoza tried several unsuccessful business ventures and was put in jail briefly for counterfeiting. He finally got a government job largely due to the influence of his uncle, Alberto Roman y Reyes, who was the Minister of Finance. In 1926 the sociable and outgoing Somoza, who spoke excellent English, met U.S. envoy to Nicaragua Henry Stimson and thoroughly impressed him. He continued to impress and gain favor with the U.S. Marine commanders and the other American officials stationed in the country. He joined the liberal rebellion that same year in support of his wife's Uncle Sacasa in his bid for the presidency. Somoza, who had once sold cars, continued to curry favor with the United States. He began to play an intermediary role between the Nicaraguans and the Americans. Somoza successfully managed the relief efforts in the aftermath of the devastating 1931 earthquake that hit Managua and was appointed Minister of Foreign Relations by President Moncada. He continued to gain even more favor among American officials. The rumor mill in Managua whispered about his very close relationship with the young wife of U.S. Ambassador Hanna. Many in Managua believed that it was she who put pressure on her husband to make sure that the ambitious Somoza became the head of the new nonpartisan National Guard.[6]

SOMOZA'S RISE TO POWER

Living up to his promise, Sandino came down from the mountains and his army surrendered its weapons when the U.S. Marines left Nicaragua. He came to Managua in February 1933 and negotiated a peace agreement with President Sacasa. Sandino challenged the constitutionality of the National Guard. The settlement included a promise to reduce the size of the National Guard and to appoint a Sandinista in charge of the northern departments with the hope of reducing the power of Somoza. The promises were never kept. Somoza viewed Sandino as an obstacle to his own political ambitions and he knew that Sandino was hated by the veteran soldiers and officers of the National Guard. Seeing an opportunity not only to gain the loyalty of the Guard but also to eliminate his opposition, Somoza ordered the assassination of Sandino. Somoza received the support of his senior staff for the plan.[7] After dining with President Sacasa on the evening of February 21, the car in which Sandino was riding was stopped by the National Guard. Sandino and two others were taken to an airfield north of Managua and executed. Sandino's brother, Socrates, was also murdered that night along with 300 other Sandino supporters, including women and children, who were massacred at Sandino's headquarters. In the short run this allowed Somoza to pursue his path to power but in the long run Sandino's ghost would haunt him and finally end his family's dynasty in 1979.

After getting rid of Sandino, Somoza continued to maneuver to gain the loyalty of the Guard's soldiers and make it a tool of his personal ambitions. As U.S. officers began leaving, both he and Sacasa appointed their loyal followers to these positions. This ignited a growing tension between Sacasa and Somoza. Somoza, whose primary strength was his personal charm, had to be careful not to raise the resentment of the professional officers of the Guard who resented his interference by making political appointments rather than professional ones. To placate an outraged President Sacasa, Somoza publicly denounced the assassination of Sandino and promised to find those who were guilty. In July 1934 he discovered a plot within the Guard to assassinate him and managed to diffuse it. Although never proven, Somoza believed that the assassination attempt had been engineered by Sacasa. The conflict between Sacasa and Somoza became public in September 1935 when Somoza announced his ambitions to become the next president.

Seeing the rise in power of Somoza, Sacasa requested support from the United States; however, Ambassador Arthur Bliss Lane and the United States chose to remain neutral and not to intervene under the new Good Neighbor Policy of President Franklin Roosevelt. In effect, the neutrality policy removed yet another obstacle to Somoza's drive for power. With the Presidential Palace surrounded by the Guard, Sacasa resigned on June 6, 1936, and the *golpe* was complete. Somoza immediately moved to replace the loyal Sacasa officers in the Guard with his own loyalists. Later that year, an election was held that conservatives boycotted. The official results indicated 107,000 votes for Somoza and only 169 for his opponent. As President and Director of the National Guard, Somoza was now the most powerful person in Nicaragua. He quickly moved to squash any opposition. The United States officially recognized the Somoza government. As the scholar John Booth points out, the United States intervened under the Roosevelt Corollary and Dollar Diplomacy to create Somoza and then under the Good Neighbor Policy of neutrality and nonintervention allowed him to assume power.

MAINTAINING THE SOMOZA DYNASTY

Somoza maintained power in Nicaragua through *continuismo* by taking care of his most important allies: the National Guard, the agro-exporting economic elites of the country, and the United States. In a process called *continuismo*, he either maneuvered to get himself re-elected or put someone in power that he could manipulate. For example, no sooner had he officially assumed the presidency in January 1937 than he realized that the Nicaraguan constitution forbade him to run for a successive term. He maneuvered to allow the Constituent Assembly or Congress to rewrite the constitution. In 1939 the Assembly then voted Somoza to an eight-year term as president. Somoza took the old Liberal Party and renamed it the Liberal Nationalist Party (PLN). It became a vehicle for his personal control of the congress, the courts, and the government bureaucracy. The press was informally censored as those who wrote unfavorable articles about Somoza and his activities were often threatened with repression.

Somoza moved to take care of the interests of his most important ally, the National Guard. He began to modernize its equipment and expand its activities. He created an air force and a navy in 1938 and began purchasing ships and planes from the United States. He continually sought better ships and planes for his forces. He re-established the Nicaraguan Military Academy in 1939. To prevent any rival military groups or organizations, he declared the Guard to be the only military of Nicaragua. He dramatically improved the pay scale of its soldiers and the pensions for its officers. A career in the National Guard was a step up and out of poverty for most *Nicas* and an officer's career with its benefits was appealing to many middle class *Nicas*. While creating incentives for its members to remain loyal to the Guard, Somoza also expected all to be personally loyal to him. He handed out personal favors to his officers in return for loyalty. At the same time he kept his spies or *orejas* within the enlisted and officer ranks. Somoza dealt mercilessly with those Guardsmen identified as malcontents or in opposition to him.

The Guard came to control the national radio, the telegraph networks, traffic control, auto and driver registration, health and sanitation inspections, the postal service, the customs office and immigration, and the railroads. It exercised all police or internal affairs activities, granted business licenses, and collected all taxes. This encouraged and allowed the growth of widespread corruption. Citizens had to pay bribes to the Guardsmen who controlled many aspects of the economy, government administration, and the legal system. The Guard also came to run the lucrative gambling, prostitution, and smuggling activities of Somoza.

Somoza was very skillful in using a combination of threats, repression, economic incentives and disincentives, and the granting of just enough political freedoms and protections to manipulate or buy off the liberal and conservative economic elites of the country. Somoza provided business owners who collaborated with him with tax exemptions, free utilities, or government contracts. Agro-exporters such as the coffee elite were given support in their attempts to bring more land under cultivation. One of his first acts as president was to devalue the currency which promoted more exports. Attractive loans and credit lines at the newly created National Bank were opened up for any potential rivals among the agro-exporting elites. Somoza also never let his opponents forget his close ties to the United States. By this time all were aware that it was the National Guard that beat up, exiled, imprisoned, tortured, and murdered Somoza's opponents. For many elites the threat of any repression led them to cooperate with or at least tolerate Somoza.

Somoza, with access to the treasury and his control of the legal system and the government, began to amass a personal fortune and became the dominant force among the *Nica* agro-exporting elite and the emerging business sector. He began seizing the best unoccupied lands. Once he gained the land he used the state to build infrastructure (roads, railroads, and utilities) to it. During World War II he seized the German-owned coffee properties. In addition to coffee he began raising cotton and cattle on his newly acquired lands. All beef, except his, that was exported was taxed and this money was used by Somoza to promote his own cattle ranches and beef industry. Somoza, who had no property in 1934, owned 51 cattle ranches and 46 coffee plantations by 1944. By that time he was the largest coffee producer in the country and the largest landowner.[8] He acquired the sugar operation at Montelimar, a major tannery, a cement factory, a match factory, the National Insurance Company, the newspaper *Novedades*, textile businesses, and rental properties in several cities.[9] Somoza granted concessions to *Nicas* and foreign investors in the gold, rubber, and timber sectors of the economy. These concessions always included kickbacks to Somoza. Booth estimates that kickbacks just from the gold mining industry amounted to 175,000 to 400,000 dollars per year in the 1940s. To open a new business, owners "contributed" to Somoza's personal economic development fund. Civil servants or government employees "contributed" 5 percent of their salaries to a fund controlled by the PLN and Somoza.

Somoza recognized that he needed the continued support of the United States and he quickly became an unwavering, public, and vocal supporter of U.S. foreign policy. U.S. enemies became Nicaraguan enemies. He visited the United States in 1939 and received a grand welcome from President Roosevelt. He returned home to Nicaragua as America's "chosen man." During World War II he quickly declared war on Japan and Germany as soon as the United States did. He allowed the United States to establish military bases in the country and received military equipment under the U.S. Lend-Lease Act of 1941. He banned all pro-Nazi materials and arrested anyone who was suspected of having pro-Nazi sympathies including his Minister of War, Rigoberto Reyes.

NICARAGUA UNDER SOMOZA

Much of the fighting during the U.S. Marine occupation of the country took place in the Matagalpa-Jinotega coffee-growing areas. As a result, coffee production on the large estates in this area fell dramatically. Demand for coffee fell precipitously during the depression and this devastated the Nicaraguan economy and the wealth of the agro-exporting elites. By 1933 coffee prices had plummeted to one-third of their 1929 values. Sugar and banana prices were similarly affected. The agro-exporters tried to make up for their lost income by expanding the amount of land under production and the volume of coffee and other cash crops. To do this they had to gain access to more land. Peasants or subsistence farmers and farmers who had small lots had their lands confiscated both legally and illegally. Land became further concentrated into the hands of the wealthy.

These now landless peasants and farmers who used to own small plots of land combined with the growing number of unemployed agricultural workers and unemployed urban workers became a potential threat to the agro-export basis of the economy. Both conservative and liberal elites saw them as political and economic threats. These groups formed the basis not only for Sandino's army but also later for the Nicaraguan Worker's Party (PTN), the Nicaraguan Socialist Party (PSN), and the growth of labor unions. Initially many economic elites including conservatives supported Somoza in his rise to power because he was viewed as the only person capable of protecting their economic interests in the face of a growing political threat from the poor. Somoza was not above using repression against any threat from organized labor and peasant groups.

Because of the global depression, the economy of Nicaragua did not fully recover until the late 1940s and the early 1950s although there was some improvement during World War II. Somoza set out to modernize the agricultural sector of the country. He created a National Bank which became the most important source of credit for the agro-export elites. He created a Ministry of Agriculture to provide technical expertise to farmers and cattlemen. He developed a state-run overseas trading company to promote *Nica* exports. In an attempt to make up for the declining exports during the depression, Somoza increased the mining and exporting of gold and silver. During World War II Nicaragua provided raw materials such as rubber, metals, and wood to the United States, but even this did not improve the national economic picture. The country became more dependent on the United States with more than 90 percent of its exports sold in the U.S. market.

CONTINUISMO, OPPOSITION TO SOMOZA, THE COLD WAR, AND THE UNITED STATES

From 1944 through 1954 a wave of progressive, democratic practices swept through the neighboring countries of Costa Rica and Guatemala. This gave some encouragement to those in Nicaragua who sought to keep Somoza from the presidency in the next election. Somoza made it known in 1944 that he intended to run again. A small group of liberals, including Carlos Pasos and Enoc Aguado, came to oppose Somoza's *continuismo*. They broke with the PLN and formed the Independent Liberal Party (PLI) that same year. The PLI consisted largely of government employees, professionals, small business people, teachers, salaried-private sector employees, and students. The party's platform consisted of policies similar to the democratic reforms that were taking place in Costa Rica and Guatemala: fair elections and an economic "New Deal" for the middle and working classes. The PLI created a student organization, the Democratic Youth Front (FJD), which successfully mobilized students, especially in the northern areas of the country which were traditional areas of liberal strength. One of its more outspoken members was Tomás Borge Martínez who later became one of the founding members of the Sandinista National Liberation Front (FSLN).

Students began to play a more essential role in the opposition to Somoza as early as 1939 by staging demonstrations in León. On June 27, 1944, students from the university in Managua peacefully protested Somoza's decision to run for his party's nomination as President. More than 500 students were arrested and jailed. The next day women dressed in black marched to protest the jailing of the students. At the same time there was a student-led demonstration in León protesting the jailing of the students in Managua. On July 4 there was a student-led demonstration in front of the U.S Embassy. Students and middle-class intellectuals who were involved in these events and other anti-Somoza activities in the next few years came to be known as the Generation of 1944. This generation included Borge and Jose Ramon Gutierrez Castro of the FJD and Pedro Joaquín Chamorro Cardenal who was a member of the conservative, elite Chomorro family from

Granada. His family's newspaper, *La Prensa*, was shut down that year and the Chamorro family fled to Mexico. Chamorro returned to Nicaragua in 1948 and would continue to play a most significant role in the struggle against the Somoza family dictatorship over the next 30 years.

Sensing the growing frustration in the country, in yet another example of *continuismo*, Somoza maneuvered to gain support of the labor unions and the PSN in 1945 by passing a series of policies designed to assist laborers. With the death of Franklin Roosevelt, President Harry Truman informed Somoza that the United States expected him to abide by the constitution and to not seek another term in office. Somoza, in an attempt to curry favor with the new American administration, not only agreed but also released political detainees from his jails, quit censoring the press, and allowed peaceful demonstrations. In the 1947 presidential election, the PLI and the Conservative Party united behind Aguado. Somoza then proceeded via a fraudulent election process to get his liberal ally Leonardo Arguello elected president in 1947. By this time, Somoza had "forgotten" about his pledges to labor unions and the PSN.

In a surprise to almost all in Nicaragua, Arguello asserted his independence and made plans to "retire" Somoza and his close allies in the National Guard. In May 1947 Somoza staged a *golpe* claiming that Arguello was plotting to establish a dictatorship and cooperating with communists. The Congress then named the *Somocista* Benjamin Lacayo Sacasa as the provisional president who served until August and was then replaced by Somoza's aging Uncle Victor Roman y Reyes. President Truman refused to recognize the new government. Somoza knew that somehow he had to regain the support of the United States. In a master stroke of timing and maneuvering, Somoza played the Cold War, anti-communist card. The PLN-dominated Congress passed a series of anti-communist laws which banned the PSN and invited the United States to set up military bases in the country to protect the hemisphere from the "growing threat of communism." In 1947 Somoza began to seek out and arrest all members of the PSN. By 1948 the United States had re-established diplomatic relations with Nicaragua. Somoza had correctly seen the changes in the world political scene and the growing Cold War tensions between the United States and the Soviet Union. Seeing the change in U.S. foreign policy, he effectively used this to his own political advantage.

In March 1950 Somoza met with leading conservatives Carlos Cuadra Pasos and Emiliano Chamorro. In still another example of *continuismo*, a deal known as the "pact of the generals" was made in which the constitution would be amended so that the Conservative Party was guaranteed one-third of the seats in the National Congress. Somoza's PLN would control two-thirds and he would be "elected" to the presidency. This was recognition and acceptance by the conservative leadership of the unchallenged power of Somoza. Elections after this pact became meaningless as all knew the outcome. Roman y Reyes died of a heart attack in May and the Congress promptly named Somoza as acting President. Later that month Somoza was elected to another term as president and the "pact of the generals" was implemented.

THE COTTON BOOM, ECONOMIC GROWTH, AND CONSEQUENCES

By the early 1950s the U.S. economy was expanding dramatically and there was a growing global demand for commodities such as sugar, bananas, coffee, and especially cotton. Somoza and the agro-export elites took advantage of this and cotton production expanded dramatically in Nicaragua, especially in the departments of León and Chinandega. By 1955 cotton was the leading export of the country and by the early 1960s it was the largest source of rural employment and earner of foreign exchange (currencies such as the dollar that are accepted anywhere in the world).[10] Between 1951 and 1955 the amount of land devoted to cotton production increased nearly 10 times. Cotton production increased more than 120 times in the northwest departments of León and Chinandega between 1949 and 1955.[11] In 1949 the country exported 379 metric tons of cotton. By 1955 it exported 43,971 metric tons.[12] Technological changes, such as chemical pesticides and the use of planes to spray the large estates, allowed the dramatic increase in production. Access to modern machinery, modern irrigation systems, as well as better roads and increased access to utilities aided the process. Sugar, bananas, and coffee production also expanded dramatically. All of this economic growth was facilitated by the provision of extensive credit from the National Bank and international lenders from the United States. From 1951 through 1952 almost 80 percent of lending for agriculture went to a few hundred producers of cotton and sugar and in 1952 more than two-thirds of all bank loans went to cotton and coffee producers. This continued through the 1960s.[13]

By the mid-1950s one could see the appearance of three networks of economic elites in Nicaragua.[14] Each network of elite families and business interests tended to coalesce around key banking and financial institutions in the country and the United States. One network of economic elites was associated with the Bank of America and came to be known as the BANAMERICA Group. It was made up of the old conservative elite families of Granada including interests in sugar, rum, cattle, coffee, export-import businesses, department stores, and supermarkets. The network had close ties to the Wells Fargo Bank and the First National Bank of Boston.

Another network of elites was associated with the Nicaraguan Bank and came to be known as the BANIC group. It was associated with León and the growth of cotton. It also included those involved in coffee, merchants and commercial enterprises, land development and construction, lumber, fish, and vegetable oil processing. This network had close ties to Chase Manhattan Bank. Yet, BANIC and BANAMERICA had connecting family ties. Pedro Joaquín Chamorro served on the Board for BANIC while his first cousin, Alfredo Pellas Chamorro, who owned San Antonio, the largest sugar mill in Central America, served on the Board for BANAMERICA. The third network consisted of the Somoza family and its extensive economic empire. The National Bank and the Central Bank financed most of Somoza's economic ventures, although later this network established its own *Banco Centroamericano*. According to Booth, even though these networks represented different families and businesses, they developed ties and relationships among them which contributed to a convergence of interest among the *Nica* elites.[15] Any business or agricultural venture that was not a part of one of these networks suffered under tremendous disadvantages. The disadvantages included the lack of access to political power and the lack of access to both national and international financial resources that were so crucial to surviving in an agro-export economy led by the Somoza economic empire.

Similar to the coffee boom of the late 1800s and early 1900s, the cotton boom of the early to mid-1950s led to a further concentration of land among the wealthy in Nicaragua. Small farmers who were not members of the three major elite agro-export networks could not gain access to credit. They were bought out by the large agro-elites who needed more and more land. Share-cropping arrangements came to an end as the growth of modern agriculture turned to wage-labor only. Peasants were forced off their lands. Those who lost their land or no longer had access to land either became seasonal wage-workers on the large plantations or moved to the urban areas to find employment or more marginal and remote lands (land that is not well-suited for agriculture) in the northeast.

THE DEATH OF ANASTASIO SOMOZA GARCÍA AND *CONTINUISMO* UNDER LUIS SOMOZA

Somoza continued to expand his economic empire in the early 1950s. He came to own the only dairy in the country that could pasteurize milk. The congress then passed legislation requiring that all milk must be pasteurized prior to being sold. He developed two textile companies, a merchant marine company, and the Nicaraguan Airline. He built and developed a new port, Puerto Somoza, on the Pacific coast. He continued to support U.S. foreign policy. U.S. military aid to Nicaragua averaged 200,000 dollars per year between 1953 and 1961. In a show of anti-communist solidarity, Somoza provided volunteers to the U.S.-sponsored group that overthrew the democratically elected Jacobo Arbenz government in Guatemala in 1954. In January 1955 he sponsored an invasion of Costa Rica with the hope of overthrowing the democratically elected government of Pepe Figureres. Somoza and many in the United States considered the government to be "communist leaning." The invasion failed largely due to lack of air support from the United States but it was clear that Somoza had established his credentials as a fervent anti-communist.

In April 1954 old-line conservative Emiliano Chamorro and the young conservative Pedro Joaquín Chamorro, editor of *La Prensa*, led an attempt to assassinate Somoza. The attempt failed and the leaders, including Pedro Joaquín Chamorro, were thrown in jail and not released until 1956. On September 21, 1956, "Tacho" Somoza was shot by Rigoberto López Pérez at a reception in León at the *Casa del Obrero*. López, a 27-year-old journalist and poet, was immediately gunned down by members of the National Guard. López insisted in a letter to his mother that he had acted alone. Somoza died nine days later in a U.S. hospital in the Panama Canal Zone. Somoza's eldest son, Luis Somoza Debayle, who was President of the Congress, was named acting president. Nearly 3,000 people were interrogated, tortured, arrested, or put on trial for the murder of Somoza García. One of the first arrested was Pedro Joaquín Chomorro who was interrogated and tortured for months, sometimes by the youngest Somoza, Anastasio "Tachito" Somoza Debayle, the new head of the National Guard. A graduate of the U.S. Military Academy at West Point, "Tachito" Somoza used all types of torture in his jails including water-boarding, the hanging of individuals by their genitals, electrical shocks, and imprisonment in coffin-sized cells. His more infamous torture was to place his opponents in animal cages open to the weather, often next to lions and panthers. These cages were placed in the garden of the presidential residence. The Somoza families including their children often "strolled" past the cages as if visiting a zoo.[16] Others that were arrested included Borge, the aging Emiliano Chamorro, former presidential candidate Aguado, and Carlos Fonseca Amador. Fonseca later became the founder of the FSLN. Most who were arrested were eventually set free while some like Pedro Joaquín Chomorro were eventually jailed in a remote prison in the southern city of San Carlos. Pedro Joaquín Chamorro managed to escape and cross the border into Costa Rica. Although many in Nicaragua wanted to get rid of "Tacho" Somoza, it was never proven that there was a conspiracy to assassinate him in 1956; more than likely Lopez acted alone.

Learning from his father, in an act of *continuismo*, Luis Somoza maneuvered to get Edmundo Amador selected as his token opponent in the

February 1957 election for the presidency. Luis Somoza's election as the next President came as no surprise to anyone. In an attempt to win back some of the liberals who had come to oppose his family, he amended the constitution to prevent any member of his family from running for president in the next election. Some *Nicas* believed that Luis Somoza was serious when he announced that his administration would be a "bridge to democracy." Yet, he represented the public and courteous side of the family while his brother, "Tachito," as head of the National Guard was the enforcer behind the scenes. Booth states that while Tachito tortured and killed, Luis made the public and courteous explanations to the families.[17] In 1958, there were conservative-led uprisings against Somoza *continuismo*. These were often led by disgruntled members of the National Guard and the older generation conservatives. Quite often these groups surrendered prior to any real combat with Somoza's National Guard. In essence, the traditional conservatives simply wanted to replace Luis Somoza with one of their own.[18] Ramón Raudales, who had fought with Augusto César Sandino, organized a small army in the Matagalpa region. He was killed in October and his army fell apart. Luis Somoza and his brother, Tachito, justified their periodic repressive actions in the name of anti-communism.

Under Luis Somoza the economy expanded with the growing textile and livestock (cattle/beef) industries. U.S. foreign aid to the country increased and was almost entirely controlled by the Somoza family. The *Nica* middle class consisting of professionals, small businessmen, teachers, government employees, and white-collar workers began to expand as the country became more urbanized. Land, access to financing, and wealth continued to be concentrated into the hands of the wealthy, in particular, the BANAMERICA and BANIC groups and the Somozas. The vast majority of *Nicas* failed to benefit from the economic growth that was taking place in their country. Economic insecurity became common among the vast majority in the countryside as peasants continued to lose access to land.

THE CUBAN REVOLUTION

In perhaps the most significant event in Latin American history in the twentieth century, Fidel Castro and his band of bearded revolutionaries rode triumphantly into Havana, Cuba, on January 8, 1959. In the name of anti-communism and the fear of more Cuban-style revolutions, the military began to play a much greater role, if not a dominant one, in the politics of almost every country in Latin America. Authoritarian governments used the military to repress anyone or any group that was considered on the political left or to be a communist. This often included union leaders and members, students, teachers, and faculty at universities. Civil rights, human rights, and political freedoms took a backseat to the struggle against communism and the fear of Cuban-style revolutions. U.S. foreign policy supported these efforts in Latin America.

At the same time the Cuban revolution stirred the passions of students throughout Latin America. It provided a model for getting rid of an authoritarian or dictatorial regime and the promise of a more egalitarian and democratic society. Radical student leaders in Nicaragua, such as Fonseca, hurried to Havana. Students began to play a much more active role in the opposition to the Somoza dynasty. On July 23, 1959, the National Guard attacked and killed unarmed student-led protestors in León. Of the 3,000 protestors that day, four students were killed while hundreds were wounded. The next day more than 12,000 people turned out for the funeral march through the city. The University did not reopen until the end of August and then students waged a successful campaign to get the National Guard expelled from campus. Later that year the first national conference of university students was held in León. The university students adopted resolutions which repudiated the pro-U.S. Bryan-Chamorro Treaty, condemned the "sell-out behavior" of the major parties, and supported issues most important to working class *Nicas*.[19] Students of this age group became known as the Generation of 59 or the Generation of the 23rd of July. Luis Somoza founded a private, Jesuit university in Managua, the Central American University (UCA), as an effort to counter the radicalization of the students at the National University in León. This proved to be unsuccessful as members of the FSLN were elected to lead the student government at the Central American University in 1963. By 1961, the stage was set for members of the Generation of 44, such as Borge, and the Generation of 59, such as Fonseca and Silvio Mayorga, to create a new guerrilla-military-political organization inspired by the Cuban revolution and based on the teachings of Sandino with the goal of toppling the Somoza dynasty and bringing about revolutionary change in Nicaragua.

CARLOS FONSECA AMADOR (1936–1976)

Fonseca stood out from his fellow Sandinistas. He was over six feet tall, fair-skinned, and skinny. Although he had striking blue eyes, he suffered from poor eyesight and almost always wore eye glasses. More importantly, Fonseca was not only the founder but also the intellectual and strategic leader of the Sandinista National Liberation Front (FSLN). Born in 1936 in Matagalpa, Fonseca was the illegitimate son of Fausto Amador Aleman. The politically powerful Amador family consisted of wealthy coffee planters and merchants. Fonseca's father was also a powerful Somoza supporter. His mother, Augustina Fonseca Ubeda, was poor but apparently very attractive. For most of his youth Fonseca lived in poverty with his mother, brothers, and sisters in a small back room in his aunt's house, although his aunt kicked them out of the house each time his unwed mother became pregnant. Fonseca's father initially paid for his illegitimate son's high school fees, lunches, and some clothes largely at the insistence of his wife. Eventually the high school awarded him a full scholarship because of his excellent grades and his ties to the Amador family. Fonseca was involved in anti-Somoza politics while at the National Institute of the North, a high school in Matagalpa known for its student activism. In his final year at high school in 1954 he and several students published a journal *Segovia* which focused on social issues, especially the lack of education among the poor and working-class conditions in the country. It represented an indirect attack on the policies of the Somoza government. According to Matilde Zimmerman, Fonseca joined the then-illegal Communist Party of Nicaragua (PSN) in 1954 and sold the party's newspaper locally.

In the spring of 1955 Fonseca moved to Managua and was hired to organize the library of the *El Goyena*, the leading secular high school in the city which gave preference to the sons of Somoza supporters and Liberal Party politicians and military officers. He recruited student-followers, published a newsletter called *Diriangen*, loaned books to kids in the poor barrios of Managua, and continued to sell *Segovia* and the newspaper of the PSN. In the spring of 1956 he moved to León and enrolled in the National University of Nicaragua as a law student. Fonseca had always been a serious student and was extremely well-read. He spent his evenings and late nights reading and discussing politics and literature. It was in León that he organized the first all-student PSN cell which included Borge and Mayorga. The cell lasted only a few months as it was largely ignored by the PSN. In the aftermath of the assassination of Somoza García in September 1956, he and hundreds of other students were arrested and thrown in jail. He was released without charges in November. In 1957 Fonseca was a delegate to the Sixth World Congress of Students and Youth for Peace and Friendship in Moscow. In 1958 he began to break with the PSN over its support for Luis Somoza's labor legislation. He organized the first nationwide student strike and demanded the release of the remaining students held in jail for Somoza's assassination. Fonseca helped to organize high school students in León. He and other young radicals flocked to Havana in 1959. Che Guevara organized many of the radicals, including Fonseca, into an armed guerrilla-force that trained in Honduras. This ill-fated group, the *Columna Rigoberto López Pérez*, was ambushed by Honduran and Nicaraguan army troops in June 1959 at El Chaparral in Honduras. Fonseca was wounded and treated in a prison hospital in Tegucigalpa. It was the Cuban Revolution and El Chaparral that led to Fonseca's complete split with the

FSN and his growing belief in Sandino's teachings and strategies as a guide for a revolution in Nicaragua.[20] He saw the development of a new revolutionary group which would finish the tasks started by Sandino by mobilizing peasants and workers into a military force with a true *Nica* identity based on self-determination and nationalism. Fonseca left Honduras for Havana and planned the formation of his new revolutionary group, the FSLN.

Virtually all of the essays, articles, and manifestos that defined the ideology of the FSLN were written by Fonseca. Fonseca's writings emphasized two themes. One was the fight for national liberation against the Somoza dynasty and the United States. Fonseca viewed this as a continuation of Sandino's earlier struggle against the United States and those Nicaraguans who collaborated with the United States. The second theme focused on the struggle for a truly socialist revolution, a revolution that would end the suffering and exploitation of *Nica* workers and peasants. According to Fonseca, social justice for the lower classes could be achieved only through a truly socialist revolution. It is important to point out that although Fonseca was an intellectual, his writings and speeches, like Sandino's, were a "language ordinary people could understand."[21]

NOTES

1. Jeffery Paige, *Coffee and Power* (Cambridge: Harvard University Press, 1999), 173.

2. Stephen Kinzer, *Blood of Brothers: Life and War in Nicaragua* (Cambridge: Harvard University Press, 1991), 29.

3. John Booth, *The End and the Beginning* (Boulder, CO: Westview Press, 1982), 44.

4. Neil Macaulay, *The Sandino Affair* (Chicago: Quadrangle Books, 1971), 111–17.

5. Booth, *The End and the Beginning*, 45.

6. Ibid., 46.

7. Richard Millet argues that Somoza was pressured by the senior officers of the Guard into giving the execution order for Sandino. See his book *Guardians of the Dynasty: A History of the US-Created Guardia Nacional de Nicaragua and the Somoza Family* (Maryknoll, NY: Orbis Books, 1977).

8. Charles D. Brockett, *Land, Power, and Poverty*, 2nd ed. (Boulder, CO: Westview Press, 1998), 44.

9. Booth, *The End and the Beginning*, 68.

10. Brockett, *Land, Power, and Poverty*, 46.

11. Matilde Zimmerman, *Sandinista: Carlos Fonseca and the Nicaraguan Revolution* (Durham: Duke University Press, 2000), 41. See also John Booth, *The End and the Beginning*, 66.

12. Thomas W. Walker, *Nicaragua*, 4th ed. (Boulder, CO: Westview Press, 2003), 84.

13. Brockett, *Land, Power, and Poverty*, 47.

14. Jaime Wheelock Roman, *Imperialismo y dictadura* (Managua: Editorial Nueva Nicaragua, 1985), 141–74.

15. Booth, *The End and the Beginning*, 66–67.

16. Ibid., 72.

17. Ibid., 73.

18. Zimmerman, *Sandinista*, 51.

19. Ibid., 59.

20. Ibid., 55–56.

21. Ibid., 10.

5

The Sandinistas and the Fall of the Somoza Dynasty (1959–1979)

Revolutions are extremely complex political and social phenomena and the Nicaraguan revolution was no different. Several key factors help to understand the fall of the Somoza dynasty in 1979. By the mid-1970s virtually every sector of Nicaraguan society including the Church, many economic elites, laborers, members of the middle class, students, indigenous people, and the urban and rural poor no longer accepted the government as legitimate. The immense corruption and brutality of the Somozas eventually undermined even the family's most ardent supporters. During the 1950s and 1960s Nicaragua experienced tremendous economic growth, especially in agriculture. Many policy makers, especially those in the United States who played a major role in financing this growth through the Alliance for Progress, believed that economic growth would promote stability and democracy. Yet, this growth contributed to the fall of the Somozas in several ways. It actually increased economic inequality in the country. More land came to be concentrated in the hands of a small group of agro-exporters. As the export agricultural sector expanded and modernized many rural poor lost their land and their own ability to meet the basic needs of their families. The gap between the wealthiest and poorest *Nicas* expanded.

These insecure peasants in the countryside turned to groups like the Sandinistas and the so-called progressive Church who promised to restore their land, economic security, and basic human rights. As the economy expanded more and more sectors of the population, especially the growing middle class, desired a greater and meaningful say in the political processes. This was met with opposition in the form of Somoza *continuismo*. With a growing economy the expectations of the Nicaraguan people increased. Expectations included the desire for better jobs, housing, and education for their children—a better life in general. The civil war escalated in the mid-1970s and when the economy suffered it was clear to most that the Somoza government could never and would never meet those rising expectations. All of these factors laid the groundwork for the revolution.

One should note that revolutions also require leadership and in the case of Nicaragua Pedro Joaquín Chamorro and Carlos Fonseca Amador stand out. Revolutions typically require at least one political organization that has adequate resources and organizational strength and provides an alternative ideology or political program to challenge the existing, illegitimate government. In the case of Nicaragua this was the Sandinista Front for National Liberation (FSLN). While waging a war against an illegitimate government, the building of a base of support in the countryside is important; it is also necessary to have an active urban underground that is willing to face extreme hardships and wage a war of terrorism against the government. The Sandinistas created both a base of support in the countryside and an urban underground. Finally, revolutions need an event or events that serve to provide a spark to ignite or accelerate the process. The 1972 earthquake that devastated Managua and the murder of Chamorro in 1978 provided the sparks that led to the success of the Sandinista-led revolution in Nicaragua.

CONTINUISMO

Opposition to Somoza's *continuismo* mounted in 1959. President Luis Somoza discovered that two major opposition groups, one in Costa Rica and the other in Honduras, were preparing invasions to topple his government. He believed that he could negotiate with the group in Costa Rica but not with the group in Honduras. In late May, Chamorro, the dissident conservative, member of the Generation of 1944, editor of *La Prensa*, and the leader of the Popular Christian Democratic Movement (MPDC) led an invasion of Nicaragua with Enrique Lacayo Farfan, a leader of the Independent Liberal Party (PLI). Chamorro had escaped prison in 1957 in San Carlos and fled to Costa Rica to organize an opposition force. The invasion went wrong from the very beginning with the planes landing at different places and a nationwide strike call that was never made. Tachito Somoza and the National Guard captured most of the invaders. Although the invasion was financed by some of the elite families in the country, Luis Somoza, who had learned politics quite well from his father, softened the repression against them. He was ever mindful of the need to placate the agro-elite families and to keep them from completely joining the opposition.[1] In June the Nicaraguan National Guard with assistance from Honduras ambushed the Cuban-led and supported *Columna Rigoberto López Pérez* at El Chaparral in Honduras. Those who were not killed were taken to a prison hospital in Tegucigalpa. Among those was Carlos Fonseca Amador who then made his way to Havana.

In November 1960 Luis Somoza announced another state of siege and used the National Guard in an effort to stifle and eliminate the growing opposition. Luis Somoza, like his father, did everything he could to maintain close ties to the United States. U.S.-backed Cuban exiles were provided an airfield and ports for their ships in their ill-fated attempt to overthrow Fidel Castro at the Bay of Pigs in April 1961. He played the anti-communist, anti-Castro card quite well in gaining continued U.S. economic aid and support for the National Guard. The National Guard benefitted from improved equipment, such as helicopters and guerrilla and counterinsurgency training conducted by U.S. military advisers. Nicaragua joined the Central American Defense Council in which the armies of all the Central American countries coordinated their anti-communist and security measures with the U.S. Central Command in Panama. At the same time Luis Somoza continued a democratic façade with some moderate reforms toward labor.

In 1962 the Alliance for Progress was initiated by President John F. Kennedy and the United States. The thrust of the Alliance for Progress was that the best way to fight communism and to prevent another Castro in Latin America was through economic growth and development largely financed by the United States. It amounted to a mini-Marshall Plan for Central America and the Caribbean. Both economic and military aid poured into Nicaragua. Economic aid doubled and military aid increased by seven times. Military aid to the National Guard played a major role in overcoming most of the organized opposition to Somoza's *continuismo*. By 1962 the young, reformist conservatives, known as the MPDC and led by Chamorro, initially supported Fernando Aguero Rocha in the 1962 presidential election. The MPDC-led Conservative Party then decided to boycott the election correctly believing that it was rigged in favor of Luis Somoza's candidate. In another example of *continuismo*, Rene Schick who had been the personal secretary to the elder Somoza and the Minister of Education under Luis Somoza was "elected" by a ten-to-one margin as president in

1963. Luis Somoza had come to believe that his family could continue to rule the country via the Liberal Nationalist Party (PLN) and its vast economic enterprises without directly occupying the presidency. Schick was seen as basically a "yes-man" for the Somoza brothers, while he kept up the façade of democratic reform. With Luis Somoza in the background focusing on the PLN and Tachito Somoza firmly in control of the National Guard, Schick also played the anti-communist card with the United States. In 1965 Nicaraguan troops assisted the U.S. invasion and occupation of the Dominican Republic. This was yet another show of support for the United States during the Cold War.

Under the Alliance for Progress both Luis Somoza and Schick began to diversify the Nicaraguan economy. From 1961 through 1967 the economy grew at 7 percent annually, the highest in Latin America. Agricultural production increased at 5 percent a year. The Unite States provided more than 43 million dollars in economic aid between 1962 and 1966. Cotton production peaked in 1965 and declined until 1970.[2] With its decline in the 1960s, cattle or beef production for export increased significantly. In 1960 the United States imported virtually no beef but by 1980 it was importing 10 percent of the beef necessary for consumption. The dramatic increase paralleled the growth of the fast-food sector in America such as McDonalds. Nicaraguan beef exports increased dramatically from 1961 through 1973 with much of it funded internationally from the United States, the World Bank, and the Inter-American Development Bank. Nicaraguan sugar and banana production increased. The country began to develop some light industries such as the packaging of fertilizers and insecticides. With U.S. support it developed a limited ability to refine oil.

President Schick increased government spending dramatically creating many jobs in the public or government sector. There were more university graduates in the 1960s and many found employment in the expanding government sectors designed to implement and oversee the Alliance for Progress programs. This also meant that they had to become members, if only in name, of the PLN which was run by the Somoza family. At the same time an expanding commercial and industrial sector caused the size of the middle class to grow with an increase in managerial, clerical, and sales jobs. Downtown Managua acquired a commercial district with shops that stocked U.S.-made goods for the growing middle class.

Although the economic growth was dramatic, it was clear that the new wealth, as in the past, was not distributed equally. By 1963 the top one-tenth percent of the rural population owned 20 percent of the land, while the bottom 50 percent owned less than 3 percent of the arable land. The growth of the cotton industry had displaced more peasants than any industry in the history of the country. Although some migrated to marginal farm land in the mountains, most migrated to Managua looking for work. The population of Managua doubled during the 1950s and doubled again in the 1960s. By 1969 more than 75 percent of the households in Managua survived on less than 100 dollars per month.[3]

Opposition to Somoza *continuismo* throughout the 1960s and 1970s came from three primary groups. The first group was the Sandinistas or the FSLN that grew out of the student movements of the late 1950s. The Sandinistas followed the legacy of Augusto César Sandino and believed that the only way to change Nicaragua was through violent revolution. Throughout the 1960s the Sandinistas were small in number and they did not become a powerful force until the mid-1970s. Another group was the so-called progressive Catholic Church whose members who had come to accept the principles and ideals of Vatican II, the bishops' conference at Medellin in 1968, and liberation theology. The progressive Church organized peasants in the countryside and the poor in the *barrios* of the larger cities. By the 1970s there was a growing alliance between the progressive Church and the Sandinistas. A final opposition group was the conservatives and, in particular, the younger, dissident conservatives led by Chamorro. It was the assassination of Chamorro in 1978 that provided the spark to unite all the opposition groups and led to the overthrow of the Somoza family.

THE SANDINISTAS

The FSLN traces its roots to the student generations of 1944 and 1959. Three of the founding members were Tomás Borge, a member of the Generation of 1944, and Fonseca and Silvio Mayorga, both members of the Generation of 1959. The forerunners of the FSLN were primarily short-lived student groups in the late 1950s and early 1960s who were inspired by the Cuban Revolution. These include the Democratic Youth Movement (JDN) formed by Fonseca and Mayorga, the Revolutionary Nicaraguan Youth (JRN) that published a small paper *Juventud Revolucionaria* from Costa Rica, and the Patriotic Nicaraguan Youth (JPN) made up primarily of the youth of members of the Conservative Party. Most of the members of these groups did not become Sandinistas but a few of note did including Julio Buitrago and José Benito Escobar of the JPN. These groups were important not only because of their youth but also because they separated themselves from both the traditional elite, family-led liberal and conservative parties and the Nicaraguan Socialist Party (PSN or the Nicaraguan communist party). These student groups were committed to organizing and taking direct action, sometimes violent, against the Somoza government.

Several student leaders who were to play a major role in the FSLN including Fonseca, Borge, Mayorga, Rodolfo Romero, and Noel Guerrero slipped in and out of Nicaragua during the 1960s and regularly traveled to Cuba, Costa Rica, Mexico, and Honduras. They helped to organize student demonstrations and regularly communicated with the Student Center of the National University in León. In 1961 Fonseca, Borge, Mayorga, and others created the Movement for a New Nicaragua (MNN) in Honduras. The MNN then created cells in Managua, Estelí, and León. With nearly the same membership, the MNN was transformed into the National Liberation Front (FLN) in late 1961 and early 1962. It was Fonseca who finally convinced his fellow revolutionaries to add the word Sandinista to the name of the group. This marked the emergence of Fonseca as the central leader of the group, and according to Matilde Zimmerman, the earliest appearance of any written documents with the name FSLN on them appeared in September and October of 1963.[4]

Several Sandinistas including Fonseca, Mayorga, Borge, and Romero gained valuable combat experience helping Castro fight counterrevolutionary forces in the Escambray Mountains of Cuba just prior to the April 1961 Bay of Pigs invasion. Taking a chapter from the Cuban revolution, the Sandinistas attempted to establish rural base camps in the remote mountains of the north. Borge and others established a camp in the village of Raiti near the intersection of the Coco and Bocay rivers in 1963. The group which lacked adequate weapons, supply lines, and peasant support did not know the local geography. It was attacked and easily defeated by the National Guard in August. Losses were heavy. With this defeat the FSLN almost ceased to exist. Its total membership was approximately 10 guerrillas in the mountains and 20 members in the urban underground.[5] Fearing the collapse of his organization, Fonseca, who had been in Honduras, returned to Nicaragua in June 1964 and was promptly arrested by the National Guard. In his public trial he effectively used the courtroom to spread the story and message of the Sandinistas. His courtroom speeches were published word-for-word in Chamorro's newspaper *La Prensa*. Fonseca's "From Jail, I Accuse the Dictatorship" was his best known prison writing or speech and it was reminiscent of Fidel Castro's 1953 prison speech "History Will Absolve Me." While in prison he fell in love with activist María Haydeé Terán. Haydeé's family members were well-known dissident liberals and members of the PLI. They owned a publishing house and a bookstore in León. In January 1965 Fonseca was exiled to Guatemala where he married Haydeé. For more than a year he and Edelberto Torres researched the anti-imperialist poetry of Rubén Dario. He did not publish any anti-Somoza writings until his return to Nicaragua.

From 1963 through 1966 the Sandinistas retreated to recruit members and develop both their urban and rural support structures. Individuals had to be asked by current members of the FSLN before they could join the organization. Senior Sandinista leaders reviewed the credentials of prospective members. Once one became a member, complete secrecy and obedience were expected. Members were given a personal contact within the FSLN and were organized into small groups called cells. Contact with Sandinistas beyond the cell was not common and the cells were purposely kept small so that if a person was captured by the National Guard, he or she would be unable to divulge much information even when tortured.

Throughout the 1960s the Sandinistas established a network of safe houses in the major cities of western Nicaragua. Typically found in working class *barrios* or small farms outside of the towns, the safe houses provided a place to hide from the National Guard, rest and recover from their wounds, or hold meetings to discuss strategy. Many of the safe houses were the homes of family members of those who were either members of or collaborators with the Sandinistas. Neighbors often provided an information network concerning movements of the National Guard for the families who lived in the safe houses. Sandinistas almost always used pseudonyms when speaking of fellow Sandinistas. Often the pseudonyms were the names of former martyrs to the cause. Fonseca was often referred to as "David" from David Tejada who had been a murdered student leader. Dora María Téllez, better known as *La Commandante* Dora, used names from young, educated, elite women like herself who had been killed in the struggle.[6]

From 1964 to 1966 the Sandinistas competed with other groups for the allegiance of those students and others who were opposed to Somoza *continuismo*. With Fonseca absent and not taking an active leadership role, the appearance of a more liberal political process under President Schick, and tremendous economic growth taking place in the country, the more moderate PSN-led Republican Mobilization (MR) provided an alternative organization for students and others to protest Somoza and promote a pro-labor agenda without supporting the violent, revolutionary option of the FSLN. The FSLN had a small number of supporters within the Federation of Revolutionary Students (FER) but even the FER lost control of student organizations at the universities in Managua and León to a student group associated with the Social Christian Party (PSC). The PSC collaborated with the MR. In fact, many of the Sandinistas such as Mayorga and Carlos Reyna worked with the moderate MR in publishing an anti-Somoza weekly. Sandinistas provided literacy classes to workers in the *barrios* of Managua. They worked to bring utilities such as water and electricity to the *barrios*. Students in the Student Center in the National University in León who normally had close contact with the FSLN worked with the Social Christians and the PSN in support for the Conservative Party candidate Aguero in the 1967 elections. In looking back at this period Fonseca argues that the FSLN strategy of working with the other groups was a mistake and accepted his own personal failure that caused the Sandinistas to "lose" their revolutionary and ideological fervor.[7] The January 1967 massacre and the *continuismo* of Tachito Somoza would return the FSLN to its violent-revolutionary strategy.

TACHITO SOMOZA COMES TO POWER

With his brother bowing out of the political processes, the ambitious and ruthless West Point graduate Tachito Somoza began to make his move for the presidency. On August 1, 1966, he announced via the government's owned and operated national radio station that he would be a candidate for the presidency in the next election. Two days later Schick died of a heart attack and the PLN which controlled the Congress selected Lorenzo Guerrero to replace him until the next election. Guerrero, for the most part, followed the wishes of the young Somoza. The united opposition of conservatives and liberals once again ran Aguero, the wealthy cattle rancher, as its candidate. Opposition rallies were often harassed and broken up by the National Guard. On January 22, 1967, Aguero organized a mass rally of about 30,000 supporters in Managua. Aguero's supporters then began marching up Roosevelt Avenue when the National Guard fired shots into the crowd and killed more than 100 demonstrators. Some in the crowd responded with their own gunfire. The National Telegraph Office was bombed and many demonstrators ran for cover into the National Palace. The battle continued through the night and the next day Tachito Somoza ordered tanks into the downtown area of Managua. Most demonstrators fled but about 600 insurgents held up in the Grand Hotel including Aguero. They took about 100 people hostage, many of them U.S. citizens, and a stand-off ensued. With well more than 200 dead, the Church and the U.S. Ambassador intervened and convinced Aguero and the other leaders to let the hostages go and lay down their arms in exchange for not being arrested. Tachito Somoza effectively blamed the event on the Cubans and local communists. He shut down all opposition radio stations, shut down *La Prensa*, and arrested hundreds. It was in this atmosphere that Tachito was elected president in early February 1967. Through the intense efforts of the Red Cross and the Church a general amnesty was granted to many political prisoners prior to Tachito Somoza's inauguration in April. Just before his inauguration, Tachito's brother, Luis, died of a heart attack.

Tachito Somoza ruled more through naked, brute force and corruption than his brother. He used the National Guard to eliminate and intimidate the opposition. He protected Guardsmen from any atrocities that they committed. While his brother was more likely to appointe individuals with the technical and educational skills into leadership positions within the governmental bureaucracies, Tachito's appointments were based strictly on family, loyalty, and the creation of expedient political allies. Knowledge and expertise were secondary considerations. Tachito Somoza began extorting money from businessmen to a degree never witnessed under his father and brother. Finally, he benefitted tremendously from the unquestioning support provided by President Richard Nixon and the U.S. government. Tachito Somoza came to power the same year that Pope Paul VI stated in his encyclical, formal statement on Church doctrine, *Populorum Progressio*, that "The Earth was made for all, not just for the rich." This theme was reflected in the growth of a progressive, more militant Church in Nicaragua, one that would organize the increasing number of economically insecure peasants in the countryside and come to oppose the Somoza family.

THE PROGRESSIVE CATHOLIC CHURCH

Historically the Catholic Church in Latin America was supportive of the political, economic, and social status quo and tolerant of the abuses that governments heaped on their citizens. A few spoke out against abuses but these brave souls represented a minority of the laity, clergy, and bishops. Penny Lernoux puts it rather bluntly, "Look behind a [Latin American] dictator; there stands a bishop." This began to change in the early 1960s with the convening of the Second Ecumenical Council in Rome or what is now referred to as Vatican II. The reforms of Vatican II had a dramatic influence on many in the Church throughout Latin America. Vatican II contributed to the image of the Church as a community of equals instead of hierarchical, power arrangements such as laity, clergy, and bishops. It focused on the need for dramatic reforms to address mass poverty and social and political injustice. Taking up the ideals of Vatican II, many members of the Church laity, clergy, and bishops began to advocate on behalf of the poor for basic human rights.

When the Latin American bishops met in Medellin in 1968, many of them openly questioned the poverty of the vast majority of people, the military repression, and violation of basic human rights that had become commonplace throughout the continent. Many came to support a theology of liberation and became social activists, even revolutionaries, and openly challenged the unjust and repressive political systems in Latin America. It should be noted that the vast majority of those who came to support liberation theology rejected violence as a means to counter the repressive political systems. In Nicaragua Jesuit priests and brothers, Ernesto and Fernando Cardenal, became spokespersons for liberation theology as young, idealistic students flocked to their lectures and classes. Ernesto Cardenal was a highly respected writer and poet who wrote *The Gospel in*

Solentiname which was based on dialogues with peasants in his Christian-based community in Solentiname. It was a brilliant condemnation of the Somoza dynasty. Fernando Cardenal, who taught philosophy at the National University of Nicaragua, testified before the U.S. Congress about the growing repression and corruption of the Somoza dynasty. The Cardenal brothers joined the FSLN. Other followers of liberation theology who also joined the FSLN included Jesuit Edgard Parrales and Maryknoll Miguel D'Escoto. Many priests and nuns worked as social workers in the poor neighborhoods of Managua attempting to teach the people their legal rights. Maryknoll nuns living and working in the poor Managua *barrio* of Open successfully staged a peaceful demonstration of more than 1,000 people which resulted in the local water company reducing its rates. They were very successful in organizing community meetings which focused on religious and civic education and political action projects.

In 1970 Miguel Obando y Bravo of the Salesian Order was named Archbishop of Nicaragua. Obando was at that time a supporter of liberation theology, although by 1982 he came to reject it. Unlike his predecessor who had supported the Somoza dynasty, Obando became a primary opposition figure. Tachito Somoza learned this early when he gave Obando a Mercedez Benz as a gift to celebrate his appointment. Obando promptly sold the car and used the proceeds to help the poor. Obando would prove to be a worthy opponent to the Somoza dynasty.

THE EBB AND FLOW OF THE SANDINISTAS

By 1966 the FSLN had become inspired once again to pursue its violent revolutionary strategy. In January, leading Sandinistas attended a conference in Havana in which Castro attacked the conservative politics of the communist parties in Latin America including the Nicaraguan PSN. They believed Che Guevara's call for "Two, Three, Many Vietnams" and by mid-1966 Fonseca returned to Nicaragua. The Sandinista urban underground in Managua, led by Daniel Ortega, waged a bloody war against the Nicaraguan government and the United States consisting of assassinations, car bombings, and robberies. In November 1966 the leaders of the FSLN published a program entitled "Sandino Yes, Somoza No, Revolution Yes, Electoral Farce No" in which they rejected the moderate politics of the PSN-led MR, the PLI, and the Conservative Party. It was signed by the FSLN leadership at the time: Fonseca, Mayorga, Rigoberto Cruz, Oscar Turcios, and Doris Tijerino.[8] The Sandinistas blamed the January 1967 massacre on both the National Guard and the opposition conservative, liberal, and communist leadership. Although there was no evidence to support it, they believed that the opposition leaders deliberately provoked the massacre believing that the United States would intervene and install Aguero as president.[9]

In 1967 the Sandinistas launched a rural military campaign in the mountains around Pancasan, east of Matagalpa. About 40 Sandinista guerrillas most who had been trained in Cuba took part in the operation. One of the participants was Gladys Baez, a former peasant and factory worker, who was the first female Sandinista guerrilla to fight the National Guard. Those *Nicas* who lived in the area were primarily subsistence farmers, many who had relocated to the area because they or their parents had lost their original property to coffee and cotton plantations and cattle ranches. Villages typically had no more than 100 to 200 people. From May through August the guerrillas tangled several times with the National Guard members who were stationed at Waslala. In August the guerrilla group led by Mayorga was ambushed by the National Guard which had effectively used helicopters to get its troops into position. Mayorga, one of the original Sandinistas, was killed. The other Sandinistas retreated to Honduras. With their defeat in the mountains and the news of the death of Che Guevara in Bolivia, the morale of the Sandinistas plummeted.

A ruthless crackdown by the National Guard against the urban underground resulted in the arrest of Ortega in late 1967. He spent the next seven years in jail. More urban militants were killed or disappeared during the crackdown than were lost at Pancasan. The losses were costly. According to former *Commandante* Omar Cabezas there were only five Sandinistas working in the León by early 1968.[10] Urban underground leader Julio Buitrago was killed by the National Guard in July 1969. The event was televised nationally as more than 100 troops and helicopters attacked Buitrago's safe house in Managua. After several hours of battle, the National Guard found the bullet-ridden body of only one Sandinista—Buitrago. His diary that was found indicated his impatience and discouragement with the FSLN leadership, the lack of money even to put together materials to protest the tenth anniversary of the 1959 student massacre, and the monotony and frustration of the inaction of the FSLN. Buitrago believed that Fonseca had not recovered from the defeat at Pancasan and had lost confidence.[11]

The Sandinistas faced a crisis in the aftermath of their rural defeat at Pancasan and the decimation of their urban underground. They were virtually unknown inside their own country, had little money, failed in two rural guerrilla operations, paid a terrible price for their urban underground resistance to Tachito Somoza, and were few in number. Some began to question the strategy of pursuing rural guerrilla warfare. Some questioned the use of violence and argued that they should focus on the student movement and work for the poor in the urban *barrios*. With the public denunciation of the FSLN by Fonseca's half brother, Fausto Amador Arrieta, in Managua on August 20, 1969, and the apprehension of Fonseca in Costa Rica on robbery charges nine days later, Tachito Somoza declared that the Sandinistas had been "smashed."

Fonseca and the Sandinistas learned a great deal about the lives of urban workers and rural peasants in the 1960s. They learned the dangers of fighting a guerrilla war in the mountains and waging an underground urban war. It was evident that the leaders differed over strategy. While in Costa Rica in 1969 Fonseca wrote the essay "Zero Hour" in which he indicated the need for the Sandinista leadership to take note of what they had learned and to chart a course for the future. He emphasized why there had to be a revolution in Nicaragua. Fonseca then completed what has come to be known as the "Historic Program." An initial draft was smuggled out to Sandinistas in Nicaragua and many who were in Somoza's prisons. In July and August 1969 the FSLN approved the "Historic Program." It specified the changes that the Sandinistas would bring about once they had toppled the Somoza dictatorship. It called for a democratic government, the seizure of the land and businesses owned by the Somoza family, and the nationalization or seizure of any foreign companies in the country. It called for the abolishment of the National Guard and replacing it with a "people's militia." There was to be a massive redistribution of land from the agro-elites to the *Nica* peasants. It called for dramatic improvements in education and an end to illiteracy. Worker's rights were to be protected as well as the rights of women and indigenous peoples. The highly nationalistic document quoted the great *Nica* poet Rubén Dario and Sandino. It was just after the publication of the "Historic Program" that Fonseca was arrested.

The FSLN regrouped and stepped up its recruitment in 1970. College campuses in León and Managua were primary recruiting areas. Novelist and poet Gioconda Belli was first asked to become a Sandinista in Managua by Camilo Ortega, the brother of Daniel and editor of *Praxis*, a magazine for artists, writers, and painters. Guerrilla commander Omar Cabezas was recruited by Juan Jose Quezada in León. Recruits were typically well read in the writings of Che Guevara and Herbert Marcuse. They often studied such texts as Marta Harnecker's *Elementary Principles of Historical Materialism*, Frantz Fanon's *The Wretched of the Earth*, and Eduardo Galeano's *Open Veins in Latin America*.[12] Many newly recruited Sandinistas were sent to the mountains for guerrilla warfare training. Guerrilla warfare training was an extremely demanding experience for many of the new student recruits.[13] It was led by the most capable Sandinistas such as René Tejada Peralta. Leading Sandinistas received military training in Cuba. A few, such as Tejada and Gustavo Adolfo Vargas and his brother Oscar-René Vargas, even traveled to the Middle East and were trained by guerrilla leaders of the

Palestinian Liberation Organization (PLO). Given the historic and strong support for the state of Israel by the Somoza family and the United States, the affinity between the PLO and the FSLN was a natural one.[14]

In October 1970 the Sandinistas hijacked a Costa Rican commercial airliner and held United Fruit Company executives, including Carlos Aguero, a member of one of the wealthiest *Nica* families and nephew of presidential candidate Fernando Aguero, as hostages. An exchange was arranged and Fonseca, Humberto Ortega, and Rufo Marin flew to Mexico City and then Havana. From 1970 through 1973 Sandinista efforts at recruitment in the urban areas paid off. Their numbers increased dramatically and their activities became more successful. In 1971 and 1972 successful Sandinista-led demonstrations, protests, and hunger strikes led to the release of prisoners.

PEASANT ECONOMIC INSECURITY: ENTER THE CHURCH AND THE SANDINISTAS

In the countryside the Church and the Sandinistas were finding greater success in organizing and mobilizing peasant support in opposition to Somoza *continuismo*. More peasants in the rural countryside of Nicaragua were facing growing economic insecurity. These insecure peasant families were susceptible and open to individuals who were capable of providing leadership, organizing them, and providing them with ways to meet their basic needs and to end their economic insecurity. Economic insecurity was caused by their constant loss of land or access to land because of the continued expansion of the agro-export economic strategy followed by the Somozas and the other political and economic elites. Between 1960 and 1975, agricultural production increased by 137 percent while the number of agricultural workers in the country declined. Much of this was due to the modernization of agriculture (use of tractors and machinery as opposed to laborers) but also because of declining wages offered to agricultural workers.[15] In 1970 nearly 60 percent of the rural families lived on 10 acres of land or less. By 1975 it is estimated that 1.8 percent of landowners in Nicaragua held 47 percent of the land and 12 percent of the landowners held 75 percent of the land.[16] The loss of land or access to land contributed to the loss of employment or, at best, the prospects of only seasonal wage-labor. It contributed to the loss of shelter or access to shelter and the inability of peasant families to meet even their basic food needs because they no longer had a piece of land on which to grow food for personal consumption. Production of food for domestic consumption declined continuously in Nicaragua from 1948 through 1978 as more and more land was converted to the production of export-only crops such as cotton and cattle or beef.[17] By the late 1970s only 13 percent of the active agricultural population had access to land to meet their basic or subsistence-level food requirements.[18] Peasants sometimes took matters into their own hands. Official records indicate that between 1963 and 1973 there were 240 "land invasions" by peasants just in the León and Chinandega departments.[19] In other words, peasants simply claimed uncultivated areas of property typically owned by wealthy elites. This often led to violent confrontations.

Insecure peasants were susceptible and open to being mobilized by the progressive Church and the Sandinistas. In the late 1960s and early 1970s, liberation theology laity and clergy from different Catholic Orders such as the Jesuits, Maryknolls, Capuchins, and Trappists began to organize Christian Base Communities (CEBs) in the rural areas. CEBs focused on not only on spiritual growth but also social organization and political action. The Jesuit-created and -led Evangelistic Committee for Agrarian Promotion (CEPA) trained peasants to organize into self-help groups, solve problems, and make demands on the government in their own behalf. CEPA began organizing initially in the coffee-growing areas near Masaya and Carazo and later León and Estelí. The so-called Delegates of the Word, who were trained by the Capuchin Order, organized Indian peasant groups in the department of Zelaya in the eastern part of the country. They built chapels with large dining halls so that all the members of the Christian community could pray and eat in a common setting. Their motto was "Love your neighbor, know your legal rights, and be proud of your Indian peasant heritage."[20] They promoted the concept of community building and democracy by electing local people to be trained at Capuchin seminars as teachers, agronomists, and lay religious leaders.

After their defeat at Pancasan, the Sandinistas began to improve their ties to the rural peasants in the northern, mountainous region of Nicaragua. By actually living in the rural areas and gaining the support and trust of influential family members, Sandinista support expanded because of the strong, traditional, *Nica* family networks. By 1970 the FSLN was strong enough in the rural areas to mount a series of attacks, known as the Zinica campaign, against National Guard outposts in the north central mountainous region. Their success against the Guard indicated that the Sandinistas had finally passed a "tactical and organizational watershed" in the mountains.[21] They were able to attack and escape from the Guard units. The Guard now recognized that the Sandinistas had developed strong ties and support among the rural peasants in the mountains. It began a campaign to deny the Sandinistas the support of the peasants in the area. The Guard used threats coupled with random and sometimes systematic executions and torture of peasants. The strategy backfired as rural support for the Sandinistas actually increased. Interactions between the members of the Progressive

Church and the Sandinistas began to appear. Some priests and laity became Sandinistas.

CONTINUISMO, EARTHQUAKE, OPPOSITION, CHRISTMAS PARTY RAID, AND REPRESSION

According to the constitution, Tachito Somoza could not run for another term in 1972. In what had now become Somoza family common practice, he maneuvered with the conservative opposition to create a three-person *junta* to run the country for 30 months. At that point in time, he would be eligible to run for the presidency again. The members of the *junta* were Aguero of the Conservative Party, General Robert Martinez Lacayo, and Alfonso Lopez Cordero. Martinez and Lopez had close ties to Tachito who remained in control of the National Guard and had very close ties to U.S. Ambassador Turner Shelton. No one doubted who was still in control of the country. Archbishop Obando of Managua openly protested the act of *continuismo* as did the younger, dissident conservatives led by Chamorro and the PLI. Fate was now ready to step in and change the nature of the political forces in Nicaragua.

A massive earthquake hit Managua on December 23, 1972, killing more than 10,000 people and leaving more than 300,000 homeless. President Nixon told Tachito Somoza that the United States would provide him with as much aid and support as he needed. For nearly two days there was virtually no order in Managua. As looting increased and order broke completely down, 600 U.S. troops were flown in from the Canal Zone. Food, medicine, and other immediate relief supplies arrived at the Managua airport and were distributed by Tachito Somoza's National Emergency Committee. Rather than being distributed for free, a large portion of the relief supplies ended up for sale in the local markets. The United States provided more than 32 million dollars in overall relief aid to rebuild Managua. The center of the city was never rebuilt as promised. Businesses had to relocate away from the center of the city to land owned by the Somoza family. Tachito charged exorbitant prices for the land. Emergency housing funds provided by the U.S. Agency for International Development (USAID) were spent on luxury housing for officers of the National Guard. Wooden shacks were built for the homeless poor. Reconstruction of roads, sewage and drainage systems, and public transportation was delayed and then assigned to companies owned by the Somozas.[22] Rising inflation in Managua made it difficult for the poor to purchase even the simplest necessities. Tachito Somoza and his friends engaged in wholesale graft and corruption by "taking advantage of the funds flowing into the country to rebuild Managua on Somozo's land, by Somoza's construction companies, with international aid funneled through Somozo's banks."[23] During the state of emergency Tachito Somoza assumed complete power.

It was Tachito Somoza's actions in response to the earthquake that changed the politics in Nicaragua. The earthquake exposed the naked brutality, insatiable greed, and tremendous corruption of Tachito Somoza. The political backlash against the Somoza family was unlike anything Nicaragua had experienced since the 1920s. Former Somoza supporters or *Somocistas*, such as Ramiro Sacasa Guerrero, left the PLN. Two major labor unions, the middle class, business elites, and dissident liberals and conservatives came to rally around Chamorro and Sacasa who organized a united opposition, the *Union Democrata de Liberacion* (UDEL). The Superior Council of Private Initiative (COSIP) which represented the Chamber of Commerce, the Chamber of Industries, and many cotton, cattle, sugar, and coffee producers became very outspoken and publicly critical of the Somoza government. COSIP, led by Alfonso Robelo Callejas, held a national meeting in 1974 for all businessmen and called for greater responsibility, honesty, and transparency within the government and the development of programs designed to meet the needs of the Nicaraguan poor. The urban poor engaged in strikes and rallies and construction workers in Managua staged a strike in 1973. The traditionally nonpolitical protestant churches became active for the first time focusing on the poor in the *barrios*. The number of recruits to the FSLN surged and its urban underground stepped up its activities against the government.

Chamorro's newspaper *La Prensa* was censored. Stories about the insurgency or criticism of the government or the Somoza family were not allowed. Reporters who dared to criticize the government were threatened, attacked, beaten, and thrown in jail. In March 1974 the PLN-led National Assembly voted in favor of a new constitution which paved the way for the presidential election in September. Recognizing the inevitable "re-election" of Tachito Somoza most parties announced they would boycott the election. These parties were promptly declared illegal. Chamorro was arrested and Archbishop Obando stated publicly that he would not vote. According to the official vote count, Tachito won in a landslide.

On December 27, 1974, Tachito Somoza held a Christmas party in honor of U.S. Ambassador Shelton at the home of Jose Maria Castillo Quant, a wealthy cotton exporter. Tachito, who could not attend the party because he was on Corn Island vacationing with his mistress, was represented by his brother-in-law, his cousin, and his nephew. It was almost 11 o'clock in the evening when Sandinistas attacked hoping to be able to kidnap the ambassador. Ambassador Shelton had already left the party but the Sandinistas took members of the Somoza family, several influential businessmen and their wives, and the ambassador from Chile as hostages. The National

Guard surrounded the home while Tachito flew back to Managua. The Sandinistas insisted that Archbishop Obando should act as mediator. In exchange for the hostages the Sandinistas received 1 million dollars in cash, the release of 14 political prisoners, a bus ride through the streets of Managua amid cheering *Nicas,* and a plane ride to Havana. In addition, a Sandinista communiqué was read over national radio.

The humiliated and outraged Tachito Somoza declared martial law and a complete censorship of the press. He asked for and received an increase in U.S. military aid to support his "anti-communist" campaign. He then unleashed an unprecedented repression. Anyone thought to be associated with the Sandinista urban underground was rounded up, questioned, and tortured. Radical students, workers, and members of the Progressive Church were also targeted. In rural areas the Church documented 400 disappearances. Amnesty International documented the disappearance of 200 peasants and the existence of at least 500 political prisoners held in Somoza's jails. American Catholic missionaries found three mass graves near Siuna with 109 bullet-ridden bodies. Capuchin monks documented at least 93 peasant disappearances.[24] Torture and murder of peasants by the National Guard was common. Catholic priests in the countryside came under suspicion. Entire villages were bombed and napalmed. Peasant homes and their fields were burned. In one sense, the repression worked. By late 1975 the FSLN had no more than a few dozen trained guerrilla fighters in the rural areas.[25] They also lacked adequate weapons to challenge the Guard. In another sense it failed because it continued to drive the middle class and many elites into the radical opposition who had come to believe that only violence would end the Somoza dynasty. According to Zimmerman "the repression of 1975 and 1976 seriously undermined the idea that Somoza had a moral right to govern Nicaragua."[26] The repression was also a failure because the human rights violations and evidence of torture and murder brought international attention to Nicaragua. Hearings were held by the U.S. Congress. Tachito Somoza threatened to try Chamorro by a military tribunal for instigating the Christmas raid. He backed down when the international press came to the defense of Chamorro. Tachito Somoza's horrible human rights record would not help him when Jimmy Carter became the U.S. president in January 1977.

THE DEATH OF FONSECA, DIVISIONS WITHIN THE FSLN, AND WIDENING OPPOSITION

Fonseca, who had been living in Cuba, made his way back into Nicaragua in November 1975. He spent time in Managua and León and then traveled into the northern mountains. On November 8, 1976, he and 11 other

Sandinistas were killed by members of the National Guard who were acting on a tip from an informer near the small town of Zinica. The Guard cut the hands away from Fonseca's body and sent them to Managua for confirmation and they took 10,000 cordobas or *Nica* dollars from his back pack and divided it among themselves. The already weakened capabilities of the Sandinistas due to the repression now coupled with Fonseca's death allowed the divisions within the Sandinista leadership to become public. By that time three identifiable groups had emerged within the FSLN leadership. Each group coalesced around particular Sandinista leaders and reflected the ideological, policy, and strategic differences among those individuals. Although differences over strategy were evident as early as 1969, they did not become public until after the death of Fonseca. Zimmerman points out that although people were drawn to the FSLN for political reasons they actually joined one of the three groups primarily "out of personal loyalty to the individual who recruited them" rather than agreement with or even knowledge of the group's specific ideology. This was especially true in the early 1970s as people tended to join because they were recruited by their own family members, lovers, classmates, or friends. All three groups portrayed themselves as Sandinistas and Marxists. They all believed that violent armed revolution was the only road to victory and none ever participated in elections. They all rejected the elite-led liberal and conservative parties of Nicaragua and they all accepted the overall leadership of Fonseca and the principles laid out in "Zero Hour" and the "Historic Program." Debates were largely within the leadership and unknown to the rank and file Sandinistas.[27]

The Prolonged People's War (GPP) grew out of the Sandinista's original rural, mountain campaign and was led by Ricardo Morales Avilés and Oscar Turcios until their deaths and then by Borge and Henry Ruiz. It was the most cautious of the three groups preferring to shore up its urban and rural forces before acting. Its student wing was the FER. Another group was the *Proletarios* (PT), who grew out of the urban underground in 1975 and were led by Jaime Wheelock Roman, Luis Carrion, and Roberto Huembes. The largest and most ideologically diverse group was the Third Tendency, better known as the *terceristas* (TI). They were led by Humberto and Daniel Ortega, Eden Pastora, Sergio Ramirez, and Victor Tirado. The *terceristas* attracted those with very different ideologies including Marxists, non-Marxists, socialists, social democrats, and social Christians. Their student wing was the Sandinista Revolutionary Youth (JRS). Militarily the *terceristas* were bolder than the GPP or the *Proletarios* as they led the broad-based insurrections of 1977 and 1978.

The opposition to Somoza *continuismo* expanded dramatically in 1977. CEPA, which had now developed close ties with the FSLN, was playing a primary role in organizing the Association of Rural Workers (ATC) in Pacific coastal areas where cotton, sugar, and coffee production had displaced large numbers of peasants. The ATC then moved into cotton, sugar, and coffee areas demanding higher wages and sponsoring some land seizures. Nearly 5000 workers at the San Antonio sugar plantation engaged in a strike in their attempt to organize a union associated with the ATC. When Tachito Somoza raised taxes on businesses many owners refused to pay. COSIP with the Church urged a national dialogue on the growing political crisis. Fearing political instability, more businessmen and elites began to turn away from Somoza. A key group of businessmen including industrialist Emilio Baltodano Pallais, lawyer-businessman Joaquín Cuadra Chamorro, supermarket magnate Felipe Mantica, and economist and international banker Arturo Cruz Porras made contacts with the Sandinista leadership to create the so-called Group of 12. From Costa Rica the Group of 12 which also included Ramirez and Father Fernando Cardenal of the FSLN began urging foreign governments not to provide assistance to Tachito Somoza.

The emphasis on the protection of human rights was one of the cornerstones of President Carter's foreign policy. In September 1977 Tachito Somoza lifted the state of siege partly due to pressure from business and elite groups, reports that the FSLN guerrillas in the countryside had been nearly wiped out, and pressure from President Carter. In 1977 and 1978 the United States significantly cut both economic and military aid to Nicaragua largely because of its abysmal record on human rights. This significant change in U.S. policy began to reduce the ability of the National Guard to contain and fight the FSLN. The government of Costa Rica throughout the 1970s had provided Sandinista guerrilla units sanctuary. Costa Rica and Panama served as the primary route for arms shipments for the FSLN. Although the Somozas and many members of the U.S. Congress frequently stated that Cuba had provided massive amounts of weapons to the Sandinistas, the evidence does not support this. Cuba had provided guerrilla training and a safe haven for Sandinista leaders and a limited amount of small arms, but Castro chose not to send massive amounts of weapons. He reasoned that aid from Cuba would more than likely lead to U.S. intervention and the defeat of the Sandinistas. He stated to Sandinista guerrilla commander Eden Pastora that "The best help I can give you is not to help you at all."[28] The U.S. State Department confirmed that Cuba had provided little assistance to the Sandinistas.

In October 1977 guerrillas from the *terceristas* faction of the FSLN launched a nationwide offensive attacking Guard units in San Carlos in the south, Ocotal in the north, and Masaya in the central part of the country. In response to the nationwide offensive and in a show of force the U.S.,

Guatemalan, and Salvadoran militaries joined the Nicaraguan National Guard and staged counterinsurgency war games in Nicaragua. By the end of 1977 all three Sandinista groups were witnessing a growing number of recruits to their urban units. The stage was now set for an event that literally would ignite the powder keg to the Nicaraguan revolution.

PEDRO JOAQUÍN CHAMORRO CARDENAL (1924–1978)

From one of the oldest elite families of Granada, Chamorro fought his entire life against the Somoza dynasty. He was the son of Margarita Cardenal Arguello and Pedro Joaquín Chamorro Zelaya, a historian who had bought the newspaper *La Prensa* in 1930. His great-great uncle was the first president of the Republic of Nicaragua and three other Chamorro family members had also held the office. As a child he loved sailing on Lake Nicaragua.

As a young law student Chamorro was jailed briefly in 1944 for protesting against Anastasio Somoza García. His family was exiled to Mexico where he studied journalism. The family returned in 1948. In 1950 he married Violeta Barrios and he became the editor of *La Prensa* in 1952 on the death of his father. *La Prensa* became the primary opposition newspaper to Somoza *continuismo*. In 1954 Chamorro was jailed and tortured and then placed under house arrest in 1955. In the aftermath of the assassination of Anastasio Somoza García in 1956 he was arrested and tortured. He was sentenced to jail in San Carlos on the southern shore of Lake Nicaragua. He escaped to Costa Rica with his wife to organize an opposition force against Luis Somoza. In 1959 he took part in an ill-fated invasion of Nicaragua. He was captured, charged with treason, and imprisoned for nine years until 1969. On his release he resumed the editorship of *La Prensa*. By 1972 Chamorro had become the leader of the younger members of the conservative party who were no longer willing to make deals with the Somoza family. He organized a non-Sandinista, united opposition, the UDEL. His editorials published almost daily were highly critical of Somoza government. The building that housed the newspaper was often fired on by thugs hired by Tachito Somoza. Reporters from *La Prensa* were intimidated, harassed, beaten, and arrested. Censorship of *La Prensa* occurred frequently.

Chamorro had become more hopeful with the election of President Jimmy Carter and his emphasis on the protection of human rights. In November 1977 he was awarded the Laureate of the Maria Moors Cabot Prize of Columbia University in recognition for his life-long work with *La Prensa* and his struggle for democracy and human rights. In late 1977 Chamorro had written an editorial about Plasmaferesis, a company owned by Tachito Somoza's son, Anastasio Somoza Portocarrero, and Cornelio

Hueck. Chamorro stated that the firm was taking blood from poor Nicaraguans in return for food. He asserted that blood plasma was then being sold to the United States for profit when it was desperately needed in Nicaragua. According to a Sandinista-led investigation, the company hired assassins to murder Chamorro. Although none of this was proven, the investigation linked Tachito Somoza's son to the order to murder Chamorro.

THE DEATH OF CHAMORRO AND THE CRITICAL YEAR OF 1978

After attending church on the morning of January 10, 1978, Chamorro approached Managua's Kennedy Avenue in his red Saab. A man driving a Chevrolet hit him from behind and their bumpers became locked. The man got out of his car and at the same time a Toyota pulled up on the left of Chamorro. Two men got out and fired on Chamorro with shotguns. All of the assassins escaped in the Toyota. Chamorro, who had ignored death threats from the Somozas his entire life, was dead. Although Tachito Somoza denied any responsibility, the entire nation was outraged. Estimates of 50,000 people turned out for Chamorro's funeral procession. Mobs burned Plasmaferesis and several other Somoza family businesses. On January 24, UDEL called for a nationwide shutdown of all businesses. It was estimated that 80 percent of the Nicaraguan economy came to a standstill through the second week of February. Less than one-third of the eligible voters showed up for the nationwide city elections in February. The residents of Monimbo, a small Indiana community in Masaya, attempted to name their town square after Chamorro. They barricaded the streets and declared Monimbo a free territory. The rebellion was met with a brutal repression by the Guard. Similar events occurred in other Indian communities such as Subtiava and Diriamba. University and high school students refused to attend classes in late March. A hunger strike was led by the mothers of imprisoned Sandinistas. Spontaneous rioting appeared in many urban areas.

Members of the Conservative Party in the Nicaraguan Congress who had traditionally cooperated with Tachito called for his immediate resignation in the aftermath of the Chamorro assassination. Perhaps most importantly, many of the agro-export elites and businessmen now turned against Tachito Somoza. COSIP widened its membership of businesses and changed its name to the Superior Council of Private Enterprise (COSEP). In March 1978 Robelo organized a new party made up of business leaders, industrialists, and other professionals called the Nicaraguan Democratic Movement (MDN). In May the Group of 12, COSEP, and the MDN formed the Broad Opposition Front (FAO). The FAO organized strikes and business shutdowns for the next 10 months.

In response to international pressure from the Organization of American States (OAS), the United States, Costa Rica, and Venezuela, Tachito Somoza allowed the Group of 12 to return to Nicaragua in July and invited the Inter-American Commission on Human Rights to the country. Tachito Somoza released political prisoners and on June 30 received congratulations from the United States for his willingness to begin to improve his human rights record. The congratulations note was released to the public in early July with more than 12 million dollars in economic development aid. This "convinced many Nicaraguan moderates that they had no ally in the U.S."[29] Yet, in fact, the U.S. State Department indicated a few days later that it opposed Tachito Somoza. According to Tachito, it was at this point that he decided he would stage a massive arms build-up and fight the insurrection to the very end regardless of the United States and any other international pressure.[30] In early August the Church and Obando called for the resignation of Tachito Somoza.

On August 23 the Sandinista *terceristas* chanced a broad-daylight attack on the National Palace in Managua. The *terceristas* believed that if they did not take immediate and public action and seize the initiative, the United States would intervene and work a deal that would allow Somoza to leave and a pro-U.S., pro-business, nonrevolutionary government would then be established. A group of guerrillas led by Eden Pastora, Hugo Torres Jiménez, and Dora María Téllez broke into the National Palace and seized virtually the entire membership of the Congress, judicial and executive employees, and other citizens as hostages. With the Church acting as a mediator, the Sandinistas received safe passage out of the country, the release of 60 prisoners including Borge, and 500,000 dollars. The Sandinistas and the released prisoners were given a bus ride through Managua with thousands of *Nicas* cheering them on as they made their way to the airport. In return the vast majority of the hostages were freed. The pictures of the procession and of Pastora, or *Commandante Cero*, raising his rifle in defiance as he boarded the plane made front page news throughout the world and in Nicaragua.

The boldness of the raid encouraged the opposition even more than expected by the Sandinistas. The FAO organized another nationwide strike that continued through late September. Uprisings in Matagalpa and Jinotega by students, women, and the poor sent a message to the Sandinistas that they could count on support for a nationwide assault. On September 9 Sandinista-led units overtook Guard stations in León, Managua, Masaya, Estelí, Chinandega, and Chichigalpa. Somoza declared martial law, ordered the Guard on the offensive, and brutally retook all the cities by the end of October. Atrocities such as rape, murder, executions, and torture committed by the Guard in September and October exceeded anything in the past. The Guard looted and destroyed churches, health clinics, hospitals, and schools.

During the months of September and October journalists from all over the world converged on Nicaragua to report what had now become a full-blown civil war. Most worked out of the Intercontinental Hotel that overlooked the city of Managua from the side of Tiscapa volcano. The small country of less than 4 million people was now on the nightly news all around the world. The United States was in a very difficult position as it wanted a Nicaragua without Tachito Somoza and the Sandinistas. The FAO insisted that that any settlement had to include the resignation of Tachito Somoza, the exile of his entire family, an end to martial law and press censorship, and a three-year interim government that would pave the way to a new constitution and elections in 1981. Tachito Somoza insisted that he should be able to finish his term, that the current constitution should remain in force, and elections would be held under OAS supervision in 1981. The U.S.-led OAS mediators proposed that Tachito Somoza should resign and give power to a group led by the PLN and the National Guard while the *Nica* Congress would elect the next president. This option left no role for the FSLN. The Carter administration underestimated the stubbornness of Tachito Somoza and the hatred that the vast majority of the people in the country had toward the Guard. Tachito simply would neither resign nor even think of exile. The Sandinistas and the FAO opposed the U.S.-led OAS agreement because it included the Guard in the interim government and it did not insist on exile for the Somoza family. By early November the Sandinistas pulled out of the negotiations and resumed their armed struggle and later that month the FAO pulled out of the negotiations. Tachito's position hardened as he purchased a large number of weapons from Israel and Argentina to reinforce the Guard and wage war against the FSLN. The United States was no longer in control of events in Nicaragua. The civil war continued while the Nicaraguan economy ground to a complete halt. Many of Tachito's wealthiest supporters fled to the United States, Honduras, Guatemala, and Costa Rica.

THE END OF SOMOZA *CONTINUISMO*

By the end of November FSLN guerrilla strength had reached an estimated 2,500 and their numbers were increasing daily. The opposition was now deep and widespread among the students, the poor in the cities, and the peasants in the countryside. Many simply organized the people in their *barrio* or small village, put on a red and black bandana, and called themselves Sandinistas. They saw the Sandinistas as the only group capable of ending the Somoza dynasty and ending the repression. Sandinista recruits simply wanted to participate in the defeat of Somoza *continuismo*. They paid little attention to the factions within the Sandinistas. It was this growing mass membership and the sense of a forthcoming victory that led to the reunification of the three factions within the FSLN. On March 7, 1979, the Sandinistas announced their reunification and the establishment of a National Directorate consisting of Daniel and Humberto Ortega and Tirado from the TI; Borge, Bayardo Arce, and Ruiz from the GPP; and Wheelock, Carrion, and Carlos Nuñez from the PT.

In April the FSLN launched its final offensive with five different fronts converging on Managua. City after city fell to the Sandinistas and their growing number of supporters. Major urban rebellions in working-class neighborhoods played a role in the fall of the cities. Tachito Somoza bombed these neighborhoods and when he ran out of bombs he dropped gasoline on the inhabitants. By May the fighting was taking place in the working-class barrios of Managua while Somoza and the remaining Nicaraguan government officials were holed up in the "bunker" in the Intercontinental Hotel. With Sandinista units controlling virtually all of Nicaragua except Managua, the Guard suffering from high desertion rates, the televised murder of ABC newsman Bill Stewart by the National Guard, and the announcement of the new Governing Junta of National Reconstruction, the United States finally got Tachito Somoza to resign. He resigned in favor of Francisco Urcuyo and fled to Miami on July 17. The next day Urcuyo also left the country while members of the National Guard took off their uniforms and fled into the countryside to escape to Honduras and Costa Rica. On July 19, 1979, the Sandinistas entered Managua and celebrated their hard fought victory.

The Somoza dynasty had come finally come to an end and the new government faced an unbelievable task. In the last two years of fighting 40,000 to 50,000 *Nicas* had died. Most of the country's economic infrastructure and commercial property had been destroyed. The final insurrection had occurred during the normal planting time for cotton and also led to a shortage of workers for the coffee harvest. The treasury was empty and Nicaragua owed 1.6 billion dollars to international creditors and foreign banks. At least 600,000 people were left homeless and 300,000 were wounded. More than 150,000 *Nicas* lived in Red Cross camps in Managua. Less than 5 percent of the children in the countryside completed the sixth grade and nearly two-thirds of the children under the age of five suffered from malnutrition. Health care in the countryside was virtually nonexistent. Yet, with all these immense problems, there was a general "can do" atmosphere among the people. The future looked bright. Even though many of the wealthy elites had fled the country, many remained and were committed to working to rebuild the country. The new Governing Junta of

National Reconstruction arrived in Managua on July 20. In the next two years the direction of the revolution would be decided and one of the members of the Junta who would play a major role in that was Daniel Ortega.

DANIEL ORTEGA SAAVEDRA (1945–PRESENT)

Daniel Ortega's father, Daniel Ortega Serda, was an active supporter of Augusto César Sandino and was imprisoned by Anastasio Somoza in the 1930s. He settled in *La Libertad*, became an accountant for a mining firm, and married Lidia Saavedra. Lidia Saavedra was also imprisoned by Anastasio Somoza because of love letters that the National Guard insisted were coded messages. Daniel, their first child, was born in 1945. The family moved to Juigalpa, then Matagalpa, and eventually settled in a poor *barrio* in Managua known as *Colonia Somoza* where his father started a small refreshment stand. His father and mother, like Sandino, blamed the poverty and lack of justice in Nicaragua on the Somozas and the United States. Anti-Americanism was a common theme in the Ortega household. Ortega once said that, "We were anti-Coca-Cola, anti-comic book, against everything good and bad, represented by the United States, except baseball." As a teenager in Colonia Somoza he organized an "anti-American street gang" and engaged in various anti-Somoza and anti-U.S. activities including blowing up National Guard jeeps, placing small bombs near homes of pro-Somoza politicians, and firebombing cars that belonged to the American Embassy. Daniel Ortega and his brothers, Humberto and Camilo, joined the FSLN almost immediately after it was formed. Daniel Ortega began giving anti-Somoza speeches in high school. In 1964 he was in Guatemala and was captured, jailed, and beaten by the Guatemalan police. Guatemalan authorities turned him over to the Nicaraguan National Guard. Daniel Ortega and the others were beaten mercilessly during the entire trip to Managua and arrived almost unconscious. He was released shortly thereafter and began to study law at the Central American University, although this was largely a cover that allowed him to recruit new Sandinistas and to direct the urban resistance in Managua. In August 1967 Ortega and others planned the assassination of one of his former torturers, Gonzalo Lacayo. Ortega participated in the successful attack but he was captured by the National Guard at the end of 1967 and spent the next seven years in prison. While in El Modelo prison he penned the poem "I Never Saw Managua When Miniskirts Were in Fashion." A scar near his right eye was one of the more visible remnants of torture inflicted on him and he was one of the prisoners freed in December 1974 as part of the ransom during the famous Christmas party raid. He spent a year in Havana recovering from his years in prison.

With the death of Fonseca in 1976, Ortega became a member of the Sandinista National Directorate along with his brother, Humberto, and Victor Tirado. By this time the ideological splits in the Sandinistas had become evident. Daniel and Humberto Ortega and Tirado had become leaders of the dominant Insurrectional Tendency (TI) or *terceristas* within the FSLN. He led the *tercerista* northern guerrilla campaign in 1977 and in 1978 and 1979 led the southern front campaign. With the numbers of *terceristas* growing he led the national popular insurrection of September and October 1978. The FSLN finally reunited. In June 1979 Daniel Ortega was named part of the five-person Junta of National Reconstruction that included fellow Sandinistas Moises Hassan, a professor of mathematics, and Sergio Ramírez Mercado, a writer. The non-Sandinistas were businessman Alfonso Robelo Callejas and Violeta Barrios de Chamorro, wife of the slain Pedro Joaquín Chamorro. As coordinator of the revolutionary junta Daniel Ortega's role and importance in the FSLN would grow dramatically.

NOTES

1. Eduardo Crawley, *Dictators Never Die* (New York: St. Martin's Press), 124–25.

2. Charles D. Brockett, *Land, Power, and Poverty*, 2nd ed. (Boulder, CO: Westview Press, 1998), 47.

3. Matilde Zimmerman, *Sandinista: Carlos Fonseca and the Nicaraguan Revolution* (Durham: Duke University Press, 2000), 90.

4. After exhaustive research Matilde Zimmerman comes to the conclusion that one of the myths of the Sandinista revolution was the often-cited July 19, 1961, meeting of Fonseca, Borge, and Mayorga that created the FSLN. Rodolfo Romero, one of the early members of the FSLN, states that the so-called three-founders meeting was a myth. See Zimmerman, *Sandinista*, 76–77.

5. Ibid., 89.

6. Ibid., 113.

7. Ibid., 94.

8. Ibid., 94–95.

9. Ibid., 95.

10. Omar Cabezas, *Fire from the Mountain: The Making of a Sandinista* (New York: Random House, 1985), 5, 14.

11. Zimmerman, *Sandinista*, 120.

12. Gioconda Belli, *The Country under My Skin* (New York: Random House, 2002), 34. See also Cabezas, *Fire from the Mountain*, 19.

13. For an honest and humorous account of guerrilla training in the mountains see Cabezas, *Fire from the Mountain*, 78–102.

14. Stephen Kinzer, *Blood of Brothers: Life and War in Nicaragua* (Cambridge: Harvard University Press, 1991), 60. See also Cabezas, *Fire from the Mountain*, 77.

15. John Booth, *The End and the Beginning* (Boulder, CO: Westview Press, 1982), 84.

16. Brockett, *Land, Power, and Poverty*, 74–75, 157.

17. Ibid., 79.

18. Ibid., 74–75, 157.

19. Joseph Collins, *Nicaragua: What Difference Could a Revolution Make?: Food and Farming in the New Nicaragua*, 3rd ed. (New York: Grove Press, 1986), 22.

20. Penny Lernoux, *Cry of the People* (New York: Penguin Books, 1984), 85.

21. Booth, *The End and the Beginning*, 140–41.

22. Thomas W. Walker, *Nicaragua, Living in the Shadow of the Eagle*, 4th ed. (Boulder, CO: Westview Press, 2003), 32.

23. John Findling, *Close Neighbors, Distant Friends* (Westport, CT: Greenwood, 1987), 139.

24. Crawley, *Dictators Never Die*, 152–53.

25. Zimmerman, *Sandinista*, 185.

26. Ibid., 211.

27. Ibid., 163–67.

28. Booth, *The End and the Beginning*, 134.

29. Ibid., 161.

30. Anastasio Somoza Debayle and Jack Cox, *Nicaragua Betrayed* (Appleton, WI: Western Islands Publisher, 1980), 412.

6

The Revolutionary Years
(1979–1990)

The forces that toppled the Somoza dynasty represented virtually every segment of Nicaraguan society. Once the Somoza family was gone it was inevitable that divisions would appear in the victorious coalition. In particular, the differences between the revolutionary Sandinistas and several of the groups representing the agro-export economic and business elites came to the forefront between 1979 and 1981. In particular, the agro-elites opposed the revolutionary land reform and agricultural policies of the Sandinistas which they saw as a threat to their property and the traditional agro-export strategy of development which had been in place since the 1860s. The fact that some Sandinistas were Marxists and interpreted the history of Nicaragua largely in terms of class conflict led many elites to believe that Nicaragua would quickly become another Cuba. By the first anniversary of the revolution many of the economic elites had already fled to the United States. President Ronald Reagan and Central Intelligence Agency (CIA) Director William Casey organized these self-exiled groups and former National Guardsmen into an opposition force, the *contras*. The *contra* forces supported directly by the United States waged a war against the Sandinistas. The decade-long war killed tens of thousands, devastated the economy, and divided *Nica* families.

Many in the United States believed that the Sandinistas had created another communist state. Yet, a closer look revealed that although the opposition press was often censored, it still operated and criticized the government throughout the 1980s. Opposition parties, groups, and politicians were sometimes harassed but they continued to work openly against Sandinista policies and ran candidates in the 1984 elections. Although the Sandinistas created Cuban-style state-run farms and nationalized many of the major businesses and utilities, most of the economy was still in the hands of the private sector. The Sandinistas admit that they made many mistakes during these years, but it is clear that the *contra* war destroyed any possibility for the success of their revolutionary agenda. It is significant that many of the agro-export and business elites did not flee the country; they chose to work with the Sandinistas and tried to influence many of their policies throughout the 1980s. These ongoing consultations, negotiations, and accommodations continued after the historic 1990 Nicaraguan presidential election. They provided the basis for not only the peaceful transition of power but also the cooperation that developed between the Sandinistas and President Violeta Barrios de Chamorro.[1] It was the revolutionary years that paved the way for the development of democracy that we see in Nicaragua today.[2]

A WATERSHED YEAR IN WORLD POLITICS

A pivotal year in world politics and U.S. foreign policy was 1979. It marked the end of the decade of détente in which the United States and the Soviet Union cooperated in areas of common interest such as nuclear weapons, arms control, and trade. There was a renewed focus on the differences between the two superpowers and return to the heightened military and political struggle with the Cold War rhetoric "heating up." Much of this rhetoric originated from the conservative base of the Republican Party in the United States led by Reagan. A revolutionary movement in El Salvador, not unlike the FSLN in Nicaragua, threatened a government supported by the United States. In Iran the pro-American Mohammad Reza Shah Pahlavi was overthrown by the revolutionary forces of the Ayatollah Khomeini and the subsequent oil crisis led to a downturn in the American economy. In November Iranian militants seized and held American citizens hostage in Teheran. The hostage crisis continued for more than a year and gave the appearance of a helpless, impotent U.S. government. The Soviet Union invaded Afghanistan in December. These events coupled with the toppling of the pro-U.S. Somoza dynasty in Nicaragua helped to create a backlash against the policies of President Jimmy Carter. Reagan seized on this public dissatisfaction with Carter's policies and was elected president in November 1980. He promised a reinvigorated and powerful United States, a Gulliver who would not be tied down by the Lilliputians and would not back down from what he called the evil empire, the Soviet Union. From the U.S. perspective, events in Nicaragua would now be viewed solely in black-and-white terms as the struggle between the United States and the Soviet Union, democracy and communism, and capitalism and socialism. President Reagan used what resources he could, both legal and illegal, to wage a low-intensity war throughout the decade in an overt attempt to topple the Sandinista-led government of Nicaragua.

THE EARLY YEARS OF THE NICARAGUAN REVOLUTION

President Carter had hoped that he could prevent the Sandinistas from coming to power in Nicaragua. Not successful in that policy, he tried to court the revolution. In September 1979 he received Daniel Ortega at the White House. The Sandinistas received assurances that the United States would not try to organize anti-Sandinista groups and former Guardsmen in the United States or Honduras. In return, Ortega assured the president that they were not providing weapons to revolutionary forces in El Salvador. Both sides kept their promises. The United States then provided a 75-million-dollar aid package to Nicaragua, although the debate over the aid package in Congress was highly contentious. Congress did insist that if evidence indicated that the Sandinistas were providing weapons to fellow revolutionaries in El Salvador, the aid program would be suspended.

The five-person Junta of National Reconstruction included fellow Sandinistas Ortega, Moises Hassan, and Sergio Ramírez Mercado and non-Sandinistas Alfonso Robelo Callejas, head of the business-dominated Nicaraguan Democratic Movement (MDN), and Chamorro. The Junta served as the chief executive body. It made decisions largely through consensus and ruled primarily through emergency powers for the first year of the revolution. Ortega was also a member of the nine-member Sandinista National Directorate (DN) which was initially recognized as the highest revolutionary authority in the country even by Robelo and Chamorro. It was Ortega who served as a link between the DN and the Junta. Policies were implemented through various government ministries such as planning, defense, interior, agrarian reform, foreign relations, telegraph and post office, and housing and human settlements. The FSLN leaders controlled the more important ministries. Ortega chaired the Junta, his brother Humberto Ortega was Minister of Defense, Tomás Borge was Minister of the Interior, Henry Ruiz was the Minister of Planning, and Jaime Wheelock Roman was the Minister of Agricultural Reform and Development. Former lower-level and middle-level government employees were called back to work in an attempt to limit the disruption in government services.

In May 1980 the Council of State, the legislative branch of government, was created. Its makeup and membership had been negotiated and agreed to by the major anti-Somoza groups at Puntarenas. The DN and the Junta changed the agreement in April by increasing the number of FSLN representatives. The new arrangements gave the FSLN 24 seats out of a total of 47. Robelo and Chamorro resigned from the Junta in protest of the change. The Council of State was largely a consultative body that was corporatist in its representation. This meant that delegates represented important groups and organizations in Nicaragua rather than geographic regions. Labor groups, business and private sector associations, women's groups, political parties, indigenous people's organizations, professional associations such as teachers and lawyers, and youth groups were all given representation. Sandinista Bayardo Arce Castaño was the first president of the Council of State. The court system was completely rebuilt due to the tremendous corruption during the Somoza years. Although the new judges and courts were autonomous or independent in most areas, in some areas they were not. In particular, Special Tribunals were created to try former members of the National Guard and Somoza supporters for war crimes. Although these courts did not follow procedures that lawyers in the United States would approve, the media had full access to the trials, prisoners were not mistreated while in jail, prisoners were given access to legal representation, and the death penalty was banned.

The first job facing the new government was to get the country's economy running again. The Sandinistas renegotiated the foreign debt it had inherited from the Somoza years and consistently made payments through 1982. The country pursued a diversified trade policy. While trade continued with the United States, it increased with western Europe, eastern Europe and the USSR or the so-called socialist bloc, and the developing world, including Cuba. The Sandinistas immediately began spending government resources in rebuilding the economic infrastructure that had been destroyed. Tax revenues actually increased and were running ahead of what was expected by the middle of 1980. Streets, roads, housing, parks, utilities, hospitals, and health centers were rebuilt and provided employment for thousands of *Nicas*. The banking, insurance, and water and electrical utilities industries were taken over by the state. The state took over the banks initially to prevent wealth from being taken out of the country, often referred to as capital flight. The insurance industry could not meet the demands of the war-torn economy so the state intervened. In 1979 and

1980 the new government invested more than 230 million dollars to rebuild the private business and manufacturing sector.

The Sandinistas had promised that once in power they would confiscate all the wealth of the Somoza family and its most ardent supporters. On July 20, 1979, the new *Nica* government seized more than 100 businesses and almost 2 million acres of prime farmland owned by the Somoza family. Unfortunately many of the managers of the Somoza-businesses fled the country. This created a shortage of qualified, skilled business managers. Most of Somoza's farmland was used to create state-run farms to continue the production of large-scale agriculture for export. It was important that Nicaragua continue to earn foreign exchange or U.S. dollars that were acceptable as payments anywhere in the world. Similar to the business sector, these large agro-export state-run businesses suffered from a shortage of qualified, skilled managers. Three hundred thousand manzanas or about 519,000 acres of land were distributed to peasants who created cooperatives. Two types of cooperatives were created: one, the Sandinista Agricultural Cooperative (CAS), in which the land was worked together as a group; and another, the Credit and Service Cooperative (CCS), where the members received credit and assistance as a group but worked the land as individuals. It should be noted that peasants who joined CCS typically already owned small plots of land.[3] By the middle of 1980, more than 2,500 cooperatives had been formed. Recognizing the importance of export agriculture to the national economy, in April 1980 the Sandinistas reassured the private owners of the large-scale estates and even the medium-sized farms that they could keep their property as long as they continued to grow crops and obeyed the labor, health, and safety regulations put in place by the new government. Most continued to worry given the increasing number of peasant land seizures and the increasingly revolutionary rhetoric of the Sandinistas.

The growth of agriculture is very much dependent on the availability of credit and loans. In the past, credit and loans were almost exclusively available to the agro-export elites associated with either Somoza or the *Banco Nicaraguensa* (BANIC) and *Banco de America* (BANAMERICA) groups. Small farms which traditionally grew the basic food grains, beans and corn, for consumption within Nicaragua were never favored under the Somoza credit system and as a result local food production suffered. The Sandinistas reoriented credit to provide a better balance between the agro-export elites and the local food grain producers with the goal of increasing local food production. From 1979 through 1980 the amount of credit available to the CAS and CCS increased by nearly five-fold. Ironically, this created a severe labor shortage on the agro-export estates because peasants on the CAS and CCS were now better off and less willing to leave their farms and work on the large agro-export estates during the harvest periods.[4]

The second phase of agrarian reform was initiated in August 1981. The state confiscated the land of any Nicaraguans who had fled the country. Private property that was idle or not planted in more than two years could be confiscated by the state. Private property that was underused or property in which less than 75 percent of the acreage was cultivated could also be confiscated. Confiscation of idle or underused property only applied the very largest agro-export estates. This process of confiscation and then redistribution to CAS and CCS proceeded slowly with 25,395 families benefitting from the land reforms by the end of 1983 and 77,430 families by the end of 1988. The development of state farms and the confiscation of properties led many *Nica* agro-elites and influential U.S. citizens to characterize the Sandinista agrarian program as Cuban style socialism. Yet, by the end of 1987, 60 percent of agricultural land was held by private individuals, 22 percent by the CAS or CCS cooperatives, and 13 percent by the state-controlled farms.[5] Agriculture clearly reflected a mixed economy in revolutionary Nicaragua.

The Sandinistas moved quickly to implement a program that represented the best of their revolutionary goals in education. In August 1979 Father Fernando Cardenal was put in charge of organizing a national literacy program. Cardenal investigated national literacy campaigns in Cuba, Peru, Brazil, and Colombia. From March through August 1980, the Year of Literacy, more than 60,000 *Nicas*, mostly women and most of them idealistic high school and university students, went into the poor *barrios* and the most remote, rural areas of the country to teach people how to read and write. While teaching they worked side-by-side with peasants and the urban poor. Journalist Stephen Kinzer writes that these volunteers represented "the best of their generation." In five months the illiteracy rate in Nicaragua was reduced from 50.3 percent to 12.9 percent. In 1980, the United Nations Education, Scientific, and Cultural Organization awarded the country with the Nadezhda K. Krupskaya Prize in recognition of the success of the campaign. The efforts continued and reached a high point in 1983 by enrolling 187,588 students in literacy classes.[6] As with most Sandinista policies, the literacy program was not without its critics as many objected to the political content of the reading and writing materials that were used by the *brigadistas*.

In the aftermath of the revolution the health care needs throughout the country were immense. Health volunteers were organized to provide assistance in the poor barrios. Over the next four years the Sandinistas completely reorganized the health care system of the country. They began to rebuild hospitals and health clinics while also emphasizing preventative health care. With assistance from the United Nations Children's Education Fund (UNICEF) and more than 78,000 volunteers they carried out several successful inoculation campaigns to focus on preventing polio, infant diarrhea, malaria, and leprosy. The oral rehydration program that was put in place was largely responsible for reducing the infant mortality rate by 30 percent. Between 1978 and 1983 health care spending by the Nicaraguan government increased by 200 percent. Both rural and urban health clinics were free to all Nicaraguans. Later the Sandinistas put in place day-care facilities and agencies to deal with the large number of orphans.

With the resignations of Robelo and Chamorro from the Junta in April 1980, many of the agro-export elites decided not to support the new government. One of the leaders of this movement was Jorge Salazar who had founded the Coffee Growers Association of Matagalpa and the Agricultural Producers Association of Nicaragua (UPANIC) which brought together many of the elite agro-exporters. He also served as vice-president of the Superior Council of Private Enterprise (COSEP). Salazar traveled to Miami to speak with *Nica* exiles. He then returned to Nicaragua and began meeting with a group of dissident army officers who wanted to launch a *golpe* or coup against the Sandinistas. Salazar agreed to help them. In November he met with two of the conspirators and was gunned down by Sandinista police. Unknown to Salazar, he was actually set up by the Sandinistas. The *golpe* plot was made up by the FSLN. Although many, especially the agro-export and business elites, protested his "murder," their protest was not too loud due to the fact Salazar had actually agreed to participate in a conspiracy to overthrow the government. Nonetheless, this pushed even more agro-elites to reject Sandinista rule, especially members of UPANIC and the coffee growers around Matagalpa.

The agro-export elites and businessmen that completely rejected the Sandinista rule viewed the world in stark contrasts, continually spoke in Cold War extremist terms, and emphasized their opposition to communism and any restrictions whatsoever on their ability to buy and sell freely. They believed that eventually the private sector would disappear under Sandinista rule. Yet, there were some agro-export elites who chose to work with the Sandinistas and were willing to compromise and less likely to adopt Cold War rhetoric. Another, even smaller supportive group known as the "patriotic producers," was associated with the National Association of Farmers and Ranchers (UNAG) who supported the overall goals of the FSLN but may have been opposed to specific policies.[7] Labor organizations grew dramatically under the revolutionary government. The Sandinista Worker's Central (CST) came to represent about 79 percent of the more than 500 industrial unions in the country. The non-Sandinista unions tended to be more militant than the CST in terms of wage demands. The Association of Rural Workers (ATC) represented more than 100,000 rural laborers and worked to reconcile their needs with Sandinista agrarian policies.

THE SANDINISTAS AND CUBA

Cuba provided inspiration, guidance, a safe haven for Sandinista leaders, and guerrilla-warfare training for many Sandinista leaders throughout the 1960s and 1970s. Although material support to the Sandinistas prior to 1979 was very limited, Cuban military aid increased substantially once it became clear to Castro that the Sandinistas were actually going to topple the Somoza dynasty. Once the Sandinistas came to power Cuban emergency relief supplies and economic and military aid increased dramatically. Economic and military aid also came from the Soviet Union and Czechoslovakia. East Germany provided specialists to help *Commandante* Tomás Borge create a state security police. It was the state security police that rounded up what remained of the hated National Guard and turned them over for trial to the Special Tribunals. Although there were leaders from across the world in Managua for the first anniversary of the Nicaraguan revolution on July 19, 1980, the most important guest was Fidel Castro. Surprising the crowd, he praised President Carter's policy toward Nicaragua and urged the Sandinistas to work constructively with the United States. Even with Castro's moderate speech, many in the United States used this as further evidence that Nicaragua would soon become a second Cuba. At no point did Cuba or the Soviet Union sign a military alliance with the Sandinista government.

PRESIDENT REAGAN, THE SANDINISTAS, THE *CONTRAS*, AND THE U.S. CONGRESS

The Sandinistas had a strong sense of revolutionary solidarity with the rebels in El Salvador. Salvadoran revolutionaries provided funding to the FSLN in 1978 and 1979. Salvadoran guerrillas fought alongside the Sandinistas in several key battles. To its credit the FSLN lived up to its promises to the Carter administration until November and December 1980. At this time the Salvadoran revolutionaries were engaged in their own "final offensive" hoping to topple the government before Reagan was sworn in as the next U.S. president. The Sandinistas, sorely wanting another successful revolution in Central America, gave in to temptation and began providing weapons they had received from Cuba to the Salvadoran guerrillas in November and December 1980. When evidence of the weapons assistance was presented to President Carter he cut off economic aid to the Sandinistas. Daniel Ortega immediately suspended all weapons shipments to El Salvador in an attempt to renegotiate with President Carter but by this time it was too late.

In 1980, Colonel Enrique Bermúdez, a cousin of Tachito Somoza and the former Nicaraguan defense attaché to Washington, met with conservatives close to Reagan. On January 20, 1981, Reagan was sworn in as president and relations between Nicaragua and the United States deteriorated. The new president, who had stated in 1978 that Somoza "has never been known as a major violator of human rights," indicated that one of his goals was to destroy the revolutionary government of Nicaragua. The remainder of the economic aid package to Nicaragua was permanently stopped, including a shipment of wheat. In March, Congress authorized 19.5 million dollars for a CIA plan to support "moderate" elements in Nicaragua and to prevent the Sandinistas from providing weapons to the revolutionaries in El Salvador. By May the CIA was sponsoring training camps for *Nica* exiles in Florida, California, and Texas. A Core Group made up of Thomas Enders, Duane Clarridge, General Paul Gorman, and Lt. Colonel Oliver North met with Nicaraguan exiles in Miami and presented them with the promise of aid if they would link up with former members of the Nicaraguan National Guard exiled in Honduras. The CIA arranged a meeting in Guatemala between former officers from the Guard and Nicaraguan exiles led by Edgar Chamorro. This meeting led to the creation of the Nicaraguan Democratic Force (FDN), better known as the *contras*. Edgar Chamorro set up headquarters in the Maya, the major hotel in Tegucigalpa, and worked with the former Guardsmen to build an entire rebel army with support bases on the Honduran border with Nicaragua completely funded by the CIA. In effect, President Reagan was planning to go to war with the Sandinistas.

In August 1981 President Reagan sent Thomas Enders to Managua to tell the Sandinistas that they must quit shipping weapons to the revolutionaries in El Salvador and break their ties to Cuba and the Soviet Union. The Sandinistas had sworn that they would not be like all other Nicaraguan governments in history, that they would not cut deals with the United States based on threats. In December President Reagan authorized the CIA to spend 19.9 million dollars to create and organize the *contras*. The administration stated publicly that the purpose of the *contras* was to interdict the arms supply from the Sandinistas to the revolutionaries in El Salvador, that the force would be limited in size, that no Americans would be involved, and that no economic targets would be attacked. Privately, officials within the Reagan administration hoped that the *contras* would evolve into a large enough force to invade Nicaragua, cause a nationwide uprising, and topple the Sandinistas. At a minimum, Reagan advisers believed that the *contras* would serve to discredit the Sandinista government.[8] On March 14, 1982, the CIA-trained FDN or *contras* blew up two bridges in Chinandega and Nueva Segovia provinces near Honduras. Between March and June 1982 the *contras* were involved in sabotaging highway bridges, destroying fuel tanks, engaging in sniper fire against Sandinista military patrols, assassinating minor government officials and a Cuban adviser, and burning a customs warehouse. By the middle of 1982 the *contra* army, led by U.S. operatives or CIA agents, consisted of 4,500 trained fighters. Fearing an invasion, the FSLN with the support of the MDN declared a national state of emergency, temporarily suspended constitutional rights, temporarily imposed a press censorship, began harassing dissidents and government opponents, and mobilized troops to the Honduran border. At this time the Sandinista Army had approximately 24,000 soldiers. President Reagan cited these actions as evidence of the totalitarian and aggressive nature of the Sandinistas and their Cuban and Soviet supporters. The *contra* war had begun.

By April the extent of U.S. involvement in Nicaragua and the purpose of the *contras* in Honduras had become hotly debated political issues in the U.S. Congress. It was clearly evident that President Reagan's policies and *contra* activities were going far beyond the original mandate to prevent weapons from being exported to El Salvador. Some Democrats in the House tried to cut off all funding for the *contras* and the covert war. In November, the cover story on *Newsweek* read "America's Secret War-Target: Nicaragua." Congress passed by a vote of 411 to zero the first Boland Amendment which prohibited the use of American funds on behalf of the *contras* or any group engaged in the attempted overthrow of the Sandinista government or facilitating a war between Honduras and Nicaragua. From December through October 1983 the *contras* launched several attacks in Nicaragua in an attempt to gain support from peasants and to set up a liberated zone. The *contras* were only successful in destroying economic infrastructure and killing peasants and government officials. Clarridge traveled to Honduras to put pressure on the *contras* to "make a better showing on the battlefield."

With the Democrats gaining seats in the Congress in the 1982 elections, they were able to be more forceful in their criticism of Reagan policies. In March 1983, more than 1,500 *contras* invaded Nicaragua. U.S. and Honduran public denials of *contra* camps in Honduras along the border with Nicaragua were exposed as a myth by reporters from the *New York Times* who found not only some of the *contra* camps but plenty of U.S. weapons. Evidence was now very clear that the Reagan administration was in violation of the Boland Amendment. In spring 1983 the House of Representatives introduced the Boland-Zablocki bill which would prohibit the funding, directly or indirectly, of military and paramilitary operations against Nicaragua. Going on the offensive against his critics in Congress, President Reagan addressed a joint session of Congress on April 27, 1983. He spoke in terms of the global struggle between the United States and the Soviet Union and stated that the future of Central America was at stake.

He spoke of Sandinista totalitarianism and their support for revolutionaries in El Salvador and raised the specter of the Soviet Union in Central America. He requested support for the *contras*. By July 1983 the *contra* forces numbered 10,000. In October 1983 the CIA prepared a manual for the *contras* that encouraged terrorism and assassination. In late 1983, Clarridge reported to the Congress in a closed hearing that the *contras*, with U.S. support, had killed "civilians and Sandinista officials in the provinces as well as heads of cooperatives, nurses, doctors, and judges." This was an admission that the administration was in clear violation of its own Executive Order which prohibited U.S. involvement in assassinations.[9]

President Reagan also began to wage an economic war against the Sandinistas. Political pressure was put on American companies that traded with Nicaragua. Standard Fruit left the country in October 1982 refusing to purchase any more *Nica* bananas. Bank of America had agreed to grant Nicaragua a short-term 30 million dollar loan in December. Pressure from the State Department led Bank of America to not grant the loan. Having already cut economic aid and blocked loans from the Inter-American Development Bank (IADB), the United States reduced the Nicaraguan sugar quota by 90 percent in 1983. The General Agreement on Trade and Tariffs (GATT) ruled that this decision violated the treaty to which the United States was an original signatory, but the United States ignored the ruling. The CIA itself carried out operations against the economic infrastructure of Nicaragua. In September CIA commandos attacked Puerto Sandino and returned later to sabotage an underwater oil pipeline. In October CIA commandos fired at oil and gasoline tanks at Corinto setting them ablaze. Hundreds were injured and the fires were so hot that 25,000 people had to be evacuated for two days while authorities put out the fires. In December President Reagan authorized the CIA to carry out more attacks against economic infrastructure. In January, U.S. personnel attacked the port of Potosi and in March the petroleum facilities at Puerto Sandino and San Juan del Norte were attacked by CIA commandos. From January through March 1984, CIA commandos planted mines in all of the major ports and shipping lanes on both the Atlantic and Pacific coasts of Nicaragua. In April, ships from Japan, the Netherlands, Liberia, Panama, the Soviet Union, and Nicaragua hit mines. The Reagan administration denied any responsibility, blaming the actions on the *contras*. Later the World Court in the Hague ruled in favor of the governments of Nicaragua, Japan, the Netherlands, Liberia, Panama, and the Soviet Union and ordered the United States to pay these countries for their losses. The Reagan administration ignored the ruling.

While the *contras* operated primarily out of Honduras another anti-Sandinista force, the Democratic Revolutionary Alliance (ARDE) led by former Sandinista *Comandante* Eden Pastora, operated out of Costa Rica. Pastora, who owned a shark fishing business and had a very close personal relationship with Panamanian leader General Omar Torrijos, was never fully trusted by the Sandinista DN. He had a reputation as a womanizer and a heavy drinker and was considered by the DN to be much too undisciplined and individualistic to be part of the leadership in the new government. In mid-1982 Pastora announced he would take up arms against his former comrades because of their growing ties to Cuba. He also indicated that he could neither support nor work with the *contras* in Honduras. *Contra* ties to Somoza's former National Guard were unacceptable to Pastora.[10]

THE CHURCH AND THE SANDINISTAS

Archbishop Miguel Obando y Bravo was most outspoken against the repression, corruption, and abuses committed by the Somoza family. Many Sandinistas viewed him as a hero because he so openly defied the Somoza government. Yet, when Robelo and Chamorro left the Junta of National Reconstruction he began to speak out against the activities of the Sandinistas and quickly became their most outspoken opponent. He rejected the belief of many Sandinistas that class conflict in society was inevitable and spoke often of reconciling "the Nicaraguan family."[11] Obando and the other bishops also spoke out against the so-called progressive Church whose members had come to believe in a theology of liberation. Obando ordered the four priests who were working in the Sandinista government to resign their positions and to return to their religious functions. Minister of Education Fernando Cardenal, Minister of Culture Ernesto Cardenal, Minister of Social Welfare Edgard Parrales, and Foreign Minister Miguel D'Escoto stated that their duty was to the Sandinista revolution and refused to leave government service.

Pope John Paul II, who had encouraged Obando in his struggle with the Sandinistas, arrived in Managua on March 4, 1983. The Pope had already indicated that he would not say anything about recent *contra* atrocities in the north and this had outraged many Sandinista leaders. One of the Sandinista leaders who met the Pope at the airport was the Jesuit priest, author, supporter of liberation theology, and Minister of Culture Ernesto Cardenal. When Cardenal kneeled and attempted to kiss the ring of the Pope, the Pope withdrew his hand, pointed his index finger at him and scolded him. Later that day when the Pope spoke in Managua in the public plaza in front of a huge crowd, he stated that it was the duty of all Catholics to obey their bishops. At this point the Pope was interrupted by an organized group of Sandinista supporters in the crowd who chanted revolutionary slogans such as "the people's power" and "we want peace." The chanting eventually died out after the Pope asked for silence several times. The event was shown on television and it turned out to be a public relations nightmare for the Sandinistas both within Nicaragua and throughout the world. President Reagan used the event to illustrate what he believed to be the totalitarian nature of the Sandinistas.

Obando denounced the censorship of the press and jailing of those who opposed the Sandinistas. The Sandinistas tried to censor Obando's sermons but were never successful; however, they were able to ban his sermons from television. It is important to point out that Obando had also pledged to speak out against all human rights abuses in Nicaragua. While he denounced Sandinista abuses, he was quiet about *contra* atrocities in the north. He never publicly identified with the *contras*, but said nothing when the *contras* justified their war in his name.[12] When the Sandinistas initiated the military draft (to be discussed later), Obando and the bishops actively opposed it and aided those who wanted to evade the draft. Several priests were forced to leave Nicaragua because of their anti-draft activities.

ECONOMIC PROBLEMS AND POLICY CHANGES

From 1979 through 1983 the economy of Nicaragua grew by 7 percent in terms of gross domestic product (GDP) per capita and local food production increased. The economic growth leveled off in 1984 and then began to decline. Much of this was due to the negative effects of the *contra* war and U.S. restrictions on credit that were once available to Nicaragua. Agro-exporters, both private and the new state-run farms, needed access to tractors, chemical fertilizers, spare parts for machinery, and other technological inputs that were no longer available due to the deteriorating relationship between the United States and Nicaragua and the lack of foreign exchange or U.S. dollars to pay for these imports. The Reagan administration's complete economic embargo imposed in April 1985 made it virtually impossible to obtain necessary imports and foreign exchange. Although increased aid from the Soviet Union, such as tractors and fertilizers, helped, there simply was no substitute for the United States. In addition, Sandinista agricultural policies were not working. The agro-exporters could not sell directly on the foreign market, they had to sell their coffee, sugar, cattle, and cotton to the government. It was the government that then sold the product on the world market. The purpose of this was to provide the government with revenue to finance its education and social programs; however, it had an adverse effect on the productivity of the agro-exporters. Jeffery Paige finds that the agro-exporters were not paid enough for their products by the state and could not realize enough profit to reinvest in standing crops, new equipment, and needed inputs to be productive the following year. There were few incentives to continue to produce under this system except for the fear that if their estates were not productive they were subject to confiscation by the government.[13] These policies further alienated the agro-export elites that had remained in the country.

The Sandinistas also overlooked the conservative nature of the peasants. Many landless peasants were assigned to cooperatives such as the CAS. The CAS farmers were told by the state-run food marketing board (ENBAS) what to plant, typically food for local consumption such as beans or corn. They had to sell much of their product to ENBAS at set prices. Although many peasants stayed with the CAS because typically the state built a school and health clinic on or near the land, some simply quit farming and migrated to the urban areas. Peasants wanted individual titles to their own land and the ability to make their own decisions as to what to plant and at what price to sell their products.[14]

In looking at the number of peasants who had benefitted from land redistribution, the number who had simply left the cooperatives, and the voting results in the 1984 election (to be discussed later), it was clear that peasants believed that the Sandinistas were not moving fast enough on land reform. At the end of 1984 only 32,844 families had benefitted from land redistribution.[15] Fearing the continued loss of political support from peasants and due to the successful lobbying efforts of the National Union of Farmers and Ranchers (UNAG), the Sandinistas moved to make more land available to the peasants and to make them more productive. It shifted toward a more "pro-peasant vision" for agriculture.[16] While they continued to favor the CAS and CCS style cooperatives, the Sandinistas increased the amount of land that was available to peasants through redistribution. The primary reforms took place in the area between the Pacific Ocean and Lake Nicaragua known as the Carazo Plateau and the plains of Masaya and Dirioma. The so-called *Los Patios* plan focused on peasants who already owned small plots of land largely in the Carazo Plateau. They were given preferential access to credit and technical assistance to modernize their production techniques. Plan Masaya implemented in the plains of Masaya and Dirioma involved redistributing more land to peasants in the form of the CAS. They were also given preferential access to credit and technical assistance to modernize their production techniques. Some were encouraged to grow basic crops such as corn and beans, while others were encouraged to grow new crops such as fruits and vegetables that could be produced in large quantities on small plots of land. Those peasants that participated in these projects saw an increase in their standard of living.[17]

Shortages of food and basic items appeared in the urban areas and continued throughout the 1980s. Although some items disappeared because they were no longer imported into the country, state-run stores were always running out of basic items and food primarily due to the price set by the government. The prices were set so low that producers simply could not make a profit and output declined. An illegal market appeared as some goods were siphoned off the legal channels and sold at higher prices. Goods were smuggled into the country and *Nicas* who had relatives in the United States were often sent U.S. dollars as the *Nica* cordoba had quickly become worthless except in the state-run stores. Some fishermen and farmers were actually paid in dollars by the government and some *Nicas* worked for foreign companies that paid in dollars. People used dollars to purchase goods on the illegal market. The government desperately needed dollars or hard currency for its foreign exchange so it could continue to purchase goods from foreign countries and pay its debts. To capture the dollars used on the illegal market, the Minister of Tourism, Herty Lewites, a Jewish candy manufacturer who had smuggled guns from California into Nicaragua during the revolution, developed the idea of dollar stores. These stores were stocked with goods that were no longer available in Nicaragua. Lewites worked through companies in Panama that imported goods from the United States and then he purchased them for sale in the Nicaraguan dollar stores. The only currency that was accepted was U.S. dollars. For those *Nicas* with dollars these stores were extremely popular. By the late 1980s the dollars stores generated 20 percent of the hard currency or dollars for the government.[18]

ELECTIONS AND THE *CONTRA* WAR

After consulting with the Swedish Electoral Commission on election procedures, the Sandinista-led Council of State passed a Parties and Electoral Law and called for national elections to be held on November 4, 1984. Seven parties ran candidates for the presidency and a new 96-member National Assembly. The right-wing coalition, *Coordinadora*, selected former banker Arturo Cruz Porras as its candidate. Cruz pulled out of the election arguing that the conditions for a free election did not exist in Nicaragua. Just before the election the Independent Liberal Party (PLI) candidate Virgilio Godoy also pulled out but his vice-presidential candidate Constantino Pereira used the party's free television campaign time to urge his party's voters to ignore Godoy and vote. More than 100,000 PLI members voted in the election. The Reagan administration tried to influence the election outcomes. American spy planes, SR-71 Blackbirds, made supersonic flights over Managua each day for a week and American warships appeared off the Nicaraguan coast in full view. The administration made false claims in the media about Soviet advanced fighter jets being sent to Nicaragua. The *contras* attacked the small village of San Gregorio and killed six children.

On election day they were able to shut down only nine of the 3,892 polling or voting stations in the country.

With three-fourths of the electorate voting in the middle of the escalating *contra* war, Daniel Ortega was elected president with 67 percent of the valid votes cast. Of the remaining one-third of the votes, half were in favor of parties to the political left of the *Coordinadora*. This refutes the contention of the Reagan administration that Cruz was the only candidate capable of defeating Ortega. While the Reagan administration declared the election to be a "Soviet-style farce," election observers representing the British Parliament, the Irish Parliament, the Dutch government, former West German Chancellor Willy Brandt, and the Latin America Studies Association all declared that the elections were basically fair with minimal problems. The Sandinistas were the first "socialist" government in history to have both revolutionary and electoral legitimacy.[19] The Sandinistas won 61 seats in the new National Assembly. The Democratic Conservative Party won 14 seats, the Independent Liberals won nine seats, the Popular Social Christian Party won six seats, the Socialist Party won two seats, the Communist Party won two seats, and the Marxist-Leninist Popular Action Movement won two seats. The primary task of the new Constituent Assembly was to write a new constitution. After two years of heated debate and compromise, as well as gathering advice from the faculty at the New York University Law School, the new constitution was enacted in 1987.

With the *contra* war disrupting more and more of the Nicaraguan economy and fearing a military escalation by the *contra* forces and the United States, Humberto Ortega, the Sandinista Minister of Defense, implemented the first-ever nationwide military draft in January 1984. By this time the Sandinista Army had grown to 40,000 soldiers and the government also began creating local militias consisting of 60,000 volunteers. Weapons from Cuba and the Soviet Union were brought into the country including artillery, propeller-driven aircraft, helicopters, troop transport vehicles, anti-aircraft guns, and tanks. The cost of fighting the *contra* war escalated dramatically and had a negative impact on the country's budget and its ability to continue to fulfill its education and social policy promises. By 1985 nearly 50 percent of the budget was spent on the *contra* war. Early that year President Reagan had asked Congress to renew aid to the *contras* using his now standard characterization of the Sandinistas as totalitarian dictators who were enabling the Soviet Union to have a base in Central America. The House of Representatives rejected his request and in retaliation President Reagan unilaterally imposed a complete trade embargo against Nicaragua in April. This meant that American companies could not export or import goods from Nicaragua. With exports declining and a shortage of foreign exchange or U.S. dollars, Ortega then visited the Soviet

Union to request more oil because Nicaragua could no longer pay for oil from Mexico and Venezuela even if it was sold at concessional rates. The timing of Ortega's visit did not serve him well as the U.S. Congress condemned his trip to the Soviet Union and voted to provide 27 million dollars in humanitarian aid to the *contras*.

Although Congress generally did not want to support the President's militaristic policy toward Nicaragua, actions by the Sandinista leadership often made it difficult for Congress not to give in to the President's wishes. With a complete U.S. trade embargo in place, the United States also put pressure on European and Latin American governments not to trade with Nicaragua. The United States continued to block loans from the IADB. Loans to purchase tractors and livestock, build roads in rural areas, and develop large-scale irrigation systems were all vetoed by the United States in 1985. In October 1985 the Sandinistas placed more restrictions on civil liberties including the press. The major opposition newspaper run by Chamorro, *La Prensa*, which was now funded by the U.S.-based National Endowment for Democracy, often lost two-thirds of its proposed articles to the censors. *La Prensa* remained uncritical of U.S. policy and the actions of the *contras*.

THE IRAN-CONTRA AFFAIR

With clear evidence of the administration's violations of the Boland Amendment, the Congress passed the second Boland Amendment in October 1984 despite the protests of President Reagan. The amendment stated that the CIA, the Department of Defense, or any intelligence agency could not provide funds to support the military operations of any group, organization, movement, or individual operating in Nicaragua. Its purpose was to end the administration's military support for the *contras*. Nonetheless, throughout 1985 flights were still made into Nicaragua and Honduras allowing the *contras* to maintain their war against the Nicaraguan economic infrastructure. With the passage of the second Boland Amendment, members of the National Security Council, including the National Security Adviser Robert McFarlane, John Poindexter, and Lt. Colonel North operating out of the White House, began to devise a grand scheme to circumvent the new legislation. The scheme was approved by President Reagan and worked in the following manner. With the help of the Israeli government Hawk anti-aircraft missiles with radar guidance systems, tube-launched, optically tracked, wire-guided (TOW) anti-tank missiles, and spare parts for jets were sold at inflated prices to Ayatollah Khomeini's government in Iran from August through December 1985. In exchange for the sophisticated weapons, Iran, a country with which the United States did not have diplomatic relations and to which President Reagan referred as "Murder

Incorporated," agreed to make sure American hostages held by Lebanese militants were freed. Iran lived up to its promise and the hostages were freed. It is not clear if President Reagan was aware of the next part of this scheme as Poindexter testified later that he made sure that the President could deny any knowledge of it. The money received from Iran was then used to create what Lt. Colonel North called "the Enterprise." This was essentially a secret government with its own funding source, money from the weapons sold to Iran. The Enterprise had its own foreign policy, providing weapons and assistance to the *contras* in violation of the Boland Amendment and the intent of Congress. It also had its own military personnel and air force, the Central Intelligence Agency's (CIA) affiliated Southern Air Transport and Corporate Air Service. Elliot Abrams, one of those who assisted Poindexter and North, sought and received extra funding for the Enterprise from Saudi Arabia, Taiwan, Brunei, and wealthy, conservative Americans. Hundreds of flights were made into Nicaragua to supply *contra* units with weapons throughout 1986. The Enterprise's actions not only violated the Boland Amendment, but also operated completely unknown to the Congress, the vast majority within the executive branch, and the American people. It was accountable to no one.

North's clandestine efforts to provide weapons to the *contras* exploded on the front pages in October 1986 when a *contra* supply plane was shot down near San Carlos along the border with Costa Rica. The surviving pilot, Eugene Hasenfus who had flown with the CIA's secret Air America group in Laos during the Viet Nam War, publicly told the details of North's military supply efforts to the *contras* during his trial. Documents on the plane carried descriptions of supply flights from El Salvador and Honduras and identified North, Robert Owens, and others as leaders of the supply effort. The Sandinistas seized the public relations opportunity and called Mike Wallace of the Columbia Broadcasting System (CBS) to come to Managua to interview Hasenfus and see all the evidence of the *contra* supply efforts. Although Hasenfus was found guilty, the Nicaraguan government released him as he was no longer needed—the damage to U.S. policy was already done. In November 1986 a Lebanese magazine published a report indicating that the United States had been selling sophisticated weapons to the Ayatollah Khomeini. North held a "shredding party" and destroyed thousands of documents that tied the administration to the diversion of funds from the sale of weapons to Iran to the *contras*. Poindexter, North, and Attorney General Edwin Meese engaged in a massive cover-up and obstructed the congressional inquiry. The Iran-Contra scandal engulfed and crippled the Reagan administration for the remainder of the president's term as one revelation after another was made public. According to Kinzer, the scandal "sounded the *contras*' death knoll."[20]

THE SANDINISTAS AND THE PEOPLES OF THE CARIBBEAN COAST

Historically the Caribbean region of Nicaragua was separated geographically, politically, economically, and ethnically from Spanish Nicaragua. Indigenous peoples in the region had always referred to *Nicas* on the Pacific side of the country as Spaniards. The area was ethnically diverse with indigenous groups such as the Miskito, the Sumu, the Ramas, and the Garifonas. With the coffee boom of the late 1800s and the cotton boom of the 1950s, mestizo peasants had also migrated from the Pacific looking for land. Throughout the 1800s British dominance in this area had fostered and promoted an autonomous region in which the indigenous peoples, especially the Miskito Indians, would be politically separate from the remainder of Nicaragua. With British and U.S. companies operating in the area, the people were oriented toward the Caribbean, Galveston, New Orleans, and Miami rather than Managua. Throughout the Somoza years this area of Nicaragua suffered primarily from neglect.

By the 1970s various organizations, such as the Miskito and Sumu Alliance for Progress (ALPROMISU), were formed that began to promote and assert ethnic identities. With more of the youth being educated by the Moravian Church and at the National University, there was a growing assertiveness in terms of their political demands toward Managua. Very little fighting during the struggle against Somoza took place in this area. There was plenty of land available and communal land was still the dominant type of land tenure pattern among the indigenous peoples. The Sandinistas, like *Nica* governments prior to them, knew very little about the region and its peoples and did not know how to interact with the different cultures found there. They treated them as less civilized and believed that it was their mission to bring civilization in the form of land reform, education, and health care to the region. Sandinista reforms were not welcome and the indigenous peoples resisted them.

Many of the Miskito Indians lived along the Coco River which is the border between Nicaragua and Honduras in the northern part of Zelaya province. Believing the Coco to be their ancestral home, the Miskitos did not recognize the international border and traveled frequently back and forth from Nicaragua and Honduras. Many lived in small villages along the river but many also lived in Puerto Cabezas on the Atlantic Coast. At Puerto Cabezas the Sandinistas hesitantly recognized the so-called Miskito, Sumu, Rama, and Sandinistas Working Together Group (MISURASATA). This group moved quickly to make sure that English and indigenous languages were included in the Literacy Crusade. MISURASATA grew as literacy volunteers joined the organization. MISURASATA leaders spoke freely of self-determination, autonomy, and sovereignty for the Atlantic Coast peoples.[21] It was clear that MISURASATA was moving too quickly for the unprepared Sandinistas. Conflicts over land and labor demands for higher wages led to violent incidents between the Sandinistas and the indigenous peoples. Miskito Indian attacks against Sandinista forces became common with the Miskitos attacking and then retreating across the Coco to the safety of Honduras. Steadman Fagoth Mueller, a MISURASATA leader, was jailed by the Sandinistas in 1981. He was shortly released when he promised to study abroad. Fagoth fled to Honduras, joined the *contras*, and began giving anti-Sandinista broadcasts over the radio. In August 1981 the Sandinistas refused to recognize MISURASATA. It was at this time that the charismatic Miskito leader Brooklyn Rivera became the primary spokesperson for the indigenous peoples' struggle. Rivera was also arrested, released shortly, and traveled to Honduras and then Costa Rica.

The Indian-led Red Christmas Campaign against Sandinista forces in the region started in November 1981. The Sandinista leadership believed that it was coordinated by the CIA and the *contra* forces. Wanting to deprive the militant Indian forces of sanctuary along the Coco River, the Sandinistas forcefully relocated nearly 10,000 Miskito Indians from their villages along the Coco River. The Sandinistas burned their villages and the stored grain and food and killed much of their livestock. The Indians were taken to a clearing in the jungle 50 miles away. They were given a few supplies and were told this is where they had to live. The relocation decision was a terrible mistake for the Sandinistas, one for which even today they continue to apologize. The relocation of the Miskitos away from their sacred homelands radicalized not only other Miskitos but other indigenous groups. The Church and foreign governments condemned the action as a clear violation of human rights. President Reagan seized on the incident as an opportunity to try to recruit the *Miskitos* as part of the *contra* effort. Reagan's efforts divided the indigenous peoples. Whereas Fagoth cooperated fully with the CIA and the *contras*, Rivera refused to do so. He saw the *contras* as just another group of Spaniards seeking to control the indigenous peoples of Nicaragua.[22] He worked with Pastora and Robelo. After Pastora "retired" from the insurgency in 1984, Rivera began negotiating indirectly with the Sandinistas with Moravian Church leaders acting as intermediaries. Talks with *Comandante* Luis Carrion failed to achieve his objective of the removal of all Sandinista military forces in the Atlantic region. He then traveled to Honduras to meet with Miskito Indians to convince them to work toward a negotiated peace settlement and to not join the *contras*. When he arrived in Honduras, he was told to leave the country. Although there is no evidence to support it, many believe that the United States approved of the decision because Rivera opposed the *contras* and Reagan's policies toward Nicaragua.

In May 1985 *Comandante* Borge announced that all those who were forcibly moved could now move back to their original villages along the Coco River. More importantly, he announced a new policy toward the entire Atlantic region. It was now to become an autonomous region within Nicaragua. Any Indian military commander who committed to stop fighting was allowed to take his men back to their villages and they would be placed in charge of local security. The Sandinista military and police would then leave the area. Many Indian commanders took his offer. According to Kinzer the Sandinistas were recognizing a type of "Indian sovereignty." They had recognized that they were outsiders in this part of Nicaragua.[23] By granting the indigenous peoples autonomy with local police powers the Sandinistas removed one of the primary reasons for their opposition and helped to contain the growing influence of Rivera. Borge also began courting the other Indian groups in the region as well. He responded to their material needs with rice and fertilizer. While he continued to try to capture Rivera, Borge's policies were effectively eliminating the need to negotiate with him. Perhaps more importantly, he was also able to turn around the public relations war in the global media as the focus on Rivera and the indigenous peoples of the Atlantic Coast waned.

THE *CONTRA* WAR CONTINUES

By mid-1985 it was estimated that at least 12,000 *Nicas* had been killed since the beginning of the *contra* war. Death touched all families, regardless of class. Sandinista leaders requested talks with the Reagan administration but were turned away each time. While North and his Enterprise provided weapons for the *contras*, there was a large fund-raising campaign led by General John K. Singlaub, the head of the World Anti-Communist League, to provide "nonlethal" aid in the form of clothing, food, medicine, and transportation vehicles. Money came from wealthy individuals, the Christian Broadcasting Company, the Unification Church, and the Veterans of Foreign Wars. Despite all of the clandestine support, the number of *contras* declined to about 12,000 by 1986. That same year the CIA provided *contra* units with land mines. The roads in northern Nicaragua became very dangerous. While the land mines were directed toward Sandinista military units, many innocent children and adults were killed or lost legs and arms to the mines. The CIA also provided *contra* units with Stinger anti-aircraft missiles which are relatively light and fired from the shoulder. These were effective against Sandinista army helicopters. CIA commandos blew up a major weapons depot near El Chipote Prison in Managua. In June 1986 after relentless pressure from President Reagan, the Congress voted for the first time to provide 70 million dollars in military supplies to the *contras*.

Reagan promised the Congress that the *contra* leadership would be reformed with new members; however, no reforms were ever initiated. Shortly after the Congressional vote in support of lethal aid, the Sandinistas shut down *La Prensa*. In fall 1986, the Iran-Contra scandal broke and Congress would never again support the *contra* cause. Throughout 1987 the CIA continued to fly support missions to the *contras* from their secret air base on Swan Island off the coast of Honduras. They flew more than 300 missions in 1987.[24]

In towns along the border with Honduras, the *contra* war was part of everyday life. Farming was virtually impossible and many simply left their land. Gunfire could almost always be heard and planes flew above carrying weapons for both the *contras* and the Sandinistas. *Contra* raids were common and they focused on destroying rural schools, clinics, day care centers, food storage facilities, and other development programs such as hydroelectric projects. Sometimes they attempted to take entire towns such as Ocotol, other times small skirmishes took place, and other times they simply assassinated teachers, nurses, doctors, technicians, or anyone associated with the Sandinistas. Sandinistas arrested anyone suspected of collaborating with the *contras*. Young men either were drafted into the Sandinista Army or fled into Honduras to join the *contra* forces. *Nica* families hated the military draft. Funerals for young people were too common and most people became weary of war.

The *contra* war was a civil war that split many families in Nicaragua regardless of economic background. *Contra* spokesperson Marta Sacasa was the sister of Captain Rosa Pasos, the spokesperson for the Sandinista Army. Luis Carrion, a member of the Sandinista DN, was a nephew of presidential candidate Cruz who was the nominee of the *Coordinadora* right wing alliance in 1984. Chamorro's family was split during the revolutionary years. Violeta Barrios de Chamorro was the editor of *La Prensa*, the major opposition paper to the Sandinistas. Her son, Pedro Joaquín, was a leader of the *Contras* and lived in exile in Costa Rica where he was the editor of an anti-Sandinista paper *Nicaragua Hoy*. Her daughter, Cristiana, helped to run *La Prensa*. Her other daughter, Claudia, became the Sandinista Ambassador to Costa Rica and Cuba. She married Edmundo Jarquín, a former economics professor at the Central American University, who served as the Sandinista Ambassador to Mexico from 1984 to 1988 and then to Spain from 1988 to 1990. Another son, Carlos Fernando Chamorro Barrios, was the editor of *Barricada*, the official newspaper of the FSLN. Her brother-in-law, Xavier Chamorro Cardenal, left *La Prensa* and became editor of *El Nuevo Diario*, an independent pro-Sandinista newspaper. The Chair of the National Bank of Nicaragua was Joaquín Cuadra Chamorro, a cousin of her husband, Pedro Joaquín Chamorro. Cuadra's son, Joaquín Cuadra Lacayo, was a Chief of Staff for the Sandinista Army.

Although the *contra* war divided families and caused tremendous hardships, it was the financial cost that played a role in bringing about the end of the Sandinista revolutionary experiment. The Sandinista government could not continue to wage the *contra* war and successfully implement its revolutionary economic and social programs. With the war effort taking up more than half the budget, Sandinista education and social reforms came to a halt. The health care system was over-burdened by the growing number of *contra* war casualties and could no longer meet the needs of the people because of the lack of medicine and drugs. Many government employees and those who were still trying to implement and carry out the Sandinista reforms saw their purchasing power reduced to the point that many simply quit. The standard of living of virtually all *Nicas* had declined. Agricultural production had declined. Government debt and inflation skyrocketed. By June 1988 the inflation rate was estimated to be 36,000 percent with war damage estimated at 12 billion dollars. In an attempt to reign in runaway inflation the Sandinistas implemented a set of severe economic austerity measures. They included drastic cuts in government spending and the dismantling of both price and wage controls. This further reduced the Sandinistas' ability to carry out their reforms and turned many of their supporters against them.

CONTADORA AND THE ARIAS PEACE PLAN

The struggle against the Somoza dynasty and the *contra* war spilled over into the other countries of Central America. In particular, Honduras to the north and Costa Rica to the south were directly involved. The Carter administration had signed military agreements with Honduras when large numbers of refugees began fleeing the wars in both El Salvador and Nicaragua. By 1981 Honduras faced growing debt problems and a decline in the world market for its major exports. Military and economic aid from the Reagan administration increased dramatically. *Contra* bases and airstrips were built along the border with Nicaragua. In 1984 the Suazo government requested a substantial increase in U.S. economic aid and was denied. General Gustavo Alvarez Martinez, who was very close to the U.S. Ambassador John Negroponte, was removed from his command based on allegations of corruption. The Suazo government wanted to lessen its military ties to the United States because many Hondurans believed that it had too much dominance and control over their country. Some feared the possibility of a military *golpe*. Honduran and U.S. relations were strained until new President José Azcona Haya, who received less than 30 percent of the vote in the elections, took office in 1986. Joint military maneuvers with the United States continued.

Costa Rica had supported the efforts to overthrow the Somoza dynasty and had provided a conduit for weapons to reach the Sandinistas. Suffering from an inability to pay its foreign debts, the Costa Rican government under Luis Alberto Monge signed a renegotiated debt agreement with the International Monetary Fund and the United States in 1982. Monge began to tolerate the existence of anti-Sandinista forces in camps along its border with Nicaragua, the most notable of which was ARDE led by Pastora. By 1985 the United States was providing more than one-third of the Costa Rican budget. With Pastora and other groups operating out of Costa Rica and providing weapons to the *contras*, diplomatic relations between Costa Rica and Nicaragua deteriorated. Significantly, Oscar Arias was elected president in February 1986 and the next month Pastora "retired" from fighting the Sandinistas indicating his displeasure with continual interference by the CIA and its insistence that he work with the *contras*.

Beginning in January 1983 the countries of Panama, Mexico, Colombia, and Venezuela, known as the contadora group, met several times in an attempt to set out the basic parameters of a regional peace settlement that included both El Salvador and Nicaragua. By October the group had come up with a 21-point proposal, and by the following spring they had developed a comprehensive regional peace treaty. It covered elections, ceasefires, arms limitations, amnesty for armed dissidents, and a prohibition on interference into the internal affairs of the Central American countries. In summer 1983, President Reagan appointed the so-called Kissinger Commission to come up with a set of recommendations for U.S. policy in the region. The commission issued its report in January 1984 and it mirrored the administration's belief that Soviet and Cuban intervention in Central America was a fundamental security threat to the United States. In essence, it supported Reagan's policies of continued military and economic aid to El Salvador's government and support for the *contra* forces against the Sandinistas.

Up to this point, President Reagan was publicly supportive of the contadora peace process and the major points of the proposed treaty largely because he believed that the Sandinistas would never accept them. On September 21, 1984, the Sandinistas agreed to sign the treaty without any modifications. By doing so, the Sandinistas agreed to expel all Soviet and Cuban military advisers, end imports of Soviet weapons, reduce the size of its military, end aid to the revolutionaries in El Salvador, enter into a dialogue with the *contras*, and allow on-site verification of the treaty. This caught the U.S. administration by surprise and forced it to reverse its initial support for the treaty.[25] The treaty clearly went against Reagan's policy in the region as it called for removal of all U.S. and other foreign troops and military aid to Central America within 30 days of its passage. The treaty forbade the use of any territory to support armed insurgents. This would deny *contra* use of bases in both Honduras and Costa Rica. Finally, the United States opposed the agreement because it did not remove the Sandinistas from power which was Reagan's primary goal. Over the next two years, the Reagan administration proposed one modification after another that was unacceptable to several of the countries involved. In the end the United States hindered and delayed the progress of the contadora peace process. The process was revived in April 1986 when the contadora group and the Central American countries met in Mexico City and worked out a similar agreement. The only country to oppose the agreement was Nicaragua. The Sandinistas insisted that the treaty could not be signed until the United States quit funding the *contras*. The United States insisted it could not cut aid to the *contras* until Nicaragua signed the treaty. In June a new draft of the peace treaty was put forward and this time the Sandinistas indicated that Nicaragua would sign the document. The United States rejected the new draft and put pressure on both Honduras and El Salvador to reject it. When the Iran-contra scandal broke in fall 1986, the contadora peace process had come to a halt.

President Arias quickly told the United States that he would no longer tolerate *contra* forces operating inside the Costa Rican border. He even refused to allow *contra* leaders, such as Adolfo Calero, entry into the country to visit *contra* bases. He shut down a secret airport that the United States had built near Santa Elena in defiance of a U.S. threat to cut economic aid. With Pastora no longer fighting the Sandinistas, Arias effectively ended all anti-Sandinista activities out of his country when he shut down the airport. Arias then began putting together another comprehensive, regional peace plan based on contadora principles. The five Central American nations met in Esquipulas, Guatemala in May 1987 to discuss the Arias Plan. All agreed in principle. In June Arias visited the United States and Reagan and his closest advisers tried to get him to change his policies. Arias said he would not change. According to Kinzer, the meeting was "sharp, tense, and blunt."

With Reagan hastily putting together a U.S.-sponsored regional peace plan, Arias met with the four other Central American presidents in August in Guatemala City in the Camino Real Hotel. Arias locked everyone in a room and would not let anyone leave until an agreement was reached. They did not even leave the room for dinner. On August 7 an agreement was announced to the world. Each government committed to an open political process for all parties, a free press, and periodic elections monitored by the UN and the Organization of American States. States of emergency would be declared over, cease-fires would be put into place, amnesty granted to enemies, and negotiations to end hostilities would begin as soon as possible. It committed the five Central American nations to require that any country outside the region should stop providing military aid to insurgents. It was a remarkable achievement and a rebuke of Reagan's policies in the region.

Ortega returned to Nicaragua to face the Sandinista DN. Many were upset that he had agreed to the Arias Peace Plan. For three days Ortega defended the plan to his fellow *comandantes*. Unable to gain their support, he flew to Havana and met with Castro. Ortega and Castro believed that the plan was the only way to end the *contra* war. With Castro publicly supporting Ortega, opposition from the other members of the Sandinista DN disappeared. The next day the Sandinista DN "unanimously" sanctioned the Arias Peace Plan. *Comandante* Tomás Borge, perhaps the most vigorous opponent of the plan, traveled to Havana in September. After meeting with Castro he never raised the issue again in public. *La Prensa* was reopened with assistance from the U.S. government-supported National Endowment for Democracy and Archbishop Obando was named as chair of the National Reconciliation Commission. That same month President Reagan asked the Congress for an additional 270 million dollars in military aid to support the *contras*. In October Arias was awarded the Nobel Peace Prize for his efforts.

THE HISTORIC 1990 ELECTIONS

In February 1988, Congress voted to deny Reagan's request for more money to support the *contras*. Nonetheless the *contra* war continued and throughout much of that year it looked like the Arias Peace Plan would not be successful as both the *contras* and the Sandinistas violated it. Archbishop Obando was unable to bring the two sides together and in December he told Ortega that direct negotiations between the Sandinista and *contra* leaders were required. With the economy in shambles, the *contra* war still ongoing, and negotiations with the *contras* not going well, Ortega offered to negotiate directly with *contra* leaders at the town of Sapoa on the Pacific coast south of Rivas. With a new U.S. president and U.S. aid no longer coming to the *contras*, their leaders finally agreed to the negotiations. In the early morning of March 24, 1989, the Ortega brothers emerged with *contra* leaders Calero and Alfredo Cesar and announced a peace agreement from a small building that once was a cafeteria. Together, they all sang the Nicaraguan national anthem. The *contra* war had, at least officially, ended. Nicaragua was officially at peace. The *contra* war had claimed the lives of more than 30,000 *Nicas*, destroyed the economy, and divided the country.

Ortega met with the opposition political parties in spring 1989. They decided to conduct the elections in February 1990 rather than the scheduled date in November. The Sandinistas believed that if they held elections, the world would know they were legitimate and would have to recognize them. In particular, the new U.S. administration would be forced to end its embargo against the country. This would allow the Sandinistas to focus on rebuilding the economy and the country. In August the five Central American nations met and established the Tela Accord. Nicaragua agreed to accept the outcome of the elections in El Salvador and the Central American nations agreed that the *contras* must be fully disarmed and demobilized. President George H. W. Bush objected but eventually accepted the accord because all the countries of Central America supported it. Ortega released 1,500 *contras* and former National Guard prisoners.

That same month the National Opposition Union (UNO) was created. It represented the following 14 parties: the Independent Liberals, the Constitutionalist Liberals, the Neo-Liberals, the National Conservatives, the Conservative Popular Alliance, the National Conservative Alliance, the Social Democrats, the National Democratic Movement, the Popular Social Christians, the National Democratic Confidence Party, the National Action Party, the Socialists, the Communists, and the Central American Integrationist Party. UNO ranged from the far right to the far left on the political spectrum. Chamorro was the only person who could unite such a coalition and the only person with enough respect and visibility among the public to actually challenge Ortega and the FSLN. Although eight other minor parties participated in the election, the real choice was between Chamorro and Ortega. Ortega had revolutionary legitimacy, represented the working class and the poor, and symbolized the desire to end the vast repression and economic and social inequality that had characterized the country since its beginning. His programs focused on improving the lot of the average *Nica*. Chamorro represented the progressive elites of the country who wanted a free market economy, free elections, electoral democracy, and closer ties to the United States. She emphasized the need for national reconciliation and promised an end to the draft and the *contra* war, a resumption of U.S. economic aid to Nicaragua, and an end to the state intervention in the economy.

On four consecutive Sundays in October a massive voter registration drive was held. By the end of the month more than 1.752 million people had registered, almost 89 percent of those who were eligible. In the same month that *Nicas* were registering to vote in record numbers, the greatest symbol of the Cold War, the Berlin Wall, was finally torn down. By this time it was evident to all that the Cold War was coming to an end and a new world order was emerging. The communist regimes in Eastern Europe had collapsed. The Soviets were pulling out of Afghanistan, and free elections had been held in Poland and Czechoslovakia. President Mikhail Gorbachev had dramatically changed Soviet foreign policy. He indicated that the Soviet Union would no longer encourage or support revolutions. Ortega and the Sandinistas knew they had to somehow adapt to a changed world. But some things had not changed. On December 20 the United States invaded Panama, captured the dictator Manuel Noriega, installed a president to its liking, and invaded the home of a Nicaraguan diplomat. Although not many were upset over the capture of the drug-running Noriega, the international community and the Central American nations were clearly upset with the invasion and the naked use of force by the United States. It was but another example in a long history of U.S. interference and intervention in Latin America. The Sandinistas condemned the invasion of Panama and the invasion of the Nicaraguan diplomat's home. Many *Nicas* believed that the timing of the invasion was such that it was really an attempt to intimidate *Nica* voters into supporting Chamorro.

There were three television channels, one weekly and three daily newspapers, and more than 50 radio stations that covered the Nicaraguan elections. While most people relied on radio for their information, the two primary newspapers, *La Prensa* and *El Nuevo Diario,* covered the campaign and by February 1990 had clearly illustrated the differences between the two candidates on issues. By this time the focus was on the possible reaction of the United States should one or the other candidate win the election.[26] It was perhaps one of the most closely observed elections in history with not only the media from virtually every part of the world scrutinizing every detail but also the presence of trained election monitors and observers from the U.S. government, the Carter Center, the Latin American Studies Association, the United Nations, the other Central American countries, and many European countries.

On February 25, 1990, more than 86 percent of those registered to vote participated in the elections. To the surprise of many pollsters and many in the world Chamorro and vice-presidential candidate Virgilio Godoy of the UNO coalition received 54.7 percent of the vote. Ortega and vice-presidential candidate Ramirez of the FSLN received 40.8 percent of the vote. A teary-eyed Ortega conceded the election and announced that he would "respect and obey the mandate of the people" while he urged *Nicas* to "respect and obey the mandate of the people." On February 28, Ortega and Chamorro called for the demobilization of the *contras*. Ortega announced a ceasefire. Representatives from President-elect Chamorro met with *contra* leaders who agreed to demobilize and disarm troops in Honduras by April 20. This demobilization and disarming process would be monitored by Cardinal Obando, the Organization of American States, and the United Nations. They further agreed that issues involving private property rights should be resolved in the courts. The UNO coalition received 51 of 92 seats in the new National Assembly which was divided among its 14 parties. The most seats held by a single party within the UNO coalition was six, held by the Social Democrats. The Independent Liberals, the National Conservatives, and the Conservative Popular Alliance each received five seats within the UNO coalition. The Sandinistas, still the single largest party in the country, received 39 seats. The remaining two seats were held by the Revolutionary Unitary Movement and the Social Christian Party.

In the interim or lame-duck period before the inauguration of Chamorro the National Assembly, which was still controlled by the FSLN, passed a series of laws. A general amnesty was given to all *Nicas*, including *contras* and military troops, who had committed any so-called crimes against the public order since July 19, 1979. The highest officials in the government were given blanket immunity from any prosecution and the government could no longer have a monopoly over the broadcast media or television. The government legalized the Sandinista holdings of property and houses that had been confiscated. Unfortunately, this was done so suddenly that many *Nicas* viewed this as simply an opportunistic grab for property and wealth before the new government came into power. It was especially visible because of certain wealthy properties in Managua that were claimed by leading Sandinistas. This came to be known cynically as *la piñata* and hurt the image of the Sandinista leadership even though a fund was set up to compensate the former owners, many who were residing in the United States.

On April 25 Chamorro became President of Nicaragua. In her acceptance speech she emphasized the need for national reconciliation and officially ended the military draft. She stated that Sandinista Humberto Ortega would remain as head of the Nicaraguan Armed Forces so that he could put together a plan to reduce the size of the army. This was most controversial and caused two of her Cabinet Ministers, Jaime Cuadra and Gilberto Cuadro, to resign. Inevitable splits within UNO had already appeared between Chamorro and her closest advisers who were Conservatives and Godoy and the PLI. This return of the classic liberal conservative struggle manifested itself in the struggle for control of the National Assembly. Chamorro preferred Alfredo Cesar of the Social Democrats but Godoy preferred Miriam Arguello.

EXPLAINING THE SANDINISTA DEFEAT

Thomas Walker, William Robinson, and other scholars argue that the defeat of the Sandinistas in the 1990 election was another in a long history of Nicaraguan submissions to U.S. dominance. The Reagan administration's willingness to wage an overt war, even in violation of U.S. laws, for eight years followed by President Bush's invasion of neighboring Panama sent a clear message to all *Nicas*. The message was that a vote for the Sandinistas would result in a continuation of U.S. support for the *contra* war and the economic embargo and the clear possibility of a U.S. invasion similar to what was seen in Panama two months before the election. The only way for an exhausted and defeated people to avoid this was to vote for Chamorro, the preferred U.S. candidate.[27] Although this argument has merit and is consistent with the history of U.S.-Nicaraguan relations, it is perhaps too simplistic to explain the electoral events of 1990.

According to Leslie Anderson and Lawrence Dodd, the argument does not take into consideration the possibility that *Nicas* actually made a reasoned and deliberate choice between Ortega and Chamorro rather than a simple submission to U.S. demands.[28] Nicaragua and *Nicas* had changed under the Sandinistas. The changes, which will be discussed in greater detail in the final chapter, include not only the creation of a more egalitarian society but also the belief and ability among all *Nicas* that they now could participate in the political process and control their own political destinies. A democratic consciousness had taken hold. During the struggle against the Somoza dynasty and under Sandinista rule the Nicaraguan people learned that they had the ability to control the elites of society and were capable of making reasoned choices through democratic processes.

Many *Nicas* came to believe in Chamorro's ability to deliver on her promises about the future. While all recognized the likelihood of the end of the *contra* war and the U.S. embargo with the election of Chamorro, they also believed that only Chamorro could unite and reconcile the fractured and divided country. This belief was based on an assessment of her ability to unite not only an extremely diverse and broad UNO coalition and but also her own politically divided family. Ortega was seen as less capable to bring about national reconciliation.[29] Interviews, surveys, and voting analyses of the 1990 elections show that many former Sandinista supporters voted for Chamorro because they believed she would better represent their interests. For example, under the CCS redistribution plan peasants who already owned small plots of land received greater access to technical, agricultural expertise, and credit through cooperative or group arrangements. These property-owning peasants benefited from the Sandinista policies and one would have expected them to continue to support the Sandinistas. Yet, many became fearful of having their property confiscated by the Sandinistas. They believed that Chamorro would provide greater protection for their private property and tended to vote for her.[30] *Nicas* were capable of clear discernment between the candidates and based voting decisions on reasoned choice.

Whereas it is clear that the desire to end the *contra* war and the U.S. embargo played a role in the vote in favor of Chamorro, it was not simply a matter of a poor, tired people capitulating to the dominant U.S. power.

Rather, through a reasoned choice the Nicaraguan people came to believe that at this point in time Chamorro presented a better future for the country than Ortega and the Sandinistas. The Sandinistas had reached a crossroads. Looking back, it is quite remarkable to see the FSLN change from a fledgling, inexperienced, revolutionary group of idealistic students and intellectuals; to an organized, well-trained, rural and urban guerrilla revolutionary army; to an idealistic, revolutionary ruling party; to an increasingly pragmatic, democratically elected-revolutionary ruling party; and finally in 1990 to a traditional, loyal-opposition party. With the election of Chamorro the FSLN would have to learn the art of compromise and the game of democratic electoral politics. Yet, at its core the FSLN had not changed. It still believed that government had a responsibility primarily to the poor, the weak, the disadvantaged, and those who did not own property. In the subsequent elections of 1996, 2001, and 2006 the FSLN would remain the single largest party in the country and would become an effective player under the new democratic electoral rules.

VIOLETA BARRIOS DE CHAMORRO (1929–PRESENT)

Known as Doña Violeta to many, Violeta Barrios de Chamorro was born into the Sacasa family and married into the Chamorro family. Both families represented the traditional political and economic elites of Nicaragua and played primary roles throughout its history. Her father was a cattle rancher and wealthy landowner. One of seven children, she was born on October 18, 1929 in Rivas and lived a sheltered, elite life in the countryside learning to ride horses. All of her brothers and sisters were sent abroad to school. She was sent to Our Lady of the Lake School in San Antonio, Texas, to learn English and attended Blackstone College in Virginia. She returned to Nicaragua in 1948 where she met Pedro Joaquín Chamorro. They were married in 1950. While her husband was perhaps the best-known opposition figure in the struggle against the Somoza dynasty, Doña Violeta raised their four children. She was often by herself while her husband was in jail. With the murder of her husband in 1978, Doña Violeta was thrust into a leadership role in seeking to bring down the Somoza government. She was one of five who served on the Junta of National Reconstruction but resigned in 1980 when she came to believe that the Sandinistas were not committed to democracy and an open economy. She stayed in the country and used her newspaper, *La Prensa*, to voice her opposition to the Sandinistas in the 1980s. She often referred to the Sandinistas as "*Los Muchachos*" or "the little boys" in her editorials. It was a difficult time for her because her own family was split with two of her children working for the *contras* and the other two committed to the Sandinista revolution. She was associated with neither the *contras* nor the United States and was viewed as an independent. Her lack of official party affiliation and her independent status led her to lead a coalition of 14 parties ranging from communists on the left to the far right in the 1990 elections. She shocked the world with her election victory over Ortega and on April 15 she was inaugurated as the first woman president of Nicaragua. She inherited a ruined economy, an ongoing *contra* civil war, a large Sandinista-led and dominated military, splits within UNO her own winning political coalition, and a country beset with wide political divisions. After accepting Ortega's concession of the election, she commented, "There are neither victors nor vanquished."

NOTES

1. Jeffery Paige, *Coffee and Power: Revolution and the Rise of Democracy in Central America* (Cambridge: Harvard University Press, 1997), 274.

2. The next chapter of this book discusses this extensively. For the best scholarly discussion of this theme see Leslie Anderson and Lawrence C. Dodd, *Learning Democracy: Citizen Engagement and Electoral Choice in Nicaragua, 1990–2001* (Chicago: University of Chicago Press, 2005).

3. See Laura Enriquez, *Harvesting Change: Labor and Agrarian Reform in Nicaragua 1979–1990* (Chapel Hill: University of North Carolina Press, 1991), 88, and Laura Enriquez, *Agrarian Reform and Class Consciousness in Nicaragua* (Gainesville: University of Florida Press, 1997), 50.

4. Enriquez, *Harvesting Change*, 88–107.

5. Ibid., 89–93.

6. Stephen Kinzer, *Blood of Brothers: Life and War in Nicaragua* (Cambridge: Harvard University Press, 1991), 75. See also Ulrike Hanemann, "Nicaragua's Literacy Campaign: Background Paper for the Education for All Global Monitoring Report" (Hamburg: United Nations Education Scientific and Cultural Organization, 2006), 1–8.

7. Paige, *Coffee and Power*, 273–79.

8. Peter Kornbluh, "The Covert War" in *Reagan versus the Sandinistas*, edited by Thomas W. Walker, 23 (Boulder, CO: Westview Press, 1987).

9. Ibid., 28.

10. Kinzer, *Blood of Brothers*, 173–74.

11. Ibid., 196.

12. Ibid., 199–200.

13. Paige, *Coffee and Power*, 287–90.

14. Kinzer, *Blood of Brothers*, 122–23.

15. Enriquez, *Harvesting Change*, 91–92.

16. Enriquez, *Agrarian Reform and Class Consciousness in Nicaragua*, 33.

17. Ibid., 19, 21–23.

18. This section is based on the experiences of journalist Stephen Kinzer while he was in Managua. See Kinzer, *Blood of Brothers*, 153–63.

19. Anderson and Dodd, *Learning Democracy*, 2.

20. Kinzer, *Blood of Brothers*, 323.

21. Martin Diskin, "The Manipulation of Indigenous Struggles" in *Reagan versus the Sandinistas*, edited by Thomas Walker, 85 (Boulder, CO: Westview Press, 1987).

22. Kinzer, *Blood of Brothers*, 262.

23. Ibid., 270.

24. Ibid., 341.

25. John Findling, *Close Neighbors, Distant Friends* (New York: Greenwood, 1987), 152–54.

26. Anderson and Dodd, *Learning Democracy*, 87–91.

27. See Thomas W. Walker, *Nicaragua: Living in the Shadow of the Eagle* (Boulder, CO: Westview Press, 2003), 56–58, and William Robinson, *A Faustian Bargain: US Intervention in the Nicaraguan Elections and American Foreign Policy in the Post-Cold War Era* (Boulder, CO: Westview Press, 1992), 140. The author of this text chatted with Sandinista supporters in Matagalpa and Jinotega and found evidence of this sentiment especially among elderly women who had sons serving in the Sandinista army.

28. Anderson and Dodd, *Learning Democracy*, 16–24. This argument is presented throughout their book.

29. Ibid., 20.

30. See Enriquez, *Agrarian Reform and Class Consciousness in Nicaragua*, 31–57.

7

Defying the Odds: The Road to Democracy (1990–Present)[1]

By the 1990 elections the groundwork had already been established for a successful, democratic transition to the government of Violeta Barrios de Chamorro. Under the Sandinistas the Nicaraguan party system became more inclusive. In addition to the traditional elite-led liberal and conservative parties, the Sandinistas (FSLN) became the party that represented the poor. For the first time in the history of Nicaraguan party politics the poor had not only a voice, but also an effective party that could run candidates for office and define and carry out policies that would meet their needs. Although the political and economic elites of Nicaragua had a long history of participating through political parties and business associations, it was the Sandinistas who mobilized groups of non-elites and empowered them to participate both during the years of challenging the Somoza dynasty and during their own revolutionary rule. In particular, students and labor were mobilized into groups that learned to challenge the Somoza dynasty. Peasants who joined the FSLN struggle in the mountains learned the advantages of political organizing. Peasant cooperatives, labor unions, rural workers, women's groups, student groups, teacher unions, professional organizations, youth groups, widows' groups, groups for families of soldiers, and others proliferated during Sandinista rule. Most of the *Nicas* who joined these non-elite or "mass" groups had never participated in politics prior to the revolution. They joined these groups and learned to select their own leaders, participate in the decision-making process, ensure the accountability of their leaders, guarantee the political equality of their members, and pursue political objectives. Gary Ruchwarger argues these groups became "schools of democracy" for the common *Nica* and that "enormous advances in political participation [took] place under Sandinista rule."[2] In addition, new groups appeared to oppose the Sandinistas. Many of the business and agro-industrial elites such as Chamorro, Arnoldo Alemán, and Enrique Bolaños did not flee to the United States. They stayed and organized groups to oppose the Sandinistas. Nicaraguans of all classes and groups had learned the practice of political organization and group participation skills. Even though many of these groups were tied to the Sandinistas and engaged in what scholars refer to as mobilized participation, it paved the way for many of these groups to break away from the Sandinistas in the 1990s and engage in autonomous or independent participation.

With the inauguration of Chamorro, it was clear that the country had a much more complicated class system than at any time in its history. It included the traditional elites, the so-called new elites, and the mobilized masses.[3] The traditional elites consisted of the elite families that historically dominated the agro-export-led economic system and created the liberal and conservative parties. As one would expect, the traditional elites not only continued to dominate the economy but also were the best educated group and had the highest standard of living in the country. The traditional elites were divided, with one group that bitterly opposed the Sandinistas and wanted to rid the country of them and a moderate group that largely stayed in the country during the revolutionary years and wanted greater democracy and an economy free of state interference. It was this moderate elite group led by Chamorro that was willing to accept and work with the Sandinistas. This group recognized that the Sandinistas legitimately represented a major portion of the *Nica* electorate. The new elites or in reality the growing middle class consisted of those associated primarily with the revolutionary Sandinistas—students, government workers, the leaders of organized groups, and the military. The new elites tended to be better educated and younger than the masses. Although many of these individuals were initially associated with the Sandinistas, many would become independent of them over the next decade. The masses continued to be the poorest and least educated *Nicas*. Because of the *contra* war women represented a majority of this group. The Sandinistas promoted a culture of political participation among all *Nicas*, elites and non-elites, male and female, which facilitated the growth of democracy with the election of Chamorro, the first female president of Nicaragua.

THE REVOLUTIONARY YEARS, THE FSLN, AND THE ROLE OF WOMEN

Although the experience of the struggle against Somoza and the Sandinista years of the 1980s encouraged and allowed women to play a greater role in the economic and political systems, it did not bring about real equality of women as many had hoped. It did not eliminate the culture of *machismo*, which is common throughout all of Latin America and is quite often misunderstood. While it is typically associated with male virility and the image of the so-called Latin lover, it is much more complex. It is tied into the cultural trait of the Latin American male's pursuit of importance, prestige, dignity, honor, and status. It has manifested itself nationally in male dominance in areas of politics and economics with women playing the more traditional roles associated with spirituality, motherhood, and child rearing. While *machismo* is more complex than most people understand so is the role of women in Latin America, especially in Nicaragua where women played a major role in the Sandinista revolution.

Most women did not actually fight in the struggle against the Somozas but nonetheless they played very active roles. Mothers of Sandinistas often visited the prisons and jails. Women often provided safe houses for the guerrillas. Safe houses were invaluable as they were a source of food, clothes, medical care, information, and hiding places. Women often organized shipments of food, medicine, ammunition, and guns. Some built bombs and carried messages. Gladys Baez was the first female to actually fight in battle with the Sandinistas in 1967 during the Pancasan operation in the mountains. She believed that the FSLN leaders—Carlos Fonseca, Silvio Mayorga, and Oscar Turcios—were fully committed to equality for women, but that most of the guerrillas did not want her on the battlefield. According to Matilde Zimmermann, the experiences of Baez are reflective of the general Sandinista beliefs about women. There was a general agreement, at least in the abstract, that women should participate on an equal basis; however, there was a lot of disagreement concerning the role of women in *Nica* society.[4] By the mid-1970s most guerrilla units had at least one female who was typically from peasant origins. Yet educated women from wealthy families also become Sandinistas. One of the most celebrated was noted author Gioconda Belli whose first poems appeared in *La Prensa Literaria*, the leading cultural journal in Nicaragua. The poems celebrated the physical and emotional sensations of love and sex and were considered scandalous. Belli was already working for the Sandinista underground.[5] Dora María Téllez, the former medical student who had been in anti-Somoza demonstrations at the age of 14, would rise to the position of guerrilla commander, participate in the famous attack on the Nicaraguan National Assembly in 1978, lead the final assault on León, and become an icon of the Sandinista revolution. Yet, it would not be until 1994 that a female would become a member of the Sandinista DN.

The Sandinistas organized the Association of Women Confronting the National Problem which consisted largely of wives and mothers who protested Somoza human rights violations. This group was later renamed the Association of Nicaraguan Women "Luisa Amanda Espinoza" (AMNLAE) named after the first female Sandinista to die in combat. Even though it was a Sandinista organization, there were disputes during the 1980s between the leadership of AMNLAE and the Sandinista leadership. Quite often the issue of women's rights conflicted with Sandinista directives. For example, AMNLAE believed that women should be drafted just like men but the Sandinista leadership believed they could better serve by providing "home" support for the combatants. This was the first of several disputes that indicated a growing separation between women's rights and the FSLN agenda. By the late 1980s AMNLAE was focusing on women's issues such as discrimination in the workplace, access to birth control, domestic violence, and unpaid labor.[6] Just before the 1990 elections, the Sandinista DN placed new leaders within AMNLAE who were considered to be anti-feminist and they cancelled the Latin American and Caribbean Feminist Meeting to be held in Managua later that year. This sent a mixed message as to what the FSLN and many Sandinista men really believed about women's rights. According to Margaret Randall, this provided the impetus for the beginning of an independent women's movement in Nicaragua.[7] In the Association of Rural Workers (ATC) and the Sandinista Worker's Central (CST), women formed their own secretariat to promote female demands in labor such as equal pay for equal work. According to the first director of the CST female secretariat, Sandinista labor unions were just like Nicaraguan society. Women in union leadership positions were opposed by men who were ". . . immersed in a world in which power is concentrated in the hands of men . . . accustomed to making all of the decisions."[8]

CHANGES IN THE FSLN

With the election of Chamorro, Sandinista groups such as the National Workers' Front (FNT) and the National Union of Farmers and Ranchers (UNAG) organized almost continual mass demonstrations and strikes in opposition to the plans to reverse what they believed to be the gains of the revolution: free education, health care, and land reform. In the middle of this turmoil in the first few months of the Chamorro government, the FSLN was faced with the question of what type of party it should be in the future. In June 1990, the Sandinistas produced the El Crucero document that publicly admitted to the errors they had committed in the 1980s. These errors included authoritarianism, the abuse of power by the civilian and military leadership, the lack of attention to demands from rank and file members, and the selection of party leaders without the use of democratic processes. One group led by Daniel Ortega argued for a more pragmatic party, one that would focus on winning elections and making compromises and alliances with other groups. Pragmatism, compromise, and alliance making were the only methods to achieve Sandinista goals in the new Nicaragua. Ortega argued that to prevent the far right—the liberals who controlled the National Oppositions Union (UNO)—from destroying all the revolutionary gains of the 1980s, the FSLN had to rule from the center and that meant a coalition with Chamorro, the Minister of the Presidency Antonio Lacayo who was Chamorro's son-in-law and closest adviser, and her other supporters. This, of course, required some compromises with Chamorro. Another group of Sandinistas argued that while the FSLN needed to expand its membership it should remain true to its ideology and focus on the struggles within the unions, the poor *barrios*, and the countryside. It should not become simply a "vote-getting machine."[9] This group saw President Chamorro, not Virgilio Godoy and the liberals, as the immediate threat to the gains of the revolution. They understood that the executive branch was more powerful than the legislative branch under the current constitution.

In October 1990, Ortega entered into a tacit alliance with Chamorro. Ortega had to agree to accept the privatization of the state-run businesses and state farms created during the revolutionary years. Although privatization typically meant that state-run businesses and farms were sold to the highest bidder, it is important to note that the PNT insisted on the ability of some current workers to become property owners of the state-run businesses and UNAG insisted that some of the land from the state farms should be turned over to its workers and returning *contra* and *Nica* army soldiers. That same year some Sandinistas cited the El Crucero document and argued that the party's National Directorate (DN) should be elected. At the 1991 party congress, the DN was elected but the so-called election simply allowed voting for or against a slate of delegates already put together. As a result, the only changes to the DN were the addition of Rene Nuñez to replace the late Carlos Nuñez and Sergio Ramirez to replace Humberto Ortega who had resigned to retain his position as head of the

Nicaraguan armed forces. This upset many, especially female Sandinistas, who expected former guerrilla commander Dora María Téllez to be elected as the first female member of the DN.[10] Daniel Ortega became the party's first secretary-general but it was evident that there was a growing dissension within the party.

The Sandinistas in the National Assembly were initially opposed to any reform of the Nicaraguan constitution and the liberal right wing wanted to rewrite it completely. The Sandinistas viewed the 1987 constitution as protecting the revolution with its guarantees of agrarian and land reform, labor rights, state ownership of natural resources, and state-run businesses and farms. In July 1993, the so-called Group of 29 called on the FSLN leaders to end its tacit alliance with Chamorro. They wanted the FSLN to return to its mass social base, the urban workers and rural poor. Daniel Ortega, who had become an astute politician, sensed a challenge from his party's left wing. He began to distance himself from Chamorro, at least in his speeches. In effect he was attempting to re-establish his revolutionary legitimacy within the party and with its mass supporters while he continued to cooperate with Chamorro. In the fall of 1993 Ramirez announced that he was interested in running for the presidency of Nicaragua. That same fall, Daniel Ortega publicly sided with a Sandinista-led national strike that had turned violent while Ramirez criticized the tactics. This caused a power struggle between Daniel Ortega and Ramirez within the Sandinista DN. Ramirez had the support of the majority of Sandinista members of the National Assembly whereas Daniel Ortega had the support of the Sandinista rank-and-file members.

POLITICS DURING THE CHAMORRO YEARS

The Chamorro presidency witnessed an on-going struggle for power between the executive and legislative branches of government that ultimately led to a constitutional crisis. Governing coalitions cut across the party lines that had been drawn prior to the election. Chamorro worked with the Sandinistas and alienated most of her UNO supporters. Under the 1987 Nicaraguan Constitution the executive was more powerful than the legislative and judicial branches of government. With the 1990 election, Chamorro and her conservative supporters came to control the executive. The UNO coalition controlled the National Assembly although there was a growing split between the liberal and conservative members of the coalition. The Sandinistas still controlled the seven-member Supreme Court of Justice and the Supreme Electoral Council, which established rules for and oversaw elections in the country. The UNO coalition moved quickly to try to gain control of the Supreme Electoral Council by increasing the number of justices and appointing UNO justices to fill the new slots. Were it not for the PTN-led labor strikes and national work stoppage in July, UNO might have succeeded. In a compromise to end the strikes, the Supreme Electoral Council was increased to nine members resulting in a balanced council with four Sandinista judges, four UNO judges, and Rafael Chamorro Mora who was appointed by the Sandinistas but viewed by many as an independent.

The conservative-liberal split in UNO became evident when it was selecting the president of the new National Assembly. Vice-President Godoy and the liberals backed Miriam Arguello and President Chamorro backed Alfredo Cesar. Arguello was nominated by UNO and Cesar turned to the FSLN for support in his bid to become president. Arguello was elected president of the National Assembly. Vice President Godoy and his liberals in the National Assembly turned against Chamorro when she decided that Sandinista Humberto Ortega would remain as the head of the army. This decision even infuriated some of her conservative supporters. This led to a growing separation between Chamorro and UNO as a whole. Ceasar was finally elected president of the National Assembly in 1991 and worked to pass a bill that would deal with the property issues that were left over from the revolutionary years of Sandinista rule. Chamorro vetoed the property bill in 1993 which pleased the Sandinistas but upset UNO. For two years Chamorro had been working closely not only with the Sandinistas to successfully reform the military but also with a group of eight moderate UNO members in the National Assembly. This new coalition of the FSLN and eight UNO moderates controlled 47 of 92 votes in the National Assembly.

In 1993 two vacancies appeared on the National Assembly's governing directorate. Cesar, the president of the National Assembly, refused to fill the appointments because he knew that the Chamorro coalition consisting of the Sandinistas and eight moderates would not allow UNO members to be appointed to the leadership positions. His refusal to make the appointments caused a walkout by the Sandinistas and the eight moderates. With 47 members absent, Cesar called a meeting of the National Assembly and passed the original property bill that Chamorro had vetoed. In November the Supreme Court ruled that the action by Cesar was unconstitutional for lack of a quorum. In 1994 the entire leadership of the National Assembly was up for re-election and the Chamorro coalition of the Sandinistas and the eight moderates voted out the UNO leaders. Christian Democrat Luis Humberto Guzman was elected president of the National Assembly with a directorate consisting of Sandinistas and moderates. It was this coalition that led to the passage of a new Military Code in 1994 that increased civilian control over the military, a change in the constitution that prohibited the reelection of the president, and the passage of Property Stabilization Law 209 in 1995 that allowed the resolution of property disputes dating back to the revolutionary era of the 1980s.[11] There was substance to the charge that Chamorro was "co-governing with the Sandinistas."

Significantly, most of the Sandinistas in the National Assembly were loyal to Ramirez rather than Daniel Ortega. By May 1994 Ramirez argued that the FSLN had to return to the center if it wanted to win the 1996 presidential elections and Daniel Ortega, playing to the Sandinista masses, questioned the strategy. At the FSLN party congress the dispute between Daniel Ortega and Ramirez became public, intense, and personal. Ramirez was left off the Sandinista DN and a split within the FSLN was certain. In the National Assembly Ramirez worked with the UNO coalition to write a moderate constitutional reform bill that would strengthen the legislative branch and lessen the power of the executive branch. It was approved by the National Assembly in November and reapproved in early 1995 as required under Nicaraguan law. Under Nicaraguan law for the Nicaraguan constitutional reform bill to go into effect the president must officially publish it. President Chamorro refused because she did not want to see the power of the executive branch diminished. Guzman, the president of the National Assembly, published the reform bill. In effect by February 1995 Nicaragua had two constitutions, one accepted by the president and the executive branch and the other accepted by the legislative branch. The Supreme Court could not act on the case due to the lack of a quorum or the required number of justices to act officially.

In April the National Assembly appointed six new members to the Supreme Court under the provisions of the new constitution. The members of the Supreme Court were hesitant to recognize their new members because by doing so they would be, in fact, recognizing the new constitution. In a masterful political move, Chamorro talked one of the appointees into serving on the Supreme Court as her appointee under the old constitution. This gave the Court the necessary number of justices to render a decision under the old constitution. The Court ruled that the National Assembly had acted illegally and stated that the old constitution was still in effect. This decision was largely ignored by the National Assembly.

The Supreme Electoral Council became part of the constitutional debate when it began to prepare for the following year's presidential elections. The Council and President Chamorro argued over which branch had the authority to register citizens to vote and create a citizen identification card system. In the end the Supreme Electoral Council won the debate while Chamorro opted to conduct a census. On June 7, the term for the members of the Supreme Electoral Council came to an end. With two constitutions in effect President Chamorro and the National Assembly could not agree on how to appoint new members to the Supreme Electoral Council. At this point in time the Nicaraguan government had come to a standstill. In late June, the International Monetary Fund (IMF), World Bank, and other international donors told the Nicaraguans that if the constitutional crisis was not settled, they would not renegotiate Nicaraguan debts. With Cardinal Miguel Obando y Bravo acting as a mediator, the legislative and executive branches finally settled their differences and came up with a new framework for reform of the 1987 Nicaraguan constitution.

Although the constitutional reforms shifted power away from the executive branch toward the legislature, it made the two branches more interdependent. The National Assembly now developed the budget, but tax laws had to be agreed on by it and the president. Future vacancies on the Supreme Court had to be approved by the National Assembly and the president. The president could no longer serve consecutive terms and the term of office was reduced from six to five years. Relatives of the president were not allowed to run for the presidency. This was passed largely to prevent Minister of the Presidency Lacayo, the president's son-in-law, from running for president in 1996. Under President Chamorro, the day-to-day running of the government and economic policy was left up to Lacayo. It was Lacayo who had helped to engineer the tacit alliance between the Sandinistas and Chamorro.

POLICIES DURING THE CHAMORRO YEARS

Chamorro with advice from the United States quickly moved to reform the Nicaraguan economy. The U.S. Agency for International Development (USAID) developed a five-year plan for the country. These so-called neoliberal or "Washington Consensus" reforms were designed to address the issue of inflation, increase exports, and reduce the role of the state in the economy. To address inflation massive cuts in government spending were announced including the lay-off of thousands of government workers, cuts in the wages of government workers who did not lose their jobs, dramatic cuts in social spending in areas such as education and health care, and the elimination of government subsidies on basic food staples such as beans and rice. Wage and price controls were ended and as a result the price of virtually everything increased while wages declined considerably. In May and July 1990, national strikes led by the PNT in opposition to these government policies brought the country to a standstill. *Nicas* successfully exercised their power to resist unpopular policies, something they had learned in the struggle against Somoza and during the revolutionary rule of the Sandinistas. Chamorro indicated a willingness to gradually implement these policies over a period of several months. In October the

Sandinistas and Chamorro came to their tacit coalition agreement. The Chamorro years would be characterized by policy implementation followed by strikes and resistance followed by compromises on the policies followed by another round of popular resistance.

The U.S. trade embargo ended, Nicaraguan tariffs were eliminated, and the value of the Nicaraguan *cordoba* was devalued to encourage exports and to earn U.S. dollars. The U.S. government approved an aid package of 541 million dollars. Nicaraguan past-due debts to private banks, the IMF, and the World Bank were paid by the United States and a new round of loans was arranged. The new round of loans from the IMF and World Bank actually led to increased debt to the tune of 11 billion dollars by 1992. This debt required Nicaragua to pay almost a half a billion dollars each year just to cover the interest. In an attempt to increase foreign investment and to provide employment, Chamorro reopened the Las Mercedes free-trade zone near the Managua airport and pushed for the creation of others. Foreign businesses that established subsidiaries in these free-trade zones were exempt from having to pay taxes. Asian and U.S. businesses quickly set up shop. The businesses were basically assembly shops called *maquiladoras*. The vast majority of the employees were women and only a minority of the workers in the free-trade zones was unionized.

State-run businesses and utilities were privatized or basically sold to the highest bidder over the next few years. Of 352 state-run enterprises, 343 were either privatized or returned to their previous owners by 1994. The PNT worked hard to give workers the opportunity to buy their factories and UNAG worked hard to make sure that some land from the former state farms were given to workers and returning military personnel. Agro-export elites regained preferential access to credit from banks and could now sell directly to the international market without having to go through the state. With increasing debt, Nicaragua was forced to emphasize the large-scale agro-export model of development as it had in the past. As in the Somoza years, medium- and small-sized farms had difficulty gaining credit and the production of food stuffs for local consumption declined. Without access to credit the owners of small- or medium-sized plots of land also had difficulty purchasing seed and fertilizer. Dramatic budget cuts also reduced the amount of agricultural extension services that the Sandinistas had put in place. This made it difficult for all farmers especially former soldiers who were given access to land but did not know how to farm. There were no state agricultural agents to provide them with the needed information to be successful.

Education policy changed dramatically under Chamorro. The Sandinistas had focused on the importance of secular education in changing inequalities based on class and gender. The Church exercised great control over the Ministry of Education under Chamorro. USAID spent 12.5 million dollars to purchase new textbooks to replace the ones used by the Sandinistas in the public schools. The new texts were selected and written by the Ministry of Education without any input from teachers. They emphasized traditional roles for males and females and the moral values of the Church. According to the USAID Director Janet Ballantyne the new texts would "reestablish civics and morals lacking in the past eleven years."[12] Sandinista texts were developed in consultation with teachers and the public. Public schools were free and student uniforms were not required under the Sandinistas. Under Chamorro two types of public schools were created. Standard public schools were free to students but they were chronically underfunded due to budget cuts and their inability to raise funds. They were attended by the poorest *Nicas*. The so-called autonomous schools could charge fees and use those fees to purchase materials and raise the salaries of teachers whose state salaries were barely above the poverty level. These schools attracted the students of families that were considered to be working- and middle-class. The children of wealthy *Nicas* attended private schools or were sent to the United States for their education. Education policy reflected the class system under Chamorro.

Health care under the Sandinistas had been a major success story and enjoyed considerable legitimacy among all segments of the population. The focus was on health care for mothers, children, and the poor. Polio had nearly been eradicated. The number of health clinics increased from 43 under Somoza to 532 by 1983 with the largest increase in the rural areas. Perhaps just as important, health care was free to all *Nicas*. Chamorro did not make many significant changes to the health care system of the Sandinistas but in 1991 she ended free health care. Payments were now based on a sliding scale but given the growing poverty level the vast majority could no longer afford medical care. The CST women's secretariat began to establish free health clinics for poor women who could no longer afford medical care. The CST also created free daycare centers to replace the ones that Chamorro no longer funded. Chamorro's primary problem in maintaining the health care system was declining resources and overall budget cuts mandated by the IMF and World Bank.

DEMOBILIZATION OF THE *CONTRAS* AND THE SANDINISTA PEOPLE'S ARMY

A major problem for the Chamorro government was what to do with the members of the *contra* army. Chamorro's election as president made it possible for the *contra* leadership to begin to demobilize its forces and in March 1990 the government began negotiating with the *contra* leaders. With the help of the United Nations (UN) and the Organization of American States (OAS) the disarming of the *contras* started by June. The reduction in size of the Sandinista People's Army (EPS) also made it easier to continue to demobilize and disarm the *contras*. Perhaps the most difficult issues facing the Chamorro administration was what to do with the EPS. It was born in the struggle against the Somoza dynasty and was the military wing of the FSLN. Prior to the 1990 elections, the National Assembly passed the Military Organizational Law 75, which officially ended the formal relationship between the FSLN and the EPS. Although the EPS was now officially the Nicaraguan armed forces, Law 75 did not state clearly that the EPS was subordinate to the authority of the executive branch of government. In March 1990 Lacayo and General Humberto Ortega, who was the head of the EPS, came to an agreement. The Chamorro government agreed to "respect the integrity and professionalism of the EPS . . . in accordance with the Constitution and the nation's laws."[13] Humberto Ortega and the EPS agreed to support the government of Nicaragua and the FSLN agreed to operate as the loyal opposition under the provisions of the 1987 constitution. This agreement helped to pave the way for a peaceful transition from Daniel Ortega to Chamorro.

Chamorro had pledged to reduce the size of the EPS which had reached more than 96,000 members by the time the Esquipulas Accords were signed. To achieve that goal she retained Humberto Ortega as the Chief of the new Nicaraguan Armed Forces. It was an extremely controversial decision and was the primary factor in the growing divide between Chamorro and the UNO coalition that led the National Assembly. This was also a practical decision based on a sober recognition of the balance of power of forces in Nicaragua at the time. The EPS was the largest, most cohesive, and most powerful force in the country. It would have rejected the selection of a non-Sandinista leader. Chamorro and Lacayo believed that the only practical way to reform it was to work with its current leadership. Humberto Ortega resigned his membership on the Sandinista DN and became the Chief of the new Nicaraguan Armed Forces. The decision was a clear reflection of Chamorro's emphasis on national reconciliation and it cost her politically.

In June 1990 Humberto Ortega submitted a plan to reduce the size of the armed forces to 41,000 by the next month. This initial downsizing affected the draftees and the enlisted personnel primarily. In November Humberto Ortega began downsizing the number of officers. By 1992 the Nicaraguan Armed Forces was reduced to 15,200 members, which made it the smallest military in Central America. The unintended consequence of this rapid downsizing is that it made the unemployment and poverty rates increase as large numbers of young men were now looking for jobs in a country that was already suffering under a poor economy with an extremely high unemployment rate.[14]

Despite the successful downsizing many within UNO believed that Humberto Ortega could not be trusted and that he could not be controlled by the executive branch. Humberto Ortega, who was fully supported by the officer corps, was very protective of the institutional interests of the armed forces. He forcefully spoke out against those who wanted to cut its budget or eliminate it completely. When Chamorro announced in September 1993 that General Humberto Ortega would be removed from his position sometime in 1994, the EPS Military Council swiftly reacted and stated that she lacked the authority to do that under current Nicaraguan law. At about the same time, Humberto Ortega had provided Chamorro with a new Military Code for the army. The code banned members of the military from joining political parties, prohibited the use of military intelligence for political purposes, and established professional norms for members of the armed forces. He believed that this had to be in place before he could step down. In August 1994 the National Assembly approved the new military code. Although it did not allow the president to appoint the chief of the Armed Forces, it allowed the president to reject the nomination made by the Military Council. Chamorro and Humberto Ortega had not only ended the relationship between the FSLN and the army, but had now made the army subject to civilian authorities within the executive branch of government. This was one of the major accomplishments of the Chamorro administration. Perhaps the best illustration of this success was in July 1993 when Humberto Ortega ordered the new Nicaraguan Army to attack former EPS soldiers who had taken over the city of Estelí.[15] They carried out their orders. On February 21, 1995, General Joaquín Cuadra became the new Chief of the Nicaraguan Armed Forces and Humberto Ortega retired.

THE ISSUE OF LAND OWNERSHIP

Chamorro was elected mainly because many *Nicas* believed she could heal the divisions within the war-torn country. She understood that resolving land ownership issues would go a long way toward peace and reconciliation in the aftermath of the *contra* war. The PLC wanted to move quickly and return all confiscated lands back to their owners. The Sandinistas opposed this, arguing that the agrarian land reforms of the 1980s were legal. Returning the land to their former owners would not only be illegal, it would cause more violence and would not be fair to peasants who had gained land in the 1980s. The peasants who had received land under Sandinista redistribution policies were not going to simply give it back to the former owners. Peasants who received land under the Sandinista cooperative arrangements were unsure as to what would happen to the land they occupied. The possibility of renewed violence over the property issue was very real. Some land had been seized illegally by peasants during the 1980s because they believed the Sandinistas were not moving fast enough on land reform. These peasants had no legal titles whatsoever to the land they occupied. Some returning soldiers from the *contra* war— Sandinistas and *contras*—had also seized land illegally. Most members of the National Assembly believed that former property owners should either have their land returned or be given compensation for their losses. Nicaragua was simply unable to compensate the former property owners. All *Nicas* and Chamorro knew that resolving these issues would be a most difficult process. In May 1990 Chamorro issued Decree 11-90 which called for a review of the confiscations and redistributions of agricultural land. Within a year the commission had heard more than 4,000 cases and had ruled in favor of the previous owners in about half the cases.[16] The Nicaraguan Supreme Court then declared much of Decree 11-90 to be unconstitutional and this further complicated the land ownership issue.

The state had to decide what to do with the land confiscated from the Somoza family and its closest supporters. This property had been turned into state-run farms for the production of sugar, cotton, and coffee. The former land owners, many of whom had fled to the United States, insisted that they had a right to reclaim the estates seized by the Sandinistas. In August 1991 it was agreed that the peasants who had worked these state-run farms would be given 25 percent of the total land for themselves. By 1993 a list of former state-run farms indicated that 35 percent had been returned to their former owners, 31 percent was given to the former peasant workers, and 34 percent was given to former military personnel.[17]

At the same time Chamorro engaged in her own agrarian land reform by making available almost 1 million *manzanas* of land to peasants and, especially, former soldiers. This was part of her agreement with the *contras* to get them finally to disarm and demobilize. Unfortunately the source of this land reform was sometimes the cooperative lands that the Sandinistas had set up in the 1980s. This often resulted in one peasant displacing another peasant or more people joining the cooperative and thus reducing the amount of land for each cooperative participant. Chamorro also created cooperative ownership of the lands rather than individual private plots. This caused resentment by the peasants and soldiers who wanted individual ownership. It was the same mistake that the Sandinistas had made in the 1980s.

In July 1995 former President Jimmy Carter, head of the Carter Center, chaired a property issues conference in Managua and brought all the major parties to the table. One of the major accomplishments was that the proceeds from the privatization of TELCOR, the Sandinista state-run tele-communications company, would be used to purchase U.S. treasury bonds. These treasury bonds would be used to provide legitimacy and backing for the so-called Nicaraguan Compensation Bonds. The Compensation Bonds would be used to pay the former property owners for their losses. Building on this momentum the National Assembly passed Property Stability Law 209 in November. The law stated that possession of and use of land acquired under previous agrarian reform under both the Sandinistas and Chamorro would be converted to a permanent land title and provided an expedited process to do so. Former owners would be compensated with the Nicaraguan Compensation Bonds. This did not resolve all property issues and the former property owners still had strong allies in UNO who sought to undermine the process; however, it was a dramatic step forward.

THE 1996 CAMPAIGN AND ELECTIONS

The split within the FSLN became official in January 1995 when Ramirez and other influential Sandinistas such as Luis Carrion, Ernesto and Fernando Cardenal, Téllez, and Mirna Cunningham left the party and in May 1995 inaugurated the Sandinista Renovation Movement (MRS).[18] The critical point was that while Ramirez controlled the vast majority of the Sandinista members of the National Assembly, he had little following among the traditional Sandinista masses, the rural and urban poor. The MRS decided that it would run Ramirez as its presidential candidate in the national elections.

Vilma Nuñez, a Sandinista with an impeccable revolutionary record, challenged Ortega for the FSLN nomination. Even though rank and file Sandinistas participated in a primary and the FSLN National Congress voted to select its nominee, there was no doubt that Ortega would be the nominee. He legitimately won the nomination, but the outcome contributed to the growing resentment among many female Sandinistas who were being locked out of power in their own party. During the campaign Ortega began to shed his Sandinista symbols. Instead of military fatigues and the red and black Sandinista kerchief, he dressed in slacks and white button-down collar shirts with the sleeves rolled up. Ortega characterized Alemán and the Liberal Alliance as "Somocistas without Somoza" while promising a "government for all." He emphasized the importance that the FSLN had always placed on social reform.

The right-wing parties had come together under the Liberal Alliance and had nominated the popular mayor of Managua, Arnoldo Alemán, who ran a campaign that focused on Sandinista rule and the civil war of the 1980s. With his campaign financed by the United States, Alemán used television commercials that focused on the hated military draft under the Sandinistas. The Church which had already increased its influence on government policy under Chamorro openly campaigned for Alemán, who served as a lector for Cardinal Obando as he celebrated mass at the National Cathedral on national television a few days before the election. Obando, dressed in a white robe fringed in red which is the color of the PLC, delivered a not so subtle, anti-Sandinista homily. It was a clear signal to all that the Church would continue to have influence if Alemán were elected. President Chamorro made it clear that she preferred Alemán to Ortega. Alemán's primary message was the promise of jobs. His television ads showed women working in the factories in the free-trade zones and he touted his creation of jobs while he was mayor of Managua.

Even though 34 parties ran candidates in the elections that were held on October 20, public opinion polls at the time indicated that the election was between Ortega and Alemán, the left and the right. The centrist conservatives and independents were forced to choose between the extremes. There were election observers from across the world including the Carter Center, the Council of Freely Elected Heads of Government, the Organization of American States, the European Union, and the U.S. government. The winners were not announced until late November. Differences appeared between the vote tallies from the precincts and the votes posted by the Supreme Electoral Council. The Carter Center worked out the irregularities to the approval of most parties and election observers and helped to organize a review of the vote count that took 19 days. Alemán and the Liberal Alliance received 46.03 percent of the vote and Ortega and the FSLN received 36.55 percent of the vote. The Liberal Alliance consisting of the Liberal Constitutionalist Party, the Neoliberal Party, the Independent Liberal Party for National Unity, and the Central American Unionist Party won 42 seats in the National Assembly. The FSLN, the single-largest party in the country, won 36 seats. The remainder of the seats was divided among the following: the Nicaraguan Party of the Christian Road won 4 seats, the National Conservative Party won 3 seats, the National Project received 2 seats, and the following parties won one seat each: the MRS, the Nicaraguan Resistance Party, the Conservative Party of Nicaragua, the Independent Liberal Party, the Unity Alliance, and the UNO-96 Alliance.

For the second time in a row Ortega was defeated in a bid for the presidency. Ortega was unable to focus the campaign on social policies which clearly favored the FSLN.[19] Most observers believed that Alemán was successful in reminding voters of the tremendous problems under Sandinista rule during the 1980s. Ortega was also dogged by continual allegations of corruption stemming from *la piñata*, when many Sandinista leaders seized houses and property prior to Chamorro's inauguration in 1990. It also did not help that many well-known and popular Sandinistas left the FSLN, created their own party, and ran a candidate against Ortega. In three fair and free elections, Nicaragua had moved from the political left under the Sandinistas to the center-right under Chamorro to the right under Alemán.

JUDGING THE CHAMORRO YEARS

The Chamorro years represent a mixed picture in terms of the economy. By 1996 inflation had been reduced to 12 percent. The economy showed positive growth of 3.2 percent in 1994, 4 percent in 1996, and 5.5 percent in 1996. Exports grew a little more than 10 percent between 1990 and 1996. Yet by 1996 Nicaragua was the second poorest country in the Americas with more than 50 percent of its population living in poverty and only able to pay for half of the cost of its basic food needs.[20] More imported foods and consumer goods were available but only the wealthy could afford them. Unemployment and underemployment stood at more than 50 percent. The gap between the rich and poor had widened. The number of those considered to be middle class or the new Sandinista elite declined as government workers lost jobs, demobilized soldiers became unemployed, and financial support for students to attend college disappeared. Nicaragua's external debt was among the highest in the world. Infant mortality rates that had declined under the Sandinistas were the highest in Central America. In the 1980s cholera, dengue, and malaria had been almost eliminated. By 1993 all had reappeared. Illiteracy rates were rising once again.

The Chamorro years were important in the history of Nicaragua primarily because they represented the transition from idealism to pragmatism, revolution to conservative backlash, limits on free speech to free speech, war to peace, mixed economy to a neo-liberal agro-export-led economy, Cold War to post-Cold War, and a country that received the intense focus of U.S. foreign policy to a country with little strategic importance for the United States. Managing that transition was probably her greatest accomplishment. Her administration was best summed up by poet, novelist, and Sandinista guerrilla Gioconda Belli.

> Violeta turned out to be a maternal figure whose simple words cradled and consoled the broken, divided country. Displaying a perceptive, nuanced wisdom few thought she possessed, she was able to appease the warring factions and force them to coexist. Risking the support of her allies, she chose to make Nicaragua a homeland for all, with no exceptions. That was how old enemies were brought together, sat at the same table, and wept over their shared sorrow. It was odd, but

incredibly encouraging, to see such a battle-scarred, defiant country capable of such civility.[21]

The stage was set for the Alemán years.

JOSÉ ARNOLDO ALEMÁN LACAYO (1946–PRESENT)

Alemán was born in Managua in 1946. His father, Arnoldo Alemán Sandoval, was an associate of Tachito Somoza and owned a coffee plantation near Managua. An excellent student he graduated from the Autonomous National University of Nicaragua in León in 1967 with a law degree. He went into practice serving large businesses, economic enterprises, and banks. He married Maria Dolores Cardenal Vargas and they had four children. In 1980 the Sandinistas charged him with counter-revolutionary activities and he spent seven months in jail. While he was in jail, his father died. From 1983 to 1986 he served as president of the National Association of Coffee Producers and president of the National Association of the Coffee Growers from 1986 through 1989. He also served as vice-president of the National Farmers Union. Throughout the 1980s Alemán stridently opposed the Sandinista government and was the primary spokesperson for the agro-exporters, large landowners, and business owners. In 1989 the Sandinistas seized three of his farms in an attempt to keep him from speaking out against them.

In 1990 he was elected to the Managua City Council who then selected him as mayor. He channeled hundreds of thousands of dollars from the USAID and Cuban and Nicaraguan exiles in Miami into highly visible public works projects designed to rebuild the physical infrastructure of Managua. Through these projects he put thousands of poor, nonorganized *Nicas* and former military personnel to work and became very popular. At the same time there were persistent rumors of kickbacks from contractors and rampant misuse of public funds. Derisively referred to as the "fat man," the charismatic and ambitious Alemán embraced the label and used it effectively in his presidential campaign. Journalist Stephen Kinzer described him as "an exuberant eater and drinker" who "hugged women, kissed babies, and remembered everyone's name."[22] He came to control the Liberal Constitutionalist Party (PLC) and worked to unite several right-wing parties under the Liberal Alliance for the 1996 presidential election.

THE ALEMÁN YEARS

For the first two years Alemán and his right-wing liberal supporters in the National Assembly were confrontational toward the Sandinistas. They had played virtually no role in the policy compromises under Chamorro and immediately challenged the 1994 Military Code, the 1995 amendments to the constitution, and the 1996 Property Stabilization Law 209. This confrontational style led to public protest and violence. Alemán also had to deal with the country's growing debt problem that required the government to come to terms with the IMF and the World Bank. More than 5,000 government workers lost their jobs in one of his first acts as president. He reduced the wages of the remaining government employees and announced that another 7,000 would lose their jobs under the IMF and World Bank debt agreement. At the same time unions demanded higher wages as the standard of living in Nicaragua had deteriorated significantly for the working class. Alemán then began to seize property of those *Nicas* who had received land under the Property Stabilization Law 209 and some of the property seized during *la piñata*. UNAG and labor unions led a national protest that resulted in the Pan American highway being blocked, daily demonstrations, and political violence. The economy came to a virtual standstill until Ortega and Alemán agreed to address these issues. This was followed in June by an attempt by Alemán to restrict certain types of political protest. In July he announced a new agreement with the IMF and World Bank that would go into effect at the end of the year as long as the country continued to cut its deficit spending.

An armed rebellion, the Andres Castro United Front (FUAC), arose in the Siuna Mountains in 1995. Many of the FUAC were former members of the Sandinista Peoples Army who were demanding access to land. By 1997 they were protesting the lack of protection for those who had gained land through Law 209, the lack of access to credit, and the absence of basic government services in health and education. In September, the chief of the Nicaraguan Army Joaquín Cuadra Lacayo warned Alemán of a "social explosion" as a consequence of growing unemployment, hunger, malnutrition, and attempts to seize land guaranteed under Law 209. Alemán and Ortega began private negotiations that fall which resulted in a deal, the Law of Urban and Rural Reformed Property Act, between the FSLN and the Liberal Alliance that resolved the property issues, in particular the urban houses and property seized during *la piñata*.

In April 1998 demonstrations by students who were protesting the cuts in the funding for universities turned violent. That same month transportation workers went on strike to oppose Alemán's plan to end the price controls on diesel fuel. Ortega was able to get Alemán to actually cut the price of diesel fuel in exchange for an end to the strike and the government increased funding to the universities. In June the FSLN deputies, 13 deputies from minority parties, and eight dissident liberal deputies walked out of the National Assembly making it unable to conduct business. At issue was another IMF and World Bank agreement that would require Nicaragua to raise taxes on water, energy, and telephone rates. The walkout ended only when Alemán agreed to have an open discussion in the National Assembly concerning the tax legislation.

One of the characteristics of Nicaragua under Alemán was the unbelievable amount of public corruption and scandal. Early in his administration traces of cocaine were found in the presidential plane. Alemán spent 300,000 dollars of public money to build a road to his home in El Chile, an isolated and sparsely populated area. He stole 4 million dollars and put it in four shell companies that he controlled outside of Nicaragua. In 2001 he and his friends spent 15,348 dollars on rooms and meals in two days in Paris while at a debt-relief conference. He then went to Egypt where the group spent more than 28,000 dollars, including 1,000 dollars for perfume. He made similar trips to India spending more than 68,000 dollars and Bali where he spent almost 14,000 dollars. Alemán had bank accounts and real estate in the United States worth 4.6 million dollars and another 10.5 million dollars of assets in Panama.[23]

In November 1999 a government audit found that Alemán's personal fortune had grown 900 percent while he was mayor of Managua and that he had not paid any city taxes on his income. Comptroller-General Agustin Jarquin who had led the government audit was thrown in jail. The growing chorus of corruption allegations and Jarquin's incarceration led the IMF to deny Nicaragua's request to enter into its Highly Indebted Poor Country (HIPC) classification. Alemán had been negotiating with the IMF since October. This denial was extremely significant because the HIPC classification carried with it the possibility of eliminating almost 80 percent of Nicaragua's external debt.

By the middle of 1998, Alemán and Ortega began working closely with each other behind closed doors. Alemán often worked with Ortega to end strikes and protests. In return, Alemán would lessen the impact of some of the economic austerity measures. This often involved raising wages of key unionized groups and lowering the prices on some staple goods. All of this was done while Alemán and Ortega publicly condemned each other. Many argued that these pacts or back-room deals undermined democracy and transparency in Nicaragua; however, they resulted in less suffering for poor *Nicas* and gave more time for the economic transition started under Chamorro to work.

EL PACTO

By late 1999 the leaders of the two major parties, the PLC that dominated the Liberal Alliance and the FSLN, were in very weak political positions.

Alemán was under intense suspicion of corruption and was criticized for his poor management of the disaster left in the wake of Hurricane Mitch in October 1998. Ortega was also struggling with charges leveled at him by his 30-year-old stepdaughter, Zoilamerica Narvaez, who stated that he had sexually abused her for nearly 20 years. Although Ortega and his wife denied the charges, the scandal received tremendous coverage in the media. This translated into declining support for their parties. In late 1999 Ortega and Alemán worked out a deal and pushed it through the National Assembly with the FSLN and the Liberal Alliance voting to support it. It has since come to be known as *el pacto*.

El pacto granted the outgoing or former president a seat in the National Assembly. This was important, especially to Alemán, because deputies in the National Assembly were immune from prosecution. Municipal elections were normally held at the same time that presidential elections were held. Under *el pacto* municipal elections were to be held the year prior to the national elections. This change benefitted the Sandinistas who were great at turning out the vote but suffered under the glare of a hostile international press during national elections. Mayoral candidates from the FSLN could now run more successfully because they did not garner the attention of the world media. In fact, Sandinistas dominated the mayoral races in November 2000 by winning in all of the major cities except two. Most significantly Sandinista Herty Lewites was elected mayor of Managua. *El pacto* allowed the two major parties to pack the Supreme Court and the Supreme Electoral Council. It made it difficult for parties that had a small following to run candidates for national office, in effect, moving the country toward a two-party system. Finally, *el pacto* reduced the constitutional requirement of receiving at least 45 percent of the votes to win the presidency. Under *el pacto* a person could win the presidency with as little as 35 percent of the popular vote as long as there was a five point difference between that person and the runner-up candidate. This voting scheme did not guarantee a victory for Ortega in the future but made it more likely. In the end *el pacto* came back to haunt Ortega. Many Sandinistas believed that Ortega had sold his soul to the devil—Alemán. They believed that he had sacrificed his revolutionary legitimacy and principles for a personal quest for power which was now being labeled *Danielismo*.

DANIELISMO AND THE FSLN

Although Ortega still used his fiery revolutionary rhetoric, many former Sandinista leaders had left the party by this time claiming that *Sandinismo* had now become *Danielismo*. According to these Sandinistas the first evidence of this took place with *la piñata* when Ortega and some Sandinista leaders benefitted from the seizure of properties and companies prior to Chamorro's inauguration. With the tacit alliance between the FSLN and Chamorro, the dismantling of the Sandinista revolution began and Ortega did little to challenge it. While he worked to soften the shift from Sandinista economics, he did not fundamentally oppose privatization and neoliberalism. In the 1996 elections Ramirez and other Sandinistas left the FSLN and created the MRS. Even though the MRS garnered very few votes in 1996, its members became vocal opponents of *Danielismo*. They believed that the FSLN had become just like the PLC and other elite-led *Nica* parties that were without ideals, guiding principles, and ethics. The FSLN had become a vehicle for the personal ambitions of Ortega and he had created a cult of leadership within the party. With *el pacto* many other former Sandinistas came to reject *Danielismo* including Victor Hugo Tinoco and Daniel's own brother, Humberto. They believed that the party had sold its soul and helped to dismember the Sandinista revolution. In fact, they argued that Ortega and his bloc of so-called Sandinista entrepreneurs benefitted under the return to privatization and the agro-export-led capitalist economy.

THE 2001 CAMPAIGN AND ELECTIONS

Nicaragua remained desperately poor by the end of the Alemán administration. The wealthy had become wealthier due to growing business opportunities and the gap between the rich and poor had widened since the Chamorro years. Yet, there were visible indications that the economy was improving. Inflation was under control and continued to fall. Gross domestic product had risen by 7 percent in 1999 with noticeable growth in construction. Infrastructure improvements, especially in roads, were noticeable. New shops selling such things as office supplies, kitchen supplies, and clothes began to appear in the urban areas. Infant mortality rates were falling once again.[24] Pizza Hut and MacDonalds opened up franchises in Managua. There was a growing sense of normalcy among many *Nicas*.

PLC losses in the municipal elections of November 2000 set the tone for the national campaign of 2001. The losses were driven by the immense corruption in the Alemán government. Alemán wielded less and less influence over the Liberal Alliance and Vice-President Enrique José Bolaños Geyer, the PLC candidate for the presidency, had kept a low profile during most of the Alemán presidency. Ortega emphasized the immense corruption of Alemán and the PLC and was critical of Bolaños for not speaking out against the corruption prior to announcing his candidacy. He focused on reconciliation and his ability to reach across party lines and govern. He chose former Comptroller-General Jarquin, a member of the Social Christian Unity Party who had initially exposed Alemán's corruption, as his running mate. Jarquin had once been jailed by the Sandinistas in the 1980s. At times Ortega shed his traditional red and black Sandinista kerchief for a pink one. Pink campaign posters proclaimed that the FSLN would "build the promised land."

In the wake of 9/11 Bolaños reminded voters of the Sandinista problems with the United States and often used the word "terrorists" in reference to the FSLN. Even though the United States was focused primarily on the horrendous events of 9/11, the State Department, including Secretary of State Colin Powell, issued press releases very critical of Ortega. John F. Keane, the Director of the Office of Central American Affairs cleverly implied that Ortega may be linked to terrorism and predicted a "vicious" response should that be borne out in fact.[25] Governor Jeb Bush of Florida ran large ads in Nicaraguan newspapers that linked Ortega to terrorism. None of these claims had any basis in fact. In a media opportunity U.S. Ambassador Oliver Garza invited Bolaños to help him deliver emergency food aid to a poor, rural village. Cardinal Obando and former President Chamorro publicly supported Bolaños.

The elections were observed by the Carter Center, the Oscar Arias Foundation in Costa Rica, the OAS, the EU, and countless other groups. There were three candidates for the presidency. In addition to Bolaños and Ortega, the Conservative Party (PC) initially had Noel Vidaurre as its candidate for president. Vidaurre wanted to form an alliance with the anti-Ortega Sandinistas, the MRS, but members of his own party rejected the move. Vidaurre was replaced with Alberto Saborio. The MRS eventually supported Ortega in the election. Bolaños received 56.3 percent of the vote to Ortega's 42.3 percent. The PC received less than 2 percent of the vote. Voter turnout was at a historic high of 87.4 percent. In the National Assembly the Liberal Alliance consisting of the PLC and the Party of Nicaraguan Resistance (PRN) received 53 seats, the FSLN received 38 seats, and the PC received one seat. The elections were deemed fair and free by all observers. The only negative statement came from former President Jimmy Carter who condemned the overt U.S. partisan involvement in the elections.

For the third time in a row Ortega had been defeated in his bid for a second term as president. The visible signs of improvement in the economy raised the hopes of many that the economy was finally turning around. This "aura of expectancy and calm in 2001" worked in favor of Bolaños who was seen as better able to deal with the economy.[26] Bolaños was able to distance himself from Alemán in the eyes of many with his anti-corruption campaign and a return to the rule of law. In 1990 the *Nica* masses or poor had begun to move away from their support of the FSLN and this trend continued through the 1996 and 2001 elections. Ortega's strongest supporters in 2001 were the middle class and the organized working class such as labor.[27] In four elections Nicaragua had moved from the political left with Ortega to the center-right with Chamorro to the right with Alemán and it remained on the right with Bolaños. Yet, the FSLN could still garner more than 40 percent of the vote with its appeals to social solidarity and greater equality.

ENRIQUE JOSÉ BOLAÑOS GEYER (1928–PRESENT)

Bolaños was born in 1928 to Nicolas Bolaños Cortes and Amanda del Rosario Geyer Abaunza. The family was wealthy and he received a Bachelor of Arts degree in industrial engineering from St. Louis University. He married Lila T. Abaunza in 1949 and they had five children. In 1952 he founded the Industrial Agricultural Services of Masaya (SAIMSA) and became one of the largest cotton producers in Central America. During the 1960s he became a member of the PLC which opposed the Somozas. During the revolutionary years of the 1980s he was active in the opposition to the Sandinistas and served as president of the Supreme Council for Private Enterprise (COSEP) for five years. His property was confiscated by the Sandinistas and redistributed to landless peasants. Bolaños then worked as a computer programmer until his selection as Alemán's running mate in 1996. He kept a very low profile as vice-president and did not speak out when allegations of corruption appeared concerning President Alemán. Bolaños, a former member of the Conservative Party, was handpicked by Alemán to run for the presidency for the PLC and the Liberal Alliance. Three months before the election Bolaños finally denounced corruption in the presidency and began to distance himself from Alemán.

POLITICS DURING THE BOLAÑOS YEARS

Bolaños was at a clear disadvantage initially because he was a former conservative and did not play much of a role in the decision-making processes during the Alemán presidency. He also did not play a role in the selection of the PLC slate of deputies for the National Assembly elections. Alemán was now a member of the National Assembly due to *el pacto* and he would be able to control the PLC deputies. Alemán believed that he would be able to continue to dominate the decision-making processes and Bolaños would merely serve as a figurehead president. However, in March 2002 the Attorney General publicly accused Alemán of corruption. The U.S and Panamanian governments froze Alemán's assets. Bolaños boldly spoke out against the former president. He told the *Nica* people that the immense government corruption and thievery kept them poor and that the country needed a "new era of moral regeneration, honesty, transparency, and accountability." Bolaños defended honesty in public life. He directly accused Alemán of stealing from the Nicaraguan people. Although Bolaños spoke the truth, it isolated him from his own Liberal Alliance. He faced a hostile National Assembly. He asked the National Assembly to end Alemán's immunity so that he could be prosecuted. The Assembly denied his request. Not to be deterred, Bolaños worked with the Sandinistas to stage a huge march on the National Assembly to demand an end to Alemán's immunity. With the glare of the national and international media, the National Assembly voted again and this time Bolaños won. In August 2002 the Nicaraguan courts filed corruption charges against Alemán. In December 2003 he was sentenced to 20 years in prison on charges of money laundering, embezzlement, and corruption. Rather than serving his sentence in prison, he was placed under house arrest due to his failing health. Ironically, he still remained the most powerful person within the PLC and continued to make decisions for the party even while under house arrest.

After Alemán was convicted the PLC voted to kick Bolaños out of the party. Bolaños went on to form his own Alliance for the Republic (APRE) which consisted of a handful of dissident members of the PLC and the Conservative Party—a total of 11 seats in the National Assembly. In October 2004 the Comptroller-General alleged that Bolaños had violated campaign finance laws in 2001 and recommended that he should be removed from office. In November/December 2004 the National Assembly controlled by PLC and the FSLN voted for constitutional reforms that would limit the power of the presidency. Under the reforms the presidential appointees to cabinet positions would be subject to a 60 percent approval by the National Assembly and the National Assembly would be able to overturn a presidential veto with a majority vote. The intent of the reforms was to shift the balance of power away from the executive branch toward the legislature. Bolaños refused to accept these constitutional reforms and for 10 months the government of Nicaragua was in crisis. In September 2005 the crisis escalated when the National Assembly voted to deny immunity to seven officials of the Bolaños administration. This would have paved the way to prosecute them on charges of violations of campaign laws. Then in October 2005 the OAS worked with Ortega and Bolaños to bring about an agreement. Bolaños agreed to support the constitutional reforms as long as they would not go into effect until January 2007, after the presidential elections. In return the FSLN would make sure that the National Assembly would protect Bolaños' immunity and that he would not be prosecuted. By the end of the Bolaños administration the Sandinistas and the PLC were still the two largest parties, but the PLC was split between Alemán supporters and those opposed to Alemán. This split among the liberals would bode well for the FSLN in the 2006 elections.

POLICIES UNDER BOLAÑOS

While Bolaños continued to work with the IMF and World Bank to manage the country's massive debt and for investment, loans, and aid to continue to come into the country, his most important policy initiative was the Central American Free Trade Agreement (CAFTA). In May 2004 the trade ministers of the United States, Guatemala, Honduras, El Salvador, Nicaragua, Costa Rica, and the Dominican Republic agreed to begin the process of implementing CAFTA. Under CAFTA tariffs would be removed on most products which could then be traded freely among the member countries. In Nicaragua most tariffs would be removed immediately, but tariffs on rice, poultry, dairy products, and yellow corn would be phased out over time. Bolaños philosophically supported free trade and believed that this would boost Nicaraguan exports and investment in his country, especially in the free-trade zones. He was committed to Nicaragua's ratification of the treaty but he faced a hostile PLC–FSLN coalition in the National Assembly. The PLC which agreed in principle to CAFTA opposed Bolaños because of his pursuit of corruption charges against Alemán. Ortega and the FSLN denounced CAFTA as an assault on Nicaraguan sovereignty. Ortega and UNAG charged that small- and medium-sized farmers and producers would not be able to compete with subsidized U.S. agricultural products and many would go out of business just as they had in Mexico with the implementation of the North American Free Trade Agreement (NAFTA). The FSLN and UNAG organized street demonstrations opposed to CAFTA.

The Bush administration began to put pressure on the PLC to support CAFTA in October 2005. U.S. Assistant Secretary of State Robert Zoellick threatened the revocation of the visas of two of Alemán's children and threatened to cut off aid designated for infrastructure projects. Under pressure from the United States, the PLC agreed to support Bolaños and the APRE on the CAFTA vote.[28] The PLC which had put Sandinista Rene Nuñez as President of the National Assembly now threatened to remove him from office if he did not bring CAFTA to a vote. On October 10, 2005, CAFTA was passed by the National Assembly with the FSLN in opposition. This was the same month that the FSLN worked with Bolaños to achieve constitutional reforms limiting presidential powers that would be implemented in January 2007.

THE 2006 CAMPAIGN AND ELECTIONS

The 2004 municipal elections favored the Sandinistas who won in 87 of the 152 municipalities. More importantly the FSLN won in Managua. This strong showing gave momentum and hope to the Sandinistas that they would finally return to power nationally in 2006. In 2005 dissident Sandinistas selected former Sandinista and Mayor of Managua Lewites to challenge Ortega for the FSLN's presidential nominee. This group represented the most vocal Sandinista critics of *Danielismo* and *el pacto*. The Sandinista DN cancelled the primary and selected Ortega as its presidential candidate again. Lewites formed the Movement for the Rescue of Sandinismo (MPRS) with the support of many former Sandinistas such as Victor Tinoco, Victor Tirado, Henry Ruiz, Carrion, Belli, Ernesto Cardenal, Monica Baltodano, René Vivas, and the revolutionary songwriter and singer Carlos Mejía Godoy. On July 2 Lewites died of a heart attack and Edmundo Jarquin became the candidate of the MPRS. José Rizo Castellón, handpicked by Alemán, was the nominee for the PLC. Eduardo Montealegre, the former banker and finance minister under Bolaños, was the nominee for the National Liberal Alliance (ALN-PC) which consisted largely of former members of APRE and anti-Alemán liberals who wanted a return to the rule of law and to rid the country of corruption and personality-based politics. His appeal was to *Nicas* who were upset with the behind-closed-door deal-making between the FSLN and the PLC. He had the support of the United States, Chamorro, and many of the wealthy in the country.

Ortega ran on a platform of reconciliation with *contras* and the Church. He selected former contra leader and banker Jaime Morales as his vice-presidential candidate. Morales won the support of some of the wealthy agro-exporters in the country. Ortega also reconciled with the Church and Cardinal Obando. He and his wife, Rosario Murillo, converted to Catholicism and were formally married by Obando. Ortega supported a controversial, comprehensive ban on abortion. He stated clearly that Nicaragua had to develop economically through market mechanisms but the government had to alleviate the suffering of the poor, the victims of what he called "savage capitalism." His campaign song, the Spanish version of John Lennon's "Give Peace a Chance," brought home his message of reconciliation between the rich and poor, the state and the Church, and the political left and right.

At the same time he openly courted President Hugo Chavez of Venezuela and many of the other growing number of left-wing presidents throughout Latin America. Even though Ortega had always received the brunt of U.S. criticism, his moves toward Chavez put the Bush administration on high alert. Ambassador Paul Trivelli openly campaigned in favor of Montealegre and encouraged all the parties on the political right to unite against Ortega. U.S. Embassy spokesperson Kristin Stewart threatened sanctions should Ortega win the election. Secretary of Defense Donald Rumsfeld was in Managua in October chairing the meeting of the Defense Ministers of the Americas. Oliver North, who had led the illegal Reagan

war against the Sandinistas in the 1980s, came to Managua and warned
Nicas of the dire consequences of electing Ortega. Republican members of
Congress threatened to end remittances or U.S. dollars sent to Nicaragua
from *Nicas* living and working in the United States. The OAS publicly condemned Ambassador Trivelli of meddling in the elections and even Montealegre, the candidate receiving U.S. support, was critical of the overt U.S.
efforts to influence the outcome of the election.

On November 5, 2006, *Nicas* went to the polls to vote in their fifth
national democratic election since 1984. Although a few irregularities
occurred, there was nothing systematic and observers from the Carter Center, the OAS, and the EU certified the election process as fair and honest.
Ortega received 38.07 percent of the vote, Montealegre received 29 percent,
Rizo received 26.51 percent, and Jarquin received 6.44 percent. The FSLN
received 38 seats in the National Assembly, the ALN-PC received 23 seats,
the PLC received 25 seats, the MPRS received five seats, and Bolaños occupied the final seat. For the second time, Ortega had been elected to the
presidency of Nicaragua. Since 1984 the country had come full circle from
the political left, to the center right, to the right, and now back to the left.
Yet, Nicaragua had changed dramatically since 1984 and so had the FSLN
and Ortega.

EXPLAINING THE SANDINISTA VICTORY

At the time of the election Nicaragua was the second poorest country in
the Americas and the gap between the wealthy and the poor was growing.
More than 50 percent of the population lived on less than two dollars a
day. Many unemployed young people believed that Ortega was the only
candidate who really empathized with them. The country was suffering
under high gasoline prices and an energy crisis that frequently caused
blackouts in Managua. Prior to the election, Ortega had discussed Nicaraguan energy issues with Chavez of Venezuela. He arranged an aid package
between the Nicaraguan Association of Mayors and Chavez. The result
was the provision of diesel fuel electrical plants for Las Brisas and Ciudad
Sandino. Ortega's relationship with the oil-rich Chavez and the promise of
oil delivered to Nicaragua at less than market prices or concessionary
terms gave credibility to Ortega's promises of easing the energy crisis. His
selection of former *contra* leader Morales as his running mate had gone a
long way in calming some of the fears of the wealthy and the agro-export
elites of the country.

Although *el pacto* with its reduction in the percentage of the vote necessary to be elected president is often cited as the reason for Ortega's victory
in 2006, it does not provide a sufficient understanding. The split between

Bolaños, who emphasized the rule of law reminiscent of his conservative party roots, and the PLC, which had become associated with personality-based politics of Alemán, ended liberal unity and provided the opening for Ortega. Two liberal candidates, Rizo, who represented the PLC and the politics of personality, and Montealegre, who represented the rule of law, split the right-wing vote. With the death of Lewites, most of the dissident Sandinistas returned to Ortega and the FSLN. At the same time it is important to point out the persistence of Ortega and his very astute political skills. He had led his party as the loyal opposition since 1990. He had "co-governed" with Chamorro and had been able to work deals to soften the neo-liberal policies of Alemán and Bolaños. Even the media critics of Ortega emphasized that he had become quite a pragmatist and realist. They believed that Ortega would do nothing to risk the agreements with the IMF and World Bank and foreign investment. Although his support wavered among the Sandinista intellectuals who opposed his authoritarian dominance of the FSLN and deal-making with opposition parties, Ortega still maintained a large national following among the organized masses, working class, and small- and medium-sized farmers and ranchers.

THE RETURN OF ORTEGA AND THE SANDINISTAS

Ortega was sworn in as president in January 2007. His party was in the minority in the National Assembly. The liberals, although divided between the PLC and the ALN-PC alliance, controlled the majority of seats. Although controlling only five seats in the National Assembly, dissident Sandinistas sometimes voted with the liberals. In addition, constitutional reforms since 1995 made the executive and legislative branches of government more interdependent. It was difficult for the chief executive to completely dominate the policy-making process due to the checks and balances between the legislative and executive branches. The legacy of *el pacto* left the Supreme Electoral Council and the Supreme Court, for the most part, evenly divided between the FSLN and the PLC.

Within this political environment, Ortega worked out new agreements with the IMF and the World Bank concerning Nicaragua's debt problems and continued access to loans. National budgets continued to be austere with virtually no funding available for necessary social programs. Much of the budget goes to repay debts. Although he had opposed the passage of CAFTA, he accepted his obligations to continue to carry out the treaty, despite evidence that under CAFTA the value of Nicaraguan exports to the United States declined by 3.1 percent and the value of U.S. exports to Nicaragua increased by more than 30 percent during 2006.[29] With the volume and value of Nicaraguan exports increasing in 2007 and 2008,

Nicaragua's participation in CAFTA was no longer an issue under Ortega. While these actions pleased foreign investors, the agro-exporters, and many wealthy *Nicas*, Ortega had to find a way to address the extreme poverty and other social problems in the country as he had promised in his presidential campaign.

Under IMF and World Bank agreements, the problem faced by Ortega was the lack of government resources to implement social programs to address poverty and related social issues. Ortega entered into the Bolivarian Alternative to the Americas (ALBA) in April 2007. ALBA is an organization of Caribbean and Latin American states created by Chavez of Venezuela. The purpose of ALBA is to provide resources for its members to address the growing inequalities, hunger, and poverty. ALBA's resources come largely from the immense oil wealth of Venezuela and the decision by Chavez to provide oil to the members of ALBA at concessionary prices. To address the growing illiteracy in the country, Ortega with support from ALBA developed a literacy campaign called *Yo Sí Puedo*. Ortega initiated a program which provides micro or small loans to small businesses in urban areas at below-market interest rates or what has come to be called "zero usury." The program focuses on businesses run by females. The Streets for the People program has provided funds to pave hundreds of kilometers of streets in poor urban areas. Houses for People has given low-income people access to low-interest credit to purchase homes. In its first year of existence, the Zero Hunger Program provided one cow, one pig, 10 hens, one rooster, and seeds to 15,000 families.

All of these programs are funded with assistance from Venezuela either through credit from the Venezuelan Social and Economic Development Bank or through ALBA. They are not funded through the official Nicaraguan budget. This is precisely why they have generated so much controversy among FSLN opponents in Nicaragua. Chavez provides 10 million barrels of oil to Nicaragua annually at concessionary terms. This is enough oil to meet the energy needs of the country. The oil is sold to the Nicaraguan State Oil Company (PETRONIC) which, by law, is an independent commercial business. Under the agreement with ALBA, PETRONIC must pay Venezuela 50 percent of the cost within 90 days. Twenty-five percent of the cost is paid to CARUNA, a nationwide credit union in Nicaragua. It is CARUNA that directly provides much of the funding for the social programs. Twenty-five percent of the cost is paid to an ALBA fund which is designed to provide low-cost loans to member countries to address problems associated with poverty and inequality. In Nicaragua, CARUNA administers these loans from ALBA. Finally, these social programs funded via ALBA are being implemented locally by the controversial Citizen Power Councils (CPC).

In the fall of 2007 Ortega attempted to get the National Assembly to support the creation of the CPC. This neighborhood entity would be made up of local citizens who would play a major role in implementing social programs at the local level. The argument was that the CPC was closer to the people who could make better decisions as to how to disperse funds to address problems of poverty in each neighborhood. The CPC is portrayed as an example of direct democracy. The liberals closed ranks in the National Assembly and rejected Ortega's proposal. They believed this was an attempt to bypass government institutions that already existed for that purpose. They did not want to see the establishment of a parallel government. Undeterred by the rejection by the National Assembly, Ortega decided to create the CPC but make them committees of the FSLN.

The fact that the National Assembly and the majority liberals had no control over the funding mechanism of these social programs led to charges of alleged corruption against Ortega and the FSLN. It was made worse by the lack of transparency as to how these funds were being spent. The CPC were controversial because they were party organizations, not governmental organizations, and they were implementing what Sandinista opponents in the National Assembly believed to be governmental social programs. The FSLN argued that the social programs were actually private programs not associated with the government because they ware not funded by the government. Underlying much of this acrimony was the fact that the United States and the liberals were upset with what they saw as interference in the internal politics of the country by Chavez and Venezuela. By 2008 soaring oil prices, even under Venezuela's concessions, and rising food costs continued to hurt the poor in Nicaragua. In June Ortega appointed his wife as Head of the Social Cabinet without approval of the National Assembly. Reminiscent of Eva Peron in Argentina, she was now directing the Zero Hunger, Zero Usury, and Streets for People programs. In October 2008 a budget could not be passed because the National Assembly and Ortega were unable to reach a compromise. By the beginning of 2009 the global economic crisis was further polarizing the political processes in Nicaragua.

DEFYING THE ODDS: THE ROAD TO DEMOCRACY

Nicaragua had now experienced fair and competitive elections in 1984, 1990, 1996, 2001, and 2006. The peaceful transfer of power had come full circle from the left-wing FSLN, to a broad center-right UNO coalition government, to liberal (right-wing) governments, and back to the FSLN. Since the Chamorro government, the Nicaraguan military had become nonpartisan, accepting of civilian authority, and increasingly professional. There was a broad array of interest groups representing virtually every segment of Nicaraguan society. Some of the groups were autonomous; others were tied to particular political parties. Yet, they were fully engaged in the political processes in the country. Turn-out in national elections reached as high as 87 percent. With *el pacto*, the country has become a two-party system with the Sandinistas and their political allies against a liberal coalition led by the PLC.

Yet, the two major parties, the FSLN and the PLC, were still tied to the personalities of their leaders, Ortega and Alemán. The authoritarian tendencies of these men within their own parties and their willingness to make back-room deals to promote their own personal ambitions were the reasons why dissident Sandinistas appeared in the 1996 national elections and dissident liberals appeared after the corrupt Alemán presidency. With Montealegre receiving more votes than Alemán's hand-picked candidate Rizo in 2006, there was a real possibility for the liberals to move away from the personal politics of the past. With Ortega unable to run for the presidency again and the growing influence of the dissident Sandinistas, it was also a real possibility for the FSLN to move away from the personal politics of the past. A more important source of change for the Sandinistas was at the local levels of government.

In 1988 the Sandinistas established city governments as locally elected governments with limited taxing powers and the ability to make decisions independent of the national government. During the 1990s city mayors, such as Alemán in Managua, practiced a style of clientelistic politics, rewarding votes with employment. Ironically, it was *el pacto* that brought about significant changes in the practice of local government. Municipal elections were to be held in non-national election years and a one-term limit was placed on mayors. The significance of these changes was that for the first time in Nicaraguan history local politics could be divorced from national politics. Municipal elections have since been held in 2000, 2004, and 2008. Since 2000 the Sandinistas have dominated these elections over the PLC. Term limits make clientelistic politics virtually impossible. Local governments have become more professional and focused on delivering primary services and being responsible to their citizens. Lewites' term as mayor of Managua is perhaps the best example of this. The Sandinista mayors elected in 2008 rose in the ranks through local party organizations and many of Ortega's most outspoken critics were the current group of Sandinista mayors, including Pedro Calderon in Estelí and Edurardo Holman Chamorro in San Juan del Sur. Leslie Anderson and Lawrence Dodd found that these mayors have encouraged a participatory civic culture at the local level.[30] Future FSLN leaders may come from this increasingly professional class of mayors. At the same time, Anderson and Dodd noted that

Ortega's use of CPCs to carry out national social policies was an attempt to undermine successful and autonomous local government and assert Ortega's power locally. Their study of voting behavior indicated that citizens voting in municipal elections viewed local government officials to be more significant than national officials in attempting to improve the lives of everyday *Nicas*. [31]

With all of its imperfections the march of democracy in Nicaragua since 1984 is quite astonishing given its long history of poverty, inequality, illiteracy, authoritarianism, elite-dominance, civil war, and U.S. intervention. Given the extreme poverty found in the country coupled with the current global depression, one might expect an attempt to return to more authoritarian government. Some would argue that is exactly what Ortega has done with his CDCs and alternative funding sources from Venezuela for his social programs. Yet, there are checks and balances that are restricting Ortega's tendencies that bode well for the future of the country. It is important to remember that democracy is an on-going process. There will be steps forward and steps backward. Since 1984 Nicaragua's steps forward have been more numerous than its steps backward. Perhaps the more important and yet unanswered question is whether this fledgling democracy can solve the problems of poverty for its people and give hope for the future to its children.

NOTES

1. For what is undoubtedly the best discussion and academic analysis of this question see Leslie Anderson and Lawrence C. Dodd, *Learning Democracy: Citizen Engagement and Electoral Choice in Nicaragua, 1990–2001* (Chicago: University of Chicago Press, 2005) and Leslie Anderson and Lawrence C. Dodd, "Nicaragua: Progress amid Regress?" *Journal of Democracy* 20:3 (July 2009): 153–67. Much of the discussion of this issue in this chapter is based on the work of Anderson and Dodd.

2. See Gary Ruchwarger, *People in Power: Forging Grassroots Democracy in Nicaragua* (South Hadley, MA: Bergin and Garvey, 1987), 116 and chapter 5.

3. Anderson and Dodd, *Learning Democracy*, 68–71.

4. Matilde Zimmermann, *Sandinista: Carlos Fonseca and the Nicaraguan Revolution* (Durham: Duke University Press, 2000), 98.

5. See the memoir of Gioconda Belli, *The Country under My Skin: A Memoir of Love and War* (New York: Anchor Books, 2002), 71–84.

6. Jennifer Bickham Mendez, *From the Revolution to the Maquiladoras* (Durham: Duke University Press, 2005), 46–51.

7. Margaret Randall, *Gathering Rage* (New Brunswick: Rutgers University Press, 1992), 52.

8. Bickham Mendez, *From the Revolution to the Maquiladoras*, 51.

9. Gary Prevost, "The FSLN" in *Nicaragua without Illusions: Regime Transition and Structural Adjustment in the 1990s*, edited by Thomas W. Walker, 157 (Wilmington: Scholarly Resources, 1997).

10. Ibid., 159.

11. Thomas W. Walker, *Nicaragua: Living in the Shadow of the Eagle*, 4th ed. (Boulder, CO: Westview Press, 2003), 61.

12. William Robinson, "Nicaragua and the World" in *Nicaragua without Illusions*, edited by Thomas W. Walker, 32 (Wilmington: Scholarly Resources, 1997).

13. Daniel Premo, "Redirection of the Armed Forces" in *Nicaragua without Illusions*, edited by Thomas W. Walker, 66 (Wilmington: Scholarly Resources, 1997).

14. Ibid., 68.

15. Ibid., 74.

16. David Stanfield, "Insecurity of Land Tenure in Nicaragua," Working Paper (Madison, WI: Land Tenure Center, 1992), 10.

17. Jon Jonakin, "Agrarian Policy" in *Nicaragua without Illusions*, edited by Thomas W. Walker, 102 (Wilmington: Scholarly Resources, 1997).

18. The author attended the inauguration ceremony of the new MRS Party in May 1995.

19. Anderson and Dodd, *Learning Democracy*, 222, 224.

20. Oscar Neira, "*Politica pro-agricola: Sera possible?*" *Envio* 182 (1997): 15.

21. Belli, *The Country under My Skin*, 357.

22. Stephen Kinzer, *Blood of Brothers: Life and War in Nicaragua* (Cambridge: Harvard University Press, 2007), 399.

23. Ibid., 399–400, 402.

24. Anderson and Dodd, *Learning Democracy*, 234.

25. Walker, *Nicaragua: Living in the Shadow of the Eagle*, 68.

26. Anderson and Dodd, *Learning Democracy*, 237.

27. Ibid., 270–71.

28. Rose Spaulding, "Post-CAFTA Trading: the Politics of Trade Capacity Building in Nicaragua." Paper presented at the XXVIII International Latin American Studies Association Meeting, Rio de Janeiro, Brazil, June 11–14, 2009, 13.

29. Ibid., 14.

30. Anderson and Dodd, "Nicaragua: Progress amid Regress?", 159–61.

31. Ibid., 164.

Notable People in the History of Nicaragua

Alemán Lacayo, Arnoldo (1946–). He was from Managua and served as an official in the Somoza government during the 1970s. Some of his property was seized and he actively opposed the Sandinista Front for National Liberation (FSLN) or Sandinista government. He served as mayor of Managua and served as president from 1997 to 2002. His administration was noted for its extensive corruption.

Belli, Giaconda (1948–). An award-winning author, novelist, and poet, she was a member of the FSLN that overthrew the Somoza dictatorship in 1979. She served as the FSLN international press liaison. Her writings emphasize the role of gender in the Sandinista revolution.

Bolaños Geyer, Enrique Jose (1928–). Born in Masaya to a wealthy business-man, he created a very successful agro-industrial company (SAIMSA) which became one of the largest cotton producers in Nicaragua. Bolaños opposed the Sandinistas. He served as president from 2002–2007 and successfully brought about corruption charges against his predecessor Arnoldo Alemán.

Borge Martinez, Tomás (1930–). The only living co-founder of the FSLN, Borge was part of the student opposition to Somoza in the 1950s. He served as the minister of the interior during the Sandinista government of the 1980s.

Cardenal, Ernesto (1925–). Born in Granada, Jesuit priest Ernesto Cardenal is an internationally acclaimed poet, author, and artist. He served as a field chaplain for the FSLN and as the minister of culture from 1979 to 1988. He was reprimanded by Pope John Paul II for spreading liberation theology and participating in the revolutionary Sandinista government.

Cardenal, Fernando (1934–). Brother of Ernesto Cardenal and Jesuit priest who supported the FSLN in the revolution that toppled the Somoza dynasty. He promoted liberation theology and served as minister of education under the Sandinista government. He was responsible for the literacy crusade of 1980.

Chamorro, Pedro Joaquín (1924–1978). From a wealthy family in Granada, Pedro Joaquín Chamorro was a writer, novelist, journalist, and opponent of the Somoza dynasty. As editor of his family newspaper, *La Prensa*, he was a frequent critic of the Somozas. He was assassinated in 1978 by Somoza and this event is often cited as the catalyst that finally led to the fall of the Somoza dynasty. He was married to Violeta Barrios de Chamorro.

Chamorro, Violeta Barrios de (1929–). Born into a wealthy family, she married Pedro Joaquín Chamorro who had a long history of opposing the Somoza dynasty. Violeta assumed control of the family paper *La Prensa* after the assassination of her husband in 1978. Initially supporting the Sandinistas, she came to oppose them. She defeated the Sandinista candidate Daniel Ortega for the presidency in 1990 and served until 1996.

Dario, Rubén (1867–1916). With international notoriety and acclaim, he is the most famous literary person from Nicaragua. Dario founded Latin America's modernist movement.

Fonseca Amador, Carlos (1936–1976). The illegitimate son of a wealthy Somoza loyalist from Matagalpa and student inspired by the Cuban revolution and Augusto César Sandino, Fonseca was the intellectual leader, strategist, and co-founder of the FSLN.

Obando y Bravo, Miguel (1926–). The former Archbishop of Managua, Father Obando was an outspoken critic of both the Somozas and the Sandinistas.

Ortega Saavedra, Daniel (1945–). FSLN guerrilla commander who became its recognized leader with the fall of Somoza in 1979. He was elected president in 1984 and served from 1985 through 1990. In 2006 he was again elected president and started his term the next year.

Sandino, Augusto César (1895–1934). Nationalist guerrilla leader led the resistance to the U.S. occupation of Nicaragua from 1927 to 1933 when the U.S. forces left the country. He was assassinated by Somoza in 1934. His anti-imperialist guerrilla activities and writings served to inspire the FSLN and many others.

Somoza Debayle, Anastasio (1925-1980). The younger of the two sons of Somoza García, Anastasio ruled Nicaragua until the FSLN came to power via a revolution in 1979. Extremely corrupt, he relied heavily on the use of violence and the National Guard to remain in power as more and more societal groups turned against him.

Somoza Debayle, Luis (1922–1967). The oldest of the two sons of Somoza García, Luis effectively ruled the country behind puppet presidents until his death in 1967. Economic growth, increasing economic inequality, a restive and progressive Catholic church, a growing revolutionary opposition, and the trend toward greater use of violence against this opposition characterized his rule.

Somoza García, Anastasio (1896–1956). The son of a coffee grower, he was placed in command of the U.S.-created Nicaraguan National Guard, he used the guard to rule Nicaragua from 1937 until his assassination. He became the wealthiest man in Nicaragua, typically ruled by "buying" off his wealthy, conservative opposition, and effectively manipulated the United States and maintained its support of his policies.

Téllez, Dora María (1956–). A medical student, who became a famous guerrilla commander for the Sandinistas, served as minister of health under the FSLN in the 1980s. She broke with the FSLN and helped to create the Sandinista Renovation Movement (MRS) in the mid-1990s. Now a historian, she recently accepted an academic position at Harvard but was denied a visa by the Bush administration.

Walker, William (1824–1860). An American adventurer invited by the Liberals to help them gain power actually declared himself to be the country's president in 1856. He legalized slavery and declared English as the official language. He left the country in 1857 due to opposition from both liberals and conservatives in Nicaragua and all the other Central American countries. He returned to Central America in 1860; the British captured him and turned him over to the Hondurans who promptly executed him.

Zelaya López, José Santos (1853–1919). The son of a liberal coffee planter, he was president from 1893 to 1909 and led the modernization of agriculture in the country through the dramatic expansion of the coffee industry. He was responsible for finally getting the British to leave the Miskito Coast. His refusal to allow the United States to have sovereignty over a cross-isthmus canal in Nicaragua and other issues led to the overthrow of his government by the Conservative Party with support from the United States.

Zeledón, Benjamin (1879–1912). Opposed to the Diaz government which he believed to be a puppet of the United States, Zeledón led a rebellion that was crushed by U.S. Marines at the Battle of Coyetepe near Masaya. Zeledón has now become a national hero and a symbol of Nicaraguan resistance to foreign domination.

Nicaraguan History:
A Bibliographic Essay

For a general history of Nicaragua there is none better than Thomas Walker's *Nicaragua: Land of Sandino* (Boulder, CO: Westview Press, 1981) or his most recent edition of that classic *Nicaragua: Living in the Shadow of the Eagle*, 4th ed. (Boulder, CO: Westview Press, 2003). John Booth's *The End and the Beginning: The Nicaragua Revolution*, 2nd ed. (Boulder, CO: Westview Press, 1985) covers the history of the country through the mid-1980s and provides a well-researched discussion of the political, economic, and social factors that led to the Sandinista revolution.

E. Bradford Burns' *Patriarch and Folk: The Emergence of Nicaragua, 1798–1858* (Cambridge: Harvard University Press, 1991) gives the reader an excellent overview of the early history of the country. For a wonderfully descriptive, entertaining, and very insightful travelogue of Nicaragua in the late 1840s, one should read the Michigan Historical Reprint Series of E. G. Squier's account *Travels in Central America, Particularly in Nicaragua* (originally published in 1853) (Ann Arbor: University of Michigan Library, 2005). Mark Twain's *Travels with Mr. Brown* (New York: Knopf, 1940) gives a brief account of his travel across Nicaragua in 1867. There are two unpublished dissertations which are excellent studies of Nicaragua under the Zelaya administration: Benjamin Terplitz, ''The Political and Economic Foundations of Modernization in Nicaragua: The Administration of José

Santos Zelaya'' (Howard University, 1973) and John Findling, ''The U.S. and Zelaya: A Study in the Diplomacy of Expediency'' (University of Texas, 1971). Neill Macaulay's *The Sandino Affair* (Micanopy, FL: Wacahoota Press, 1998) is still the best study of Sandino's struggle against the U.S. occupation. Sergio Ramirez' compilation *Sandino: The Testimony of a Nicaraguan Patriot 1921–1934* (Princeton: Princeton University Press, 1990) translated by Robert Conrad gives one invaluable access to Sandino's letters and materials. Richard Millett's *The Guardians of the Dynasty: A History of the US-Created Guardia Nacional de Nicaragua and the Somoza Family* (Maryknoll, NY: Orbis Books, 1977) gives a good account of the creation of the National Guard and the Somoza government. Jeffrey Gould's *To Lead as Equals: Rural Protest and Political Consciousness in Chinandega, Nicaragua 1912–1979* (Chapel Hill: University of North Carolina Press, 1990) covers the history of peasant movements up to the Sandinista revolution. Mark Everingham's *Revolution and the Multi-Class Coalition in Nicaragua* (Pittsburgh: University of Pittsburgh Press, 1996) explains why many elites (capitalists) allied with the Sandinistas in the overthrow of Somoza. Joseph Mulligan's *The Nicaragua Church and the Revolution* (Lanham, MD: Sheed & Ward, 1991) provides an excellent overview of the role of the Catholic Church in the revolution.

The significance of agriculture in the history of Nicaragua and its impact on politics cannot be overstated and it has profoundly influenced most who study the country. Academic studies of the impact of agriculture can be found in several well-written and meticulously researched texts including Charles D. Brockett's *Land, Power, and Poverty* (Boulder, CO: Westview Press, 1998), Laura Enriquez' *Harvesting Change: Labor and Agrarian Reform in Nicaragua 1979–1990* (Chapel Hill: University of North Carolina Press, 1991) and *Agrarian Reform and Class Consciousness in Nicaragua* (Gainesville: University Press of Florida, 1997) and Jeffery Paige's *Coffee and Power: Revolution and the Rise of Democracy in Central America* (Cambridge: Harvard University Press, 1997). Marta Harnecker's interview with Jaime Wheelock Roman in *Nicaragua: the Great Challenge* (Managua: Alternative Views, 1984) gives one insight into the agricultural policies that he put in place as minister of agrarian reform during the revolutionary years of the 1980s and Joseph Collins' *Nicaragua: What Difference Could a Revolution Make?: Food and Farming in the New Nicaragua* (New York: Grove Press, 1985) provides an overview of agricultural and food policy under the Sandinistas. Max Spoor's *The State and Domestic Agricultural Markets in Nicaragua: Opposition and Accommodation, 1979–1993* (New York: Macmillan, 1995) compares the Sandinista agricultural policies with those of Violeta Chamorro.

There are many books that cover the 1980s when Nicaragua was governed by the Sandinistas. Stephen Kinzer's *Blood of Brothers: Life and War in Nicaragua* (Cambridge: Harvard University Press, 2007) gives one a first-hand journalistic account. Alejandro Martínez Cuenca's *Sandinista Economics in Practice: An Insider's Critical Reflections* (Cambridge, MA: South End Press, 1999) gives us a sober reflection of an insider's knowledge of economic policy during the revolutionary years. Bruce E. Wright's *Theory in the Practice of the Nicaraguan Revolution* (Athens: Ohio University Center for International Studies, 1995) explains how the revolution changed over time due to the realities of Nicaragua. Robert Arnove's *Education as Contested Terrain: Nicaragua, 1979–1993* (Boulder, CO: Westview Press, 1994) provides an overview of the education policies of the Sandinistas. Michael E. Conroy's edited volume *Nicaragua: Profiles of the Revolutionary Public Sector* (Boulder, CO: Westview Press, 1987) looks at the state-run enterprises of the Sandinistas.

There is a broad literature that focuses specifically on the Sandinista leaders. Tomás Borge's memoirs *The Patient Impatience* (Willimantic, CT: Curbstone Press, 1992) received the 1989 Casa de las Americas Prize for Testimony. Matilde Zimmerman's *Sandinista: Carols Fonseca and the Nicaraguan Revolution* (Durham: Duke University Press, 2000) is the best researched study of the life of the founder of the Sandinistas. Omar Cabezas' *Fire from the Mountain: The Making of a Sandinista* (New York: Random House, 1985) gives a lively and honest first-hand account of becoming a guerrilla and supporting the Sandinista revolutionary cause. Margaret Randall's *Sandino's Daughters: Testimonies of Nicaraguan Women in Struggle* (New Brunswick: Rutgers University Press, 1995) provides interviews with key women in the Sandinista Revolution. Gioconda Belli's *The Country under My Skin: A Memoir of Love and War* (New York: Knopf, 2002) discusses how a woman from an upper-class family comes to be a Sandinista guerrilla. Teofilo Cabestrero's *Ministers of God, Ministers of the People* (Maryknoll, NY: Orbis, 1983) focuses on the Roman Catholic priests (Ernesto and Fernando Cardenal, and Miguel D'Escoto), who played such a significant role in the Sandinista government. Books of poetry by Ernesto Cardenal, such as *Golden UFOs: The Indian Poems* (Bloomington: Indiana University Press, 1992) or *Apocalypse and Other Poems* (New York: New Directions Publishing, 1977), clearly indicate his importance as a voice of the revolution.

Leslie Anderson and Lawrence C. Dodd's *Learning Democracy: Citizen Engagement and Electoral Choice in Nicaragua, 1990–2001* (Chicago: University of Chicago Press, 2005) is without a doubt the best scholarly analysis of the development of democracy in post-revolutionary-era Nicaragua. David Close' *Nicaragua: The Chamorro Years* (Boulder, CO: Lynne Rienner, 1998) gives one an overview of the country under Violeta Chamorro. *Dreams of the Heart: The Autobiography of President Violeta Barrios de Chamorro of Nicaragua* (New York: Simon & Schuster, 1996) is an excellent read. Thomas Walker's edited volume *Nicaragua without Illusions: Regime Transition and Structural Adjustment in the 1990s* (Wilmington: Scholarly Resources, 1997) provides an insightful overview of Nicaragua during the 1990s. Jennifer Bickham Mendez' *From the Revolution to the Maquiladoras* (Durham: Duke University Press, 2005) is a wonderful study of women and the women's labor movement in the post-revolutionary era of globalization.

There is a very large body of literature on U.S. policy toward Nicaragua. Walter LeFeber's *Inevitable Revolutions: The United States in Central America* (New York: W. W. Norton, 1993) provides an overview of the extensive U.S. intervention in Nicaragua and the other countries of Central America. John Findling's *Close Neighbors, Distant Friends* (Westport, CT: Greenwood, 1987) is a well-written and well-researched overview of U.S. policy toward Central America and Nicaragua through the mid-1980s. Roy Gutman's *Banana Diplomacy: The Making of American Policy in Nicaragua 1981–1987* (New York: Simon & Schuster, 1989) and Thomas W. Walker's edited volume *Reagan versus the Sandinistas* (Boulder, CO: Westview Press, 1987) provide the best critiques of President Reagan's policy toward the country.

For a study of the attempts to integrate indigenous communities into Hispanic Nicaragua one should see Jeffrey Gould's *To Die in This Way: Nicaraguan Indians and the Myth of Mestizaje, 1880–1965* (Durham, NC: Duke University Press, 1998). Charles R. Hale's *Resistance and Contradiction: Miskitu Indians and the Nicaraguan State, 1894–1987* (Stanford: Stanford University Press, 1994) also covers the history of relations between the Nicaraguan state and the Miskito Indians of the Caribbean side of Nicaragua.

Index

About the Author

CLIFFORD LEE STATEN, PhD, is professor of political science and international studies and dean of the School of Social Sciences at Indiana University Southeast in New Albany, Indiana. He is the author of Greenwood's *The History of Cuba*.